About My Sister's Business

❖ ❖ ❖

THE BLACK WOMAN'S
ROAD MAP TO SUCCESSFUL
ENTREPRENEURSHIP

Fran Harris

A FIRESIDE BOOK / PUBLISHED BY SIMON & SCHUSTER

FIRESIDE
Rockefeller Center
1230 Avenue of the Americas
New York, NY 10020

FIRESIDE and colophon are registered trademarks
of Simon & Schuster Inc.

Designed by Junie Lee
Illustration by Laurie Reed Davis

Manufactured in the United States of America

1   3   5   7   9   10   8   6   4   2

Library of Congress Cataloging-in-Publication Data

Harris, Fran, date.
About my sister's business: the Black woman's road map to
successful entrepreneurship / Fran Harris.
p.   cm.
Includes index.
1. New business enterprises—Management.   2. Women–owned business
enterprises—Management.   3. Afro-American business enterprises—
Management.   I. Title
HD62.5.H3737   1996
658.02'2'08996073—dc20   96-19526
CIP

ISBN 0-684-81839-6

Acknowledgments

Thanking someone is one of life's greatest honors and it's not something I take lightly. I am so grateful for the life I've had and the people who have touched me in so many ways.

So many people helped write this book, and some of them don't even know it. I would like to have a memory that would enable me to recognize all of you, I'm sorry I can't. Just know that . . . if we have met, crossed paths, kissed, argued, shaken hands, shared a meal, prayed together, taken a class together, laughed, traveled together, exchanged a glance, loved, reasoned, spoken on the phone, cried together, learned together, taught each other something, made love, worked on a project together, gone to the movies together, disagreed, broken up, gotten back together, worshipped with one another, listened to music together, realized we have a common friend, acquaintance or interest, played ball together, run on the same track, shared an ice cream cone, misunderstood each other, done theater together, shared more meals, run lines with each other, partied together, shared life's lessons, fallen on our behinds at the same time, gotten to the top around the same time, smiled at the same greeting card, watched television, practiced together, dated the same person, slow-danced, high-fived, mourned the loss of a loved one together, marched for the same cause, referred business each other's way, given each other a cold, forgotten each other's birthday, played cards together, shopped together, fought over stupid #%*#, fought over important stuff, written to each other, made up after a fight, spoken a foreign language to one another, helped each other in business, been there for each other, cursed or blessed each other, and most importantly, if we've shared a smile along this spiritual journey, I say from the bottom of my heart . . . you have been an important part of my life, and you had something to do with this book being written . . . and I thank you.

To Kellye Richardson, who literally bugged me daily for years about writing in general, thanks Shawn. Thanks to Martha Iglehart, who let me ask her 1,001 "black business women" and "sister" questions whenever I wanted to and never got tired of me asking (at least I think). To Cynthia Taylor-Edwards, thank you for being a ball of fire and such a positive force through your dramatic expression. To Gail Raben, one of my soul mates, thanks for being a great friend, a confidante and true inspiration to me.

To the black women I've met during the process of writing *About My Sister's Business:* You've shared your stories, triumphs and pains, and I applaud and thank you again.

Then I have to go way back and thank the many great language arts and English and grammar educators in my past. Beginning with my mother, who began teaching me to read before I could even walk. Believe it or not, it just so happens that every English teacher I've had was a woman. These women taught me to appreciate the beauty of language, conversation and prose; to be able to speak to a reader or audience so that they can see, feel, taste or smell just what I'm writing or saying. You'll have to forgive me if I can only call you Ms. so and so. In those days all teachers were referred to in this way. In fact I don't think I even knew that some of my teachers had first names! Anyway, to my teachers—I am jogging my memory—forgive me if I forget one of you. Here goes. Thanks to Ms. Johnnie Jackson, who had the distinction of being my first grade teacher for only one day before I skipped ahead to second grade into the stern, yet loving care of Ms. Vivian Taylor; to Ms. Haynes in third, to Ms. Betty Glover in fourth, to Ms. Carnedia Mulkey (my fifth *and* sixth grade teacher, poor soul), and on into the terrific and terrible teen years. There I continued to be blessed with teachers who loved language, reading and expression and who introduced me to writers such as James Baldwin, Phyllis Wheatley, Robert Frost, Mark Twain, Lorraine Hansberry and William Shakespeare—my high school English and literature teachers Sonya Tyler, Diane Cox, Addie Helen Lee and Carolyn Willis.

I am also grateful to other teachers who never had the chore or pleasure of teaching me English but who taught me a great deal about life, success and what those two things mean to me. My dear, sweet Barbara Bardwell; Ms. Fuquals; Christine Walker; Lillian Reeves; Ms. Sanders; Carolyn Bush; Ms. Casey; Celia McKinney; Clementine Brown; Susan Stephenson; Ms. Jessup; Marva Jordan; Ms. Rolla; Ms. Poston and my fourth grade student teacher Ms. Hannah.

To the great women at New Birth Baptist Church in Dallas, Texas— Alma Pryor, Pamela Pryor, Arlelia Harrison, Louise Monroe, my other mom, Jean Caldwell, Alice Johnson, Florence Wilson, Jackie Haggerty and Virgie Grant: I thank you for your encouragement and, of course, all the Easter, Christmas and special recitals.

And thanks to my special friends Rochelle Williamson, Cora Lewis and Quitha, Elizabeth Whitaker, Kim Basinger, Gert Baker, Vicki Faust, Kimber Cavendish, Jennifer and Lee Walker, Kamie Ethridge, Annette Smith-Knight, Audrey Smith, C. J. Jones, Beverly Williams, Shannel Curtiss, Belinda Hare, Beth E., and my two adopted brothers, Willie V. Tatum and Charles Caldwell.

And last but not least, thanks to all of the wonderful men who have inspired me, loved me and supported me.

In tribute to the Honorable Barbara Jordan

B.J., thank you for a rousing Welcome Home speech after the undefeated, '86 national championship season . . . for sitting courtside at our home games and sharing your incredible energy with me and my teammates . . . for your eternal words of personal encouragement . . . for your contributions of peace, power and perseverance to people everywhere . . . and most importantly, for exemplifying the finesse and fortitude that we African American female entrepreneurs will always admire and treasure.

We will miss you.

In memory

My dear friend and coach, Mike Stevenson, for teaching me that life is every bit of what you make it.

Dedication to my family

My mom, Bessie, thank you for taking flight and charge of your life during a time when society told you to glorify in your role as mother and wife and never aspire to be anything more or different. Thank you so much for breaking the rules. Miss you.

Dad, John W., you were my first portrait of entrepreneurship . . . thanks for never working for anyone.

Debra, you have been an encouraging force since the rice, Charlie Brown and bad school-picture days. Thanks for respecting my choices and individuality.

Mike, you entrepreneur extraordinaire, thanks for your unfailing enthusiasm and for being one of the reasons (along with Miki and Jon) my sister smiles each day.

Alonzo, you lighted the entrepreneurial flame. Thanks for the *Black Enterprise* subscription at age twelve.

Larry, you have always inspired me with your talent and zest for life.

Chris, what a gift from God you are. Thanks for your undying love and devotion.

To my cherished and so loved chosen family, Apryl, you have given me your support, love, friendship and sense of humor through some of the toughest times, thank you. And Brittany, thanks for being such a brilliant example of unconditional love.

Special thanks

Terrie Williams, thanks for being so generous with your time and resources.

My agent, Denise Stinson, for believing in my work and most importantly, for recognizing the opportunity.

My editor, Dawn Daniels, for saying the magic words, "Give up the manuscript," and for guiding this project to completion.

And finally, to all the sisters who have broken the rules in the name of change, success and empowerment, thanks.

Contents

Foreword

So, you have decided to take the plunge—and be the mistress of your destiny. Buckle up and get ready for the roller coaster ride of life! Black women in America have always had to be tenacious and resourceful, if only for their own survival and that of their families. Tenacity is the first step toward entrepreneurship; the second step is a game plan. Sure, if you want a business you can call your own, as a woman and an African American there will be added boulders placed in your path. What Fran Harris shares with us in this book is just how you can get over and around those boulders and move forward.

In the pages of this treasured guide—both in her practical advice and in the words of women who have done it—Fran has provided a road map to take you on the journey from that notion floating around in your brain about starting your own business to the point on the grid called "success." She's done it. Your sisters have done it. You can do it.

How I wish I had this guide when I first started out—something that would have helped me understand what it takes to chart the course. Even almost a decade after I took the leap, I find that I learned a lot from the lessons of this book. I also revisited many mistakes and frustrations and even more of my triumphs.

I first met Fran Harris through a letter she wrote to me about my book, *The Personal Touch, What You Really Need to Succeed In Today's Fast-Paced Business World.* Her spirit leaped off the page. I could sense the warm, confident, giving smile I have now come to know. I was drawn to her immediately as someone extraordinary: someone I could bounce ideas off and someone who would share the storehouse of knowledge within her.

I recently read a book celebrating the spirit of entrepreneurship in this country. In comparing our country to those in Europe, the author said the one reason America has succeeded is because of the chances it offers even its most apparent outsiders. During most of the industrial revolution in Europe, if you had an idea for, say, an invention, you had to be accepted by a great established institution and pass all the rigors of education and social class standing just to be heard.

But in America, the greatest inventions have come from the little guy—or the woman—working out of a garage or kitchen. Seamstress Elizabeth Keckley bought her freedom from slavery from the proceeds of her system of fitting and cutting dresses. Madam C. J. Walker had no federal grants, no university endowments. She washed floors while struggling through trial and error to concoct a formula for a hair straightener. Madam Walker became the first female self-made millionaire of any color. These women believed!

Take hold of Fran's words and the experiences of the women in this book. Make them work for you. There is no reason on the planet why you cannot have your own business. Of course, there will be many moments when you question your sanity, even consider throwing in the proverbial towel (don't *even* go there!). If you want it badly enough, it's yours for the asking, the praying and the doing. You must be willing to stay in the race. Many of the sisters whose words Fran has compiled for us were going through difficult times when they began. Some were caught up in the cycle of generational welfare, others in sex, drugs and rock 'n' roll. Neither place offered much of a future. But they persevered. And they drew on the experiences of those who came before them.

Knowing that you're not alone or the first is precisely what will pull you through. That's why this book is invaluable! At a young age, gifted, athletic and disciplined Fran Harris is leading the way. She has asked these sisters and others to share their experiences with you. They have done so willingly and from the heart. Allow their examples to lift, guide and inspire you. The best way to thank them is to let someone else know the book's out there. We are on the planet to support one another, to hold each other up. We must keep the cycle going.

Digesting Fran's simple and down-to-earth wisdom and the stories of these courageous sisters will help you discover the principles that you need to guide your own life. We have always revered those who came before us. We have not forgotten their struggle and especially their pain. The stories of our grandmothers and our mothers are vivid. Where would we be without their wisdom and inspiration? How could we have made it through the maze without their spirit and guidance?

We can't argue that women of color are not yet fully part of mainstream America, but that never stopped a good idea. If you have focus and passion, you will find a way. Don't even think about allowing age, the economy, racism, sexism and all those other pesky irritants to stop you. The best argument against them is excellence. Maybe you want your business to be one that services your immediate community. Maybe you want to go national, or global. The sky is the limit. There are several formulas for you in these pages. You can't go wrong if you follow them.

Dive into this book without hesitation—thought and contemplation are fine but remember the Lord helps those who help themselves. He will help you find your way. In my most difficult moments, I remind myself that "He did not bring me this far to leave me." You must learn to walk on faith. Arm yourself. When you've read this book once, develop your own game plan and keep the book handy for reference. You'll want to check back time and time again. Then get started on what will be a ride with no boundaries except the ones you create, a life experience that will enhance you and allow you to reap extraordinary benefits.

Don't be intimidated if the women who speak in this book sound "so together" and you're just learning how to walk. They're works in progress, just like all of us. Know that if we can, you can. Know that the fear you have — that knot you have in your stomach—is a good thing. It propels you to greater heights and achievements. If you're *not* scared, it means you're either six feet under or going nowhere through life—pathetic and slow. Jump in with both feet and all your senses. Commit with all your heart and soul, and your dream will become a reality. It won't be long before you'll have a success story of your own to share with Fran.

You have the information. The rest, as they say, is up to you. Listen to your heart. Go forth. Stay strong and in the race, and you will conquer all things. God bless. And don't forget to say "Thank you, Fran."

Terrie Williams

DAILY AFFIRMATION

I am a beautiful black woman. I know that today, right now, I have all the talent and resources to build a healthy, successful business venture. I am assertive and proactive in my pursuit of excellence and this entrepreneurial reality.

I will not back down when I face challenges. Instead I will welcome them and acknowledge them as growth opportunities.

This business is not a dream, it's a reality. I've seen it, I've tasted it and I love it! I am responsible for my emotions, reactions and most important, my choices. I am a good decision maker. I hold myself accountable no matter what the outcome of my decisions.

I release these positive, powerful affirmations into the universe, peacefully having faith that they are already happening.

Fran Harris, 1996

Introduction

Dr. Martin Luther King, Jr., told a story of an older woman who was walking one day during one of the 1960s marches. "Ma'am you don't have to walk, you are old," he said. The woman smiled and said, "Son, I ain't walking for myself. I'm walking for my grandchildren. My feets is tired but my soul is rested."

I've read this story at least twenty times and each time I get chills. What a compelling, victorious story of courage and faith. What I've done and what you are either doing or are about to do is also a leap of faith. We are walking on this entrepreneurial journey because black women before us walked. Our daughters will walk this way because of the roads we are paving. Throughout this book you will be reminded of the triumphs of pioneer black women entrepreneurs such as Madam C. J. Walker, Harriet Tubman, Phyllis Wheatley and Sojourner Truth. I would be remiss to forget the contributions of the thousands of black women who cooked, cleaned and cared for other folks' families to provide for their own—our ancestors. Although I don't know them by name, their spirit gives contemporary entrepreneurs like you and me the courage to run on and the peace of mind to believe that the earth and all of its abundance is ours, if we want it.

Opening Ceremonies

Entrepreneurship is nothing new to African American women. It's a part of our history. Or as George Fraser's book so eloquently outlines, success runs in our race. Black women gave "succeeding on a shoestring" new meaning. So, when I hear black women express self-doubt, I wonder where that came from. I wonder, don't they know who we are? Don't they realize that we are *already* successful and that we have a tradition to uphold? Can't this sister see that the road, though different now, was paved for her over two hundred years ago? So, why aren't there more black female entrepreneurs? Isn't business ownership and, moreover, entrepreneurship the Black American dream? Of course it is.

Why do I believe that entrepreneurship is the ultimate? Reason number one: When there's a local or national conference that interests me, regardless of where it is or how much it costs, I know that if I want to be there, I can be there. I don't have to get clearance from management or check to see how many vacation days I've used. Reason number two: When my sister thought she might have a serious health issue, I knew that I could close shop and be with her if I needed to. Reason number three: When the forecast says Friday is going to be a great day for golf, I know that if I work real hard I can take Friday morning off to play a round and then get a massage right after lunch. That's why entrepreneurship is the ultimate. Who wouldn't want total freedom to come and go as she pleases, to schedule vacations around your personal commitments, to work overtime and always see the benefits of that kind of work ethic? Entrepreneurship affords all of this and more.

So, I ask you again. Do you want to control your destiny by creating the career opportunity that matches perfectly with your skills, talents and desires? Then fasten your seatbelt; you've just gotten on the ride of your life. Trust me, you'll love it!

PART ONE

❖ ❖ ❖

On Your Mark

GETTING OFF TO A GREAT START

As in any race, preparation is the key. Ask Oprah. Before she ran that 19th Marine Corps. Marathon in Washington, D.C., she studied, investigated and prepared to run it. She didn't just decide to sign up a week before. The race you're about to run is the most important race you'll run. Before you go to the track, let's be sure you know a little bit about the race. The entrepreneurial race (E-race) is a long one. Whether you realize it or not, you're an athlete. And your sport is your business, literally.

You have become an athlete, a runner. A distance runner. The race before you is a long, sometimes grueling one. It's not one of those itty bitty strides to the twenty-yard line. If you're going to enter this race, you must be ready. You must train, train, and train some more. You must prepare until you are reciting your stuff in your sleep. You must be ready to go the distance. Ready to endure the heat, the cold, the rain and the snow. Ready for those rare hurricanes and tornadoes. Ready for the runner in Lane 4 to cut you off unexpectedly. You see, this race is anything but predictable. I wish I could promise you great weather, perfect conditions and a cheering section that would rival that of Michael Jordan, but that wouldn't be true to the game. I wish I could tell you that your friends, family and loved ones will be the perfect support system that you need, but that wouldn't necessarily be true. I wish I could tell you that the first time you approach a banker for a business loan he or she will say, "Yes, we will give you $10,000," but I can't. I would love to tell you that in your first year of business you will have nothing but smooth sailing, but I can't even make that promise.

So what *can* I promise? I can promise you that if you are 100 percent committed to your business it will be difficult for you to fail. I can promise that if you believe in your ability to succeed you'll be more likely to do so. I can promise you that if you will surround yourself with good, positive influences good things will literally fall into your space. And I can promise you that if you work long and hard you will win the entrepreneurial race and become a huge business success.

By writing this book, I've entered into a contract with you, even though we may never meet. My pledge to you is to try to cover all of the bases. Your part of the deal is that you will never, never, never, never, never, never NEVUH . . . quit! Deal? Deal.

Are You Ready?

So, you want to start your own business? I guess so, since you bought this book. Or maybe you've already started your own business. Regardless of which group you fall near or into, thank you. This book is about faith and courage. It's about building empires, and it's about empowering yourself personally, financially, spiritually and psychologically. When I started writing this book, I wondered what the final product would look like. As I talked to sisters from around the world about entrepreneurship and business success, it all fell into place.

Your decision to go into business for yourself is a huge step, so let me give you a big high five right now. You should feel good about yourself. When I started this journey about twenty years ago, I had no idea where I'd end—that's one of the nice things about being an entrepreneur—you just never know to which place you'll rise. The fun is the ride. I invite you to put your seatbelt on. I have to warn you that my approach may be different than what you're accustomed to—I'm a sorta in-yo'-face-here's-the-deal-fix-your-life-if-you-don't-like-it person. I don't apologize for this approach, I'm merely warning you.

Yes, you're taking a major step toward your personal development. Pretty brave considering what you've been prepared and encouraged to do. I commend you and, in the same breath, warn you. Warn? Warn. Entrepreneurship is many wonderful things. But it can also be many horrific things, too. If you already own your business then you probably have a few war stories to share already. If you're in that "getting ready to" stage, take heed of the advice you'll be given in this book. You are no doubt a capable, competent sister who believes in herself and her enterprise. Unfortunately, belief and confidence are only two of the main ingredients for successful entrepreneurship. The others you'll learn before you finish this book. For now, the doctor is in.

Open Wide and Say "Ahh"

Unlike the doctor who tells you that the shot you're about to take won't hurt, I'm honest. If this exercise doesn't hurt or at least sting then you're not ready. Why? Because we're about to dissect your mind and body to get you ready to *win* this race. Remember when your mom or dad said that they were doing this out of love? Well, same here. Besides, if you're considering taking the entrepreneurial plunge, you need to prepare for battle, so consider me your drill sergeant for the next few hours. First let's decide why you're considering starting your own business. Place a check beside each reason that applies to you.

	YES
Freedom from the 9–5 routine?	_____
Being your own boss?	_____
Improving your standard of living?	_____
Are you bored with present job?	_____
You have a product or service for which there's demand?	_____

Okay, so you answered yes to those. Going into business still requires certain personal characteristics. Let's get into your head. You didn't know you were buying therapy when you bought this book, did you?

	YES	NO
Are you a leader?	_____	_____
Do you like to make your own decisions?	_____	_____
Do others turn to you when making decisions?	_____	_____
Do you enjoy competition?	_____	_____
Do you have willpower and self discipline?	_____	_____
Do you plan ahead?	_____	_____
Do you like people?	_____	_____
Do you get along well with others?	_____	_____

If you answered yes to most (90 percent) of them, then you're probably ready for the E-race. If you batted only .500 you may need to reassess your decision to start a business.

Okay, the questions will get a little harder . . . answer yes or no:

> Do you realize that owning your own business may require working twelve to twenty hours a day, six days a week, sometimes on Sundays and holidays?
> Are you willing to get yourself in the physical shape it takes to run a business successfully?
> Are you prepared to temporarily lower your standards of living until your business is established?
> Is your family/significant other prepared for the ride?
> Are you prepared to lose your savings?

If you answered no to any of these you need to get that area of your house in order. If you are not prepared, for instance, to contribute and potentially lose your personal savings, stop the presses! Your heart and soul are probably not into starting a business.

Personal Skills and Experience

❖ Do you know what basic skills you will need to have a successful business?
❖ Do you possess those skills?
❖ When hiring personnel, will you be able to determine if the applicant's skills meet the requirements for the position you are filling?
❖ Have you ever managed or supervised before?
❖ Have you ever worked in a similar business organization?
❖ Have you had any business training in school?
❖ If you don't have the training, are you willing to delay your plans until you've acquired those skills?
❖ Do you have doubts about starting your own business?

The Idea

> Can you briefly describe the business you plan to start?
> Can you identify the product or service you plan to sell?
> Does your product or service satisfy an unfilled need?
> Will your product or service serve an existing market in which demand exceeds supply?
> Will your product or service be competitive based on quality, selection, price or location?

Answering yes or positively to most of these questions means you're on the right road. A no or unsure answer means the road may be rockier than it needs to be. You may want to reevaluate your readiness and consider getting help to develop in those areas where you weren't as strong.

Where Are All the Sisterpreneurs?

In September 1994, I was featured as one of five entrepreneurs in *Essence* magazine. After that article ran, I spoke with sixty to seventy sisters of all ages, backgrounds and situations who said that they wanted to start their own business. What's stopping you? I asked. Well, of course we had to go through the usual slow dance about the spouse, kids, parents or day jobs, but eventually we got to the heart of the matter—fear. Can you believe that? Fear was immobilizing all of these bright, articulate sisters. I honestly was shocked to hear more than 75 percent of the women I spoke to were not living their dreams because they were afraid to take this quantum leap. I knew then that I'd have to do something about it. So, I developed a relationship with a few of them (a few I've even met), and I've taken a personal interest in helping them realize their dreams. Sound like a crazy undertaking? It's not. It's one of the most rewarding decisions I've ever made. And the return on the investment stays right in our community!

If *About My Sister's Business* moves or shakes you, brava! If it makes you angry, I'm sitting somewhere fired up. If it helps you to get out of the missing in action mode and into the action, I am psyched. If *About My Sister's Business* provides that swift kick in the rear you've been needing lately, you're welcome. Although this journey of entrepreneurship may not always be exactly sentimental, it never fails to be exciting, exhilarating and unpredictable. Remember one thing: If while running the E-race, your legs get a little weary, look over in Lane 2. I'm sure there's a sister there who believes, as you do, that you can make it, and if she's not there, call me.

Fran's Story

When I was nine years old, I wanted to sing like Aretha Franklin. No, I wanted to be Aretha Franklin. I fell in love with "Natural Woman" and "Chain of Fools" and drove my family crazy playing these 45s over and over and then some more.

It was Aretha, Ms. R-E-S-P-E-C-T herself, who had gotten me through most of those turbulent early years. If it weren't for "Bridge Over Troubled Water," I still don't think I would have survived being run over by Jimmy Clay, a twelve-year-old bicycler who warned me to get off of the sidewalk because he didn't have any brakes.

Yep, Aretha was my idol. But for some reason, I had put my dream of being her backup on the shelf for five years. I finally got the courage, at age nine, to dust it off and approach my mom about pursuing the stage—in the church choir. You have to understand that by this time, my mom had seen about a hundred of my dreams come and go. First, I was going to be the next girl NFL wide receiver (I had no clue that by being the next, I would also be the first). So, when I bolted through her bedroom door that steamy summer day, she was anything but surprised with my business proposition.

"Mom, I want to sing in the choir at church and I need your help," I said.

"Yep, what do you need?" she asked.

"I need a choir robe and it costs $110," I said with the enthusiasm of someone who had obviously never worked a day in her life.

"One hundred and ten dollars, huh? That's a lot of money, Fry (as in French)," she said.

"Yeah, but I really wanna do it," I said, wrapping my wiry chocolate arms around her milky, walnut-colored neck while repeatedly kissing her thin lips.

"Well, then I think you should," she said, resting her head on the back of her favorite chair. "How are you gonna get the money?"

Wait a minute, I thought. She misread her lines. This doesn't sound like it did when I needed that fifty dollars for the shoes or the two hundred dollars for the soccer equipment.

"Yyyyouuuuu," I squealed, "You're gonna give it to me," I said, flashing that usually winning smile.

"I don't think so," she said as she kept smiling and looking at *Green Acres*.

"Quit playing, Mom," I said.

"Mommy's not playing, Fry," she answered, still smiling.

"Well, how am I suppose to get my robe?" I whined.

"I don't know, you're my little genius, I know you'll figure it out," she said.

That day my mom gave birth to an entrepreneur. Maybe she knew something I didn't. I stormed to my room without making a sound and did my normal rites of pouting, but when I left my bedroom that day, I left with more than just puffy lips and eyes. I went outside to play and as usual the ice cream truck came by. I wanted a snow cone because I luuuuvved snow cones, but he was out of them, so I didn't buy anything. In fact, all of my playmates wanted snow cones.

While we were sitting on the curb playing what had to be our 315th game of jacks and trying to figure out just how many licks it did take to get to the center of a Tootsie Roll Pop, one of my playmates said, as we often said about almost everything, "I would do anything for a snow cone." I had it!

I took off running down the street to my house like there was no tomorrow, burst into my mother's room and said as only a child out of breath could, "IknowhowtogetmyrobebutIneedyourhelp." There I was. Nine years old, with no collateral and only an impeccable five-star credit rating to my name. Nevertheless, I was determined to get that choir robe and become one of Aretha's ah-oopers.

I said, "Mom, can I . . . may I borrow twenty-five dollars to buy ice and syrup to set up my snow cone stand?" She told me to make a list; she said she'd pick up the items for me. That was Saturday evening. By Monday afternoon, I was selling ten snow cones an hour and weighing the benefits of franchising.

That was over twenty years ago. Today, I'm not much different from the nine-year-old who used to drive her mother crazy. I still have boundless energy. I still love snow cones—coconut. I still love Aretha, but my new idol is Anita Baker. I've fine-tuned my sales approach a bit, and I've learned that as profitable as the snow cone business was, my calling is for enterprises that are much more exciting—and lucrative!

The last twenty years of my life have been anything but boring, and I hope that as you read and hear some of my stories and those of other sisters like us you'll be inspired to reach new heights, go out on more limbs and discover new worlds. Take it from a very round the way sister: Life is what you make it. Remember, it's never what happens to you that matters—it's how you respond.

Best advice ever given: *Life goes on . . . never sweat the small stuff.*

Advice to you: *Life is like a card game. We're all given a hand to start the game. What you make of that hand depends on your next move.*

> Fran Harris
> President, Nouveau Sports Marketing
> Principal, ExecuTips, motivational products
> Principal, The Fran Harris Agency
> Austin, Texas

Can You Hang?

Before you go out and purchase your sneakers and water bottle for the race, you need to know if you can hang. This is not a twenty-yard dash. It's a marathon, a long distance race. Long distance races take months of training and preparation. Going into business for yourself is not something you just wake up and do, not if you want to be successful. This race is rigorous and chronically fatiguing. There will be people who will start the race but won't finish. You may be one of those people if you don't plan. There will be people who will try to cut you off in your lane. There will be heavy winds, maybe even snow and blizzards. Sometimes you will be the only cheering section you have. You need to know that you can hang. So take this test, and you'll have a good idea of where you are.

- Do you feel comfortable being the only black woman in an all-white environment?
- Are you comfortable working with white males over fifty?
- Would you attend a conference/seminar alone?
- Would you attend a conference/seminar alone in a city several hundreds of miles away?
- Do you allow personal tragedies to set you back for prolonged periods of time?
- Do you do what you say you're going to do?
- Do you hold yourself accountable for the choices you make?
- Are you good at asking for help?
- Are you comfortable saying "I'm sorry?"
- Do you allow your personal life to interfere with your goals?
- Do you worry about what others think of you?
- Are you uncomfortable making decisions alone?
- Are you self-confident?
- Do you like for things to go your way?
- Do you believe you're cut out for entrepreneurship?

Count the number of yeses you have. How did you do?

12–15	Go for it, you're ready.
8–11	You're getting there. Work on those areas where you're not as strong.
7–8	Keep your day job. You will drive yourself insane being in business for yourself.
0–6	You're being quite unrealistic at this point in your life. Don't leave your job.

If it sounds as though I'm trying to discourage you from taking this quantum leap into entrepreneurial bliss, I'm not. As the owner of three businesses, I'm simply trying to help you succeed. If the pieces are in place from an emotional, physical and mental perspective, you are more likely to land on both feet. If too many things are off balance, there's no telling how you will land. You are getting the benefit of the experiences of at least twenty other successful sisters who all want you to make it in this elite sorority.

If Not You, Who? If Not Now, When?

How many times have you sat around and thought about starting your own business? A few? A hundred? If you are like about 50 percent of the sisters I've spoken to, you have an excuse as your answer: children, spouse, parents, health, death, money, taxes and timing just to name a few. The funny thing is that you can do something about *all* of these factors, except someone else's death. "Yeah right, how can I start a business when my children just started school?" Well, this is the perfect time to start a business. Chances are your children have been your life for most of their lives. So, you probably have tons of time on your hands. Use that time to find out what you're good at, give yourself and your kids an opportunity to grow and see Mommy in another light.

You say you don't have the money? Bologney! Money's floating around right between the pillows on your sofa! Raising money is not hard if you set your mind to it. As children, we were the ultimate fund-raisers. When that ice cream truck drove by didn't we find a way to raise twenty-five cents? You bet we did!

Your spouse/mate won't hear of it? Then get a new one. Yes, it's time for us to start realizing that anyone who doesn't want us to be whole individuals doesn't deserve us. If that partner refuses to love and support your entrepreneurial dream, you tell them that your love is not deep enough to meet their selfish needs at the expense of yours. This is some in-your-face stuff for your own good. This book was meant to inspire you, not make you feel good. I don't want you to be comfortable staying out of action. As my mother used to say, you may as well buckle down and go with the flow.

A Look Back at Black American Entrepreneurship

If you want to keep blaming the system and white America for our business woes, that's one party I won't attend. There are many great examples of entrepreneurism in the black community.

My favorite sisterpreneur is Rosa Parks. Her courage, savvy and conviction model what black women need to succeed in business. I often think about what motivated her to refuse to give up her seat that day in Montgomery. She wasn't the first to do it but, because she was so active in the community, when *she* did it, it got people's attention. If she was like you and me, she was tired. Tired of the status quo. She knew she deserved a better life. But the most important quality that Rosa Parks exhibited that steamy day was courage. In a time when black women were relegated to silence and the back burner, Ms. Parks created a winning and empowering situation, not just for herself, but for black people everywhere. Believe it or not, not much has changed since 1955. People still believe that we belong at the back of the bus—even some of us. It still takes tremendous courage to start a movement—your own business. Ask anybody who's done it.

It's Not the Idea, It's You

There are millions of great ideas floating around out there. The key element in getting those ideas into motion are the people—*you*. If you have a sound business idea and you are a committed, hard-working woman, then it's going to be difficult for you to fail. But good ideas don't necessarily make good businesses. They aren't even particularly important to success. In fact, having a good idea is the wrong reason to start a business, because good ideas shimmer and shine and make great beginnings but lousy finishes.

A Letter to Fran

Right now, I want you to take out a sheet of paper, doesn't matter how small it is.

Answer the following:
What do I want from my life?
What is it I want to experience before I die?
What gives me the greatest satisfaction in life? (Money, freedom, etc.)
When I have nothing to do I usually _____.

Then, seal this in an envelope with a self-addressed stamped envelope and send it to:

Fran Harris
P.O. Box 5806
Austin, TX 78763
Attn: The Sisterpreneur Connection

Cynthia's Story

It was the spring of 1990 when I was leaving a local newspaper where I was a receptionist. I had been told by the editor that auditions were being held at Dr. Anderson's office for *A Raisin in the Sun*. I went to meet Dr. Anderson and Frederick Johnson, founders of First Stage Productions. I auditioned and got the part of Ruth—which surprised me. During one of our conversations Mr. Johnson mentioned that he was going on location for a film. He said that he was concerned that the film would take him away from the theater company for long periods of time. I offered to work as his secretary/receptionist while he was away and assured him that I would "hold down the fort while he was away." He was shocked that I would offer to help him in this way, yet he gave me the thumbs up sign. Mr. Johnson in the meantime decided to go back to college— which meant that he wouldn't have too much time to run First Stage. So, he asked me if I had any interest in being the Executive Director of FSP. I prayed about it and in two days I said yes.

Since that glorious day, FSP has developed into a wide cross-section of actors that caters to a diverse audience. My goal is to help empower the community by giving people—children and adults of all ages, ethnicities and other differences—the opportunity to appreciate their own special talents. First Stage Productions is about giving back, and I'm proud to be associated with a company that truly values people.

I'd never really thought about leading a theater company. I guess great things are right at our finger tips; we just have to look in some not so obvious places to find them. Aim high, sister, and go get 'em, girl!

Cynthia Taylor Edwards, Executive Director
First Stage Productions
Austin, Texas

Your Personal Wake-Up Call

❖ ❖ ❖

The trouble with being in the rat race
is that even if you win, you're still a rat.
—Lily Tomlin

You're tired and you've had it. You work from seven till seven. You never have holidays, and you haven't seen a night out since college. Your supervisor thinks he's your boss. Your raise is way over due. You're a young sister who dreams in color but you can't see a pot of gold at the end of that company's rainbow. Or, you're a seasoned sister, who's done the children and marriage thing and now you want a life to call your own. Only thing is, if you enter the world of pin stripes and attachés you know that you'll be treated like a polyester suit.

Face it, life for black women in corporate America ain't been no crystal stair. So, leave it. Black women have worked too long for low pay, puny rewards and no respect. In your heart, you know that the only way you will ever have everything you deserve is if you create it for yourself. But don't let me talk you into it. Consider the following statistics, quoted in *Work, Sister Work*:

- Black women comprise only 3 percent of corporate management and less than 1 percent of female corporate officers.
- Of the highest paying professions in 1990 including lawyers, physicians, engineers, marketing, advertising and computer systems analysts, only 2.5 percent of them were women. And of those women, only 6.6 percent were Black women.
- Since the 1950s, African American income has remained at about 50 percent of white America's income.

- We are more likely to be divorced and heads of households. Fifty-three percent of all working black mothers are living in poverty.

Looking at those statistics, why would you ever want to work for anyone but yourself? I'm not talking about self-employment here. We're talking entrepreneurship. There's a difference. Self-employment is believed to be the process of providing employment for yourself. When you think of entrepreneurs which words come to mind? Bold, imaginative, creative, risky, right? When someone says, "I'm self-employed" what comes to mind? I bet not the same words that ring through your mind when you hear "entrepreneur." The perception of people who are self-employed is that they are simply providing themselves with a job, a way to support their family and pay their bills. Entrepreneurs are thought to be people who concentrate on opportunities missed by others. Entrepreneurs enjoy making money, though they're not necessarily driven by it. Ask yourself again. Are you entering a world of self-employment or entrepreneurship?

WHAT GLASS CEILING?

Anyone who knows me knows that I do not, will not and never have believed in a glass ceiling. Who created it anyway? No doubt it was a woman. We *had* to give it a name, didn't we? If you want to leave your job because you're tired of the crap and skinny paycheck, say that. If you're considering leaving your day job because your management doesn't recognize your incredible ability and performance, then say that. But please, please, stop perpetuating this glass-ceiling schizpot—it's something we've created to make us feel better about sitting on our proverbial behinds instead of making something happen. Yes, we do live in a patriarchal society—one that values and celebrates masculinity and all that it embraces. Or do we? It's not whether we do or not, it's how you create your own reality. If you choose to relate to the world as though it's a man's world, one that stops you every time you try to rise above, then you'll continue to hit your head on any old obstacle—a glass, Formica or some psychological ceiling.

If I sound a bit fanatical, good, because I want you to hear this loudly and clearly—if you thought there was a glass ceiling while you worked for someone else, to what name will you relinquish your power as an entrepreneur on her own? The cement ceiling? I assure you, you will face challenges and road blocks that will *appear* insurmountable. I'm living proof that those obstacles exist only as strong and viable as you create them in your mind.

Each day we must rid ourselves of the lies we've been told about ourselves. . . .
—Maya Angelou

CHOOSING ENTREPRENEURSHIP

There's no such thing as a born entrepreneur, leader or anything else. Successful people are made. Do you realize that your life today, now, is a result of the choices you've made?

A CURRENT LOOK AT BLACK ENTREPRENEURSHIP

According to a 1992 Census Bureau survey, there were more than 620,912 African American-owned businesses in the United States, with a total revenue of $32.2 billion. Do you think it's safe to estimate that at least half of those were also women-owned? I wonder. I'd guess that maybe 35 to 40 percent of those were owned by sisters. I wonder how many of the people involved in those ventures are entrepreneurs as opposed to self-employed.

Why am I lobbying so hard for entrepreneurship? Well, just by the sheer nature of the profile, it has a far more long-term potential. Since entrepreneurs are often leaders who try to be on the cutting edge of technology, business or social trends and professional development, they will probably find a way to thrive and not merely survive in today's competitive environment. That's why I hope you will learn to understand and value the importance of entrepreneurship.

Speaking of entrepreneurs, what do they look like? They come in all shades, sizes and shapes. Despite these differences there seem to be common traits that run through most black female entrepreneurs.

They don't mind living on the edge.
Notice that I didn't say all of us love living on edge. I do, I thrive on it. But most entrepreneurs will admit the excitement that often accompanies living on the edge is exhilarating and challenging.

They are turned on by making money.
Successful entrepreneurs enjoy making money. To some people, money is like a four-letter word, and to others it runs and rules their lives. Although money may not be the primary motivation for all entrepreneurs, few will dispute that the process of making it gives them a natural high.

They believe that while others are dreaming they're scheming.
Scheming here is not meant to conjure up thoughts of dishonesty and deceit. It means that you're strategically minded, always looking for a way to outdo and out-maneuver. Too much emphasis has been placed on dreaming, so much so that some people are perpetual dream chasers, yet they never get out of bed to make them realities.

They believe that the three Cs usually prevail.
Confidence, competitiveness and competence are hard to beat, I don't care what color you are. Successful black women understand that if you're good at what you do, you'll win. If you offer a quality product or service that is competitive in the marketplace, you'll get some business. If you exude confidence, people will gravitate to you and want to do business with you.

They have incredible energy.
People ask me all the time "where do you get all of your energy?" I say I'm active, enthusiastic and I have a wonderful life—that, in itself, creates energy. Entrepreneurs are usually excitable and high-energy people, otherwise how could they possibly fuel their dreams?

They are positive people.
When I go to meetings with other entrepreneurs, the energy in the room is magnetic and awesome. There is nothing like being around people who seem to have given new meaning to "I can and I will."

They are visionaries.
Talk about thinking outside of the box. Entrepreneurs adopt the philosophy that there are no boundaries, so they often achieve what others think is impossible.

They are clear about their purpose.
Some people think that entrepreneurs lack focus because they do so many things. I'm sure there are people in every camp who have a difficult time focusing, but that's hardly the case for many entrepreneurs. We almost always know what we want.

They don't mind traveling solo.
My mother used to tell me to be prepared to do things without people. Sometimes entrepreneurship involves a bit of isolation but that doesn't generally bother most of us. People who don't share our enthusiasm and vision may not readily see the benefits or logic of our actions.

They are self-motivated.
What motivates the most successful entrepreneurs? Most of my research reveals that successful black women entrepreneurs are motivated to begin ventures for three reasons: money, goodwill and independence.

THREE REASONS FOR ENTREPRENEURSHIP

The Motivation of Money

The Root of All Evil?

Most of us have heard this at least ten times—money is the root of all evil. Well, yes, money may be what we argue, fuss, fight and kill about, but *it* is not the problem. It appears that money is a dirty word in our community— the black community. Although I don't personally identify, I do understand. We haven't been trained to have healthy relationships with money, yet it is one of the focal points of most of our lives. I'd bet that everyone has had a conversation, good or indifferent, about money. If you haven't, you will. Why is that? Because face it, money is an important resource. Black people in particular have had very unhealthy experiences with money and financial independence, so money and the acquisition of it often gives us indigestion.

Dealing with Bills

Face it. Bills are a reality and most of us have them. One of the most obvious questions a budding entrepreneur asks herself is how am I going to pay my bills during my start-up months? Good question. You must develop a plan to handle your financial situation during the early years. It's no secret, black women luuuuv to shop. Ask yourself, "am I willing to stay out of Bloomingdale's in the name of my enterprise?" The answer for me was a resounding yes. To be honest, I was so proud of me, because I can wear a mall out! I went shopping only twice during my lean months, one time to get a suit (I really needed it) and the other for a gift. You say, stop shopping? Not me. Then I say you need to rethink your decision to go into business if shopping means more to you. Your financial situation deserves your undivided attention. I poured in thousands of dollars into my businesses, which meant my personal livelihood suffered. Only you can determine where and how you'll make the necessary adjustments. Let's analyze your situation.

Financial Health Check

Fill in your monthly expenses for each category:

Mortgage/rent	_____
Utilities	_____
Phone	_____
Transportation/gas	_____
Car payment	_____
Medical	_____
Insurance (health, life, home, car)	_____
Food	_____

Clothing	_____
Entertainment	_____
Personal Grooming	_____
Credit Cards	_____
Cleaning	_____
Education	_____
Other	_____
TOTAL	_____

Now look at your expenses. Which of them can you reduce? Do you really need to eat out every weekend? Probably not. Could you rent a movie and cook at home, versus going to the theater and dinner on the town? Probably so. Could you pay cash for items that you continually whip out the old plastic for? I think so. Only you know how you can cut your expenses. Believe me, being in business requires your total commitment—that includes your money. If you're not willing to cut into your personal finances, keep your day or night job until you are.

Dealing with Your Money Issues

It's time you faced your own money issues, for your personal and business' sake. You are in business to be profitable, and if you can't come to terms with your money issues, your business is going to suffer. There are basically three types of female African American money profiles.

From Poverty to Prosperity. Rene (fictitious name, of course) wasn't accustomed to having large sums of money. She's always worked minimum-wage jobs. When she started her writing services she was making almost $700 a week—twice what she'd ever made as someone's employee. The money was rolling in so easily and quickly Rene forgot that it takes money to run a business. Instead she got into the habit of pocketing everything as "net" and just figured that when it was time to buy paper and computer supplies she'd be fine. Rene got a firsthand experience with Murphy's Law. Her computer broke down and had to be repaired, costing her nearly $1,000—that she incidentally didn't have when she went to the old pocketbook.

I don't think I have to do what all of our parents probably did to us—remind us over and over again that we goofed. Rene is only an example of what happens when we go from rags to riches. There's no way to prepare someone who has never had money to have money. Although Rene made a classic mistake, at least she wasn't afraid to make it.

I'm destined to be destitute. Sadly, some of us are still afraid to leave the cotton fields. We've been emancipated but we're just not sure that the free world is the place for us. It's true, there are some of us who are afraid of success. Is it because we know that once we leave the nest we'll be seen for who we truly are? Or is it that we don't think we *deserve* money and financial abundance? I did a seminar where I asked five people to share their dreams, personal and professional. The exercise, entitled, "What Do You Want?" is designed to get people to define in the most intricate details their heart's desires.

All of the participants talked about living comfortably and being able to provide for their families. None of them cited money as something they wanted. When I brought up money: "what about money—how much would you like or does it take to live comfortably?," not one could give me an answer without squirming or losing eye contact. This was a seminar of all professional, well-educated, well-spoken African Americans in a Fortune 200 company. I rest my case.

Money Makes Me. Some of us think that because we have money we don't face the injustices of racism or sexism. We think that by acquiring money, we're elevated to a higher status. Maybe you think you have a perfectly healthy relationship with money—you may even be right. This exercise is to prepare you for what could possibly happen as you venture into this crazy, sometimes unpredictable world of entrepreneurship. All of us have a way in which we relate to money. Think about your relationship to it. Do you spend it freely or do you hold on to it like a woman on a New York subway? Are you the type of person who reaches for the check when you and your friends are at a restaurant? In your intimate relationships do you believe that everything should be fifty–fifty? How do you pay your bills? Are you going to die if you can't go out to lunch everyday as you have for two years?

The Motivation of Goodwill

Starting your business because you want to give back or help people is a great reason to do it. The book *Do What You Love, the Money Will Follow* says that we can build businesses by pursuing the things that truly create internal peace and happiness for ourselves. It's so true. At least, I believe it. That's how I became a writer. The first thing you must do is identify what it is you wish to do for the world, your community or family.

Let me be a damp blanket on the goodwill issue. We have historically been so concerned with giving back and helping others that our businesses have suffered in the worst ways. I'm all for philanthropy and investing in the black community, yet I'm also a serious businesswoman who doesn't believe that those two concepts have to be mutually exclusive. Just because you are in a service business doesn't mean you shouldn't turn profits. In fact, you *are* in business to make a profit—that's what business is. Be careful not to fall into the old trap of making plenty of friends and no money.

The Motivation of Independence

I went into business for myself for the energy and independence. I wanted complete freedom to work and play as I saw fit. Other black women will tell you that they went into business to control their own futures. Being in business for yourself, though difficult, affords you the freedom to build a solid financial future and at the same time a strong, healthy sense of self-reliance, self-worth and self-esteem.

If black women are going to create wealth of mind, spirit and bank accounts, we must do it on our own. I've been an entrepreneur since I was nine years old when my mother and I ran a snow cone stand from our garage in Dallas, Texas. My story is unique but so is yours. In fact, this book is filled with inspiring stories of women just like you and me: women who have had everything from humble to horrific beginnings; women who've realized that the corporate world offers nothing to them but a basket full of heartaches and disappointments; women whose vision for their lives means having a room with a view and some Anita Baker glaring through the pipes if she wants; and women who are committed to building empires and enterprises and who won't stop until they have both.

FROM EMPLOYEE TO EMPLOYER

What? Leave the Security of a Corporation?

What security, girlfriend? Most large companies are run mostly by white males. We know how the powers that be take care of their own. It's no secret that the general consensus of the majority is that we're inferior. So why would someone promote someone who doesn't quite cut it anyway? Well, you say, you're terrific at building relationships, you'll just break right into the good ol' boy network, right? I say that's impossible because you won't even be made aware of the meetings. Few black folks and especially black women are in the loop when it comes to information that could propel their careers to the top. If you don't know what's going on how can you succeed? You can't. Oh, sure, there are a teaspoonful of black women who do hold powerful, decision-making positions in major companies, but I'd be willing to bet that some of them have a few war stories I don't even want to hear. The rewards of being on your own are too numerous to mention. However, I will tell you that when you're doing what you love in an environment that promotes success and cultivates positive energy, there's no match.

A Black Woman-Owned Business? Puh—leez

Believe it or not, that's what some people say. People, us included some-times, can't believe that we start and build thriving enterprises, that we are presidents and CEOs of companies. I can't tell you how many times I've been at expos or conferences and been in a discussion with people—mostly men—but sometimes women, unfortunately, who've said: "So, what do 'ya'll' do?" "I'm a professional development trainer," I say. "Oh, how long have you been working for (glance at my business card) NARF?" "Since I started consulting ten years ago." Ding, ding, ding. The light finally comes on (looks at card again and notices the word president on my card). "Oh, you're . . . ohhhh, this is *your* company?" they exclaim. Nine out of ten times people automatically assume that we, black women, work for some-body else. It can be infuriating.

Are You a Con or a Pro?

We've all done that exercise where you draw the line down the middle of the paper. Compare advantages and disadvantages. Know the one? Well, let's do it again. Rather than just listing them, I'd like for you to counter the ad-vantages of staying in your job with a solution for leaving. There's room on this page for you to do it right here, right now.

Advantages of Working for Someone   **Advantages of Being on My Own**

_____   _____
_____   _____
_____   _____

For me, the advantages of working for someone greatly outweighed the dis-advantages. I had a company car so I didn't have a car payment for almost four years. The flip side of leaving that situation was that I could drive a car that I actually liked! It's different for everyone, but your list oughta give you an idea of what you're missing out on by working for someone else.

How Do I Leave Thee? Let Me Count the Ways

After looking at your comparisons you're thinking about seriously taking the plunge, right? Only problem is that you do still have a day job. Moon-lighting as some people call it, simply means starting your business while you're still working for someone else. All I have to say is *tiene cuidada, chica*—be very careful, girl. Some companies frown terribly on employees working on the side, especially when black people do it. My own experience with this wasn't horrible, but it really made me angry a time or two.

You have to know that if your side venture is highly visible, you stand the chance of being scrutinized more than, say, a writer. I am an ESPN analyst, which means that you may turn on your TV and see my face splattered across it. That is precisely what happened to me. I'd done a basketball game on a Saturday night. In this day of technology you'd think that people would get a clue and understand the concept of rebroadcasting (reruns).

ESPN replayed the game on a Tuesday in the middle of the day! You can imagine what ensued. At a company function, someone (no doubt, a non-black person) said, "Hey Fran, I was flipping through the channels on television yesterday around two o'clock and I heard this voice." I'm sitting there knowing what he's about to say. "And I said, I *know* that voice. It's Fran! And then they showed you—it's awesome." He says all of this in the presence of some people who were not thrilled that my smiling face was on the tube in the middle of a workday. So, be careful. Not everyone in your workplace is an ally. I wasn't fooled by the people who were always talking about how neat it was to be an ESPN analyst because I'd heard too many comments such as "how do you have time for that?" So, be careful. While having a side business can be a wonderful escape from the world, it can present a unique set of issues if you intend to work in a company at the same time.

Be Seen, Not Heard

Normally, I tell black women in corporate America to make sure they're visible. If you're not planning to leave your job soon, you don't want to draw attention to yourself. This is something that most business owners have to face in their lives. Unless you have a side business, such as quilting, that in no way conflicts with doing business in your organization, then I say be as quiet as possible about your venture. You don't want people to start talking about it. The first thing they'll say is "how wonderful it is." The next sentence is that you're not doing your job and now they understand why. Even if you think everyone loves you and would never do anything to hurt you—don't discuss your business. Even if you just shattered all of your department's records and won a trip to Honolulu—don't do it. The last thing you need is more pressure.

Now that you've convinced yourself you need to leave, the question now is how will you leave. Very, very carefully. Leaving an employer can be a sticky, sometimes painful, ugly situation. You don't want to do it in a way that you'll regret later. First you need to evaluate your work situation. Are you in good standing or are you on everybody's bad list? If you're the star of your organization, you couldn't be in a better position. You may even be able to leverage your good standing by getting a raise, say, for the next year, if you're planning to make your exit within a year. Or you may be able to take your organization on as a client if applicable.

However, if you're not a star performer and you've messed up a few times lately, I would advise the following. Don't be a brat. Don't go around announcing your departure or flaunting your soon-to-be independence. This is not the time to be a bit loose with the tongue. Simply prepare a professional-looking resignation. Depending on your job level and situation, your notice should be between two and four weeks. Then schedule a meeting with your immediate supervisor if it's appropriate. Tell him or her that you have decided to leave for a better opportunity. Depending on your relationship with this person, you may want to fully disclose your plans, if you're comfortable. It's your call whether you want to say that you're starting your own business. I wouldn't use this time to rag on the company. I would use this opportunity to provide feedback if you can deliver it well. This is something you'll need to think about beforehand. You won't want to come across as a person who's been waiting to dump on your coworkers, your former manager or the company. If asked simply say, "Actually there are a few issues that I'd like to discuss. I really felt that the environment was hostile for black people in this company." I'm a big advocate for being forthright and truthful particularly when it involves improving work environments for all people, especially sisters and brothers coming behind us. If you're fortunate to have what some companies call an exit interview, I would keep it as short and sweet as possible unless, of course, you've been dogged in the workplace. Then I say tell 'em, they need to know.

If you're not absolutely positive that it's the right move for you, you're already one leg behind in the race. Let's talk about some of the things that might make you believe you're not ready. They are real issues, I know, so we need to address them.

Don't Leave Home Without It

A plan, that is. As much as I am an advocate of being on your own, you should never leave a job or start a business without a solid plan. A plan is your blueprint for success; without it, you're whistling with crackers in your mouth. Developing that plan takes time and effort. It requires you to think of several alternatives to everything. Even contemplating leaving your job could make you feel worn out and worn down. It's important to weigh all the options.

Timing is everything. Believe me, it can be one of the toughest parts of leaving your employer. Just when *is* the right time? Well, the right time depends on you and what's going on in your life and your employment situation. Are you about to be promoted? Is your company going through a restructure or layoffs? If so, this may be the perfect time to leave. Did you just get a new manager who has a reputation of being a bigot? Avoid the potential frustration and leave. *If* you've just made some major financial commitments, such as a house, car or college tuition, I wouldn't advise starting a business *unless* you have sufficient resources to handle your mortgage or car payment.

Why Black Women-Owned Businesses Fail

While I want this book to be an empowerment tool and one that encourages you to knock 'em dead, the reality is that a great percentage of us who try this fail. Unfortunately an even greater percentage of those failures could be avoided. This whole section is about not making the same mistakes sisters around the globe have made. If you've ever wondered why black women-owned businesses don't succeed, wonder no more.

Poor Planning
I bark at all the people who keep downplaying the importance of business planning. Stop fooling yourself. You need a business plan if you plan to be a serious player.

Non-Quantifiable Plans
Everything that can be communicated in words should also be communicated in numbers. If you're telling the banker that your business will grow by 200 percent over the next year, you need to be able to show this on your financial statements.

No Practical Implementation Plan
Sometimes we set out to discover the world but we don't have a clue as to where we're going to start. Remember to break up your plan into small baby bites. That way they'll never seem too big for you.

Lack of Checks and Balances and Quality-Control Tools
We don't ask ourselves or each other how we're doing until it's too late. We don't know where the day's gone because sometimes we're poor project managers. We spend too much time on the wrong things.

Lack of Discipline with Finances and Forecasts
We either overspend or misspend. We don't learn to pick our finances apart. We dip into our business funds for personal use. We're afraid of balance sheets and profit and loss statements, when they're our strongest allies.

Giving Up Too Easily

When the going gets tough, sometimes we get out. When your month doesn't go as well as you would have liked, hang in there. Being in business is tough and unpredictable. Successful entrepreneurs don't quit and neither can you.

Lack of Experience

Sometimes we start businesses that we really don't know much about. It's like me trying to start a business as a wall and floor covering consultant. I know what looks good and I know about textures and fabrics, but I don't know the first thing about the best adhesives for your wall or floor! Unless I brought in a partner who did, I'm destined to fail.

Mismanagement

When you're on your own it's tempting to do the wrong thing. You're out and you want to get some lunch but you don't have any personal cash, so you write a company check. You figure one time is not going to hurt much. Then you start making it a habit, and pretty soon you're $350 in the hole in only one month.

No Niche

As a small business consultant, one of the things I do is help entrepreneurs define and fine-tune their business ideas. Currently I'm working with a service-oriented entrepreneur who faxed over a sheet of information describing her business. In it she said she was truly unique. Never say you're truly or very unique, it's overly redundant. In our initial consultation I got her to talk about what was so unique about her business. She began to list a few things. After each I said, "And no one else in town is providing this service?" Each time she said, "Well, yeah, there's so and so." Each time I'd say, "Then you're not that unique, are you?" Finally, she got to one thing that was actually unique, and it was a biggie. I explained to her that I wasn't being a cynic, I was simply trying to help her gain a competitive edge in her field. If she didn't let her prospective clients know what distinguishes her from similar operations they wouldn't become clients.

Not Meeting a Market Need

I once heard a story of a writer who wanted desperately to write. However, whenever she read her samples in her class, her classmates always made suggestions for improving the piece. She never listened to their recommendations and just kept churning out the same kinds of stories. Finally, her instructor asked, "Are you incorporating any of the great ideas you're getting in class?" "No," she said matter-of-factly, "I like it how I write it, if they don't like it, too bad." This would-be writer to this day is unpublished because she wasn't willing as the O'Jays said to "Give the People What They Want."

Undercapitalization
This is one of the biggest obstacles of black women-owned enterprises. No money and no chance of finding any. If you don't have the money to start a business then you don't have a business. There's no money and then there's no money. When I went full time into my business, I had the first kind of no money. In other words, every penny was accounted for. I knew how much I could use for food and gas.

Not Asking for Help
Another killer of black women's businesses. Look, no one really thinks you're superwoman, I don't care who calls you that. Superwoman is a figment of our imagination. You are human, incredible as you may be, you are not invincible and from time to time you'll need help. If your business means as much as you're saying it does, ask for help.

Not Interacting with the Outside World
If you operate with blinders on, you'll kill your business. Even if you sell to a predominantly African American market, you still need to mix and mingle with other types of businesses and other people as much as possible. If nothing else, you'll get some ideas for how to do business.

Get Your Mind Outta the Gutter— and Keep It Out!

Before you consider starting a business, you need to make sure that your house, your body, mind and soul are in order. For the next few pages, we're going to talk about your mind, since it's the thing that needs to be in check before you do anything. It deserves your immediate and absolute attention. Since you're probably over the age of eight, I'm going to assume that you've already been programmed to think and believe certain things. We're going to reprogram you. Yes, reprogram your mind.

Realizing the Power of the Mind
Did you know that how far you go on this entrepreneurial journey depends on the condition of your mind? My greatest challenge in the black women's empowerment movement is getting you and the rest of our sisters to take a step in the right direction. It's getting you to realize that everything begins with a thought. If you can get that initial thought to be powerfully positive the rest is easy.

You basically have two minds: a conscious and subconscious mind. Your conscious mind is what I call your logical factor. It's what's reading this book and processing the information on the pages. Once your logical factor has decided how the information should be interpreted, your subconscious mind takes over. Your subconscious is a computer, it doesn't make judgments. It was programmed a long time ago. When your mother told you that you were beautiful at age two, you didn't know what beautiful meant, you just accepted the message, right? Your subconscious mind is like a computer—if you hit backspace, it backspaces. Later on you started to see pictures of women who other people said were beautiful and your conscious mind started to process it all. This magazine says that short, neat hair and small noses are beautiful. Okay, I believe it. If your conscious mind's job is to determine what to believe and accept, can't you see why it's so important to get your subconscious messages right?

Programming Your Mind

When you get messages from other people, the media and books and you accept them as truths, that's programming. When you talk to yourself, tell yourself that you are beautiful or ugly, that's called self-programming. I know people who ask me, "How are you so good at remembering names or numbers or pieces of conversations from years back?" It's because I program myself to remember. I say to myself, "I have an incredible memory." It's the same for people who constantly tell themselves, "I have a bad memory." No wonder they can't remember squat! As you read on, we'll continue to revisit the essentials of subconscious reprogramming. You'll learn how to clean up your language and get rid of habits that are sabotaging your greatness.

Training Your Conscious Mind

What? How can I train my own mind? Easy. First you must understand how the mind works. All the tapes, books and seminars in the world will never take you any closer to success until you get your mind right. People think that the body leads, when it's actually the mind that takes the first step. When people say they can't stop smoking because they need cigarettes, I say as long as you embrace that thought you won't stop. Your body needs what your mind tells it. When I played ball in college, I told myself that because I was so active I needed to eat like a horse. So, you guessed it, I ate like a horse—sometimes two! When I could barely move up and down the floor in the Pan American Games tryouts, the top U.S. basketball team in 1987, I had to check my programming. Guess what? I discovered that when I told myself that a double-cheeseburger and large fries were truly unnecessary for satiety, I no longer ate them. I told myself that in order to be my best self, best athlete, I needed to be lean not plump. Notice I didn't say that I wanted to be skinny, I said lean. Lean means that I'm giving my body what it needs to function like a fine-tuned machine. But before I could achieve leanville, I had to understand the way the mind functions. Here are five principles of training the mind. Learn them and you too can experience phenomenal business success.

1. *It believes what you tell it.*

   Remember, the subconscious mind is a computer. When I was working on my MBA, a friend and classmate would say, "Fran Harris, I have the greatest marketing mind in the world," and I'd say, "Nice try, but actually, I have the greatest marketing mind in the world." We both believed it, consequently we both have incredible and exciting marketing aptitude. He's risen to the top of the marketing department of a Fortune 500 company in less than three years. And I? Well, you know I got it going on!

2. *Your subconscious mind plays second fiddle to your conscious mind.*

   Have you ever wanted desperately to go to sleep but couldn't? Your subconscious mind needed to be focused on something other than sleep, like the details of your glorious first day as a business owner. If you would just focus on one thing, you'll discover that falling asleep is a breeze. Again, allow your subconscious mind to focus on peaceful thoughts.

3. *Your body is waiting on your mind's command.*

   Ever been attracted to someone? What happened? Your initial response to the person you were attracted to was in your mind. You *thought,* "what a neat person," and then it was probably followed by some physical reaction—a shiver, a warm feeling, a smile. The same thing happens when you concoct negative thoughts in your mind. You say, "I always get nervous before I speak to a group of people," and then you wonder why you come close to having a cardiac arrest before your presentations. Ever wonder why feeling bad physically is always preceded by your saying, "I'm starting to feel bad"? It is impossible to have a thought and not have your physical being respond on some level. Change your thoughts, and you change the reality.

4. *The mind wants you to add credibility to your thoughts.*

   Since your mind moves in the direction of its dominant thoughts, it can only respond to the things that you think about. It responds the quickest to things that you've already thought previously. Another way to look at it is to say that what you seek, you'll surely find. If you think the whole world's rotten, then you'll focus your thoughts on death and destruction in the universe. Conversely, if you believe that some good lies in all of us, then you'll immediately see the good in us all.

5. *Imagination is the key.*

   Albert Einstein said that imagination, not knowledge, is powerful.

What he meant is that if you believe something, then that is your reality. If you think that everybody is trying to use you, then you relate to and, more important, treat the world like everyone's trying to use you.

As black women, there is some foundational programming that you may have fallen prey to. We have a picture of who we are that has been painted by the media, our families and history. As an entrepreneur you have to decide which of those messages will propel you to greatness and conversely which habits and beliefs to stay away from. Here are ten mind traps you should be aware of.

1. *I wasn't raised to be a (fill in the blank).*
    A friend once told me that the reason she was an ineffective communicator was because her family didn't talk much when she was growing up. "In my family, if we talked it meant things had gotten really bad." I looked at my friend who had obviously bought right into this excuse and said, "Well, it's time to stop blaming your upbringing for your communication deficiencies." My friend agreed and got ready to offer yet another excuse. "Yeah, but . . ." No buts, ya'll, just assume responsibility for yourself.
2. *My parents didn't (fill in the blank).*
    We're all products of somebody, somewhere, who didn't give us the love, attention and nourishment we believe we needed. That's a given, but what's stopping you from getting the love you need NOW? Stop blaming your mother, father, sister, brother, cousins, boyfriend, girlfriend, manager or slavery for what you haven't become. If you haven't become it, it's because you haven't wanted it . . . until now.
3. *It's not my fault, so it's not my responsibility.*
    The world wants you to blame everybody else because it keeps you out of action—one less black woman to compete with. We've all shrugged responsibility onto other people. My favorite story involves my younger brother who got a speeding ticket. He called the judge to arrange to handle the ticket. When the judge didn't return his call he replied, "It's not my fault, they didn't return my call!" Can you believe that? I laughed so hard. He really believed that once he made the initial effort it was no longer his responsibility.
4. *They'll never let a black woman . . .*
    You're right. Nobody *lets* you do anything, you have to take what's yours. Nobody wanted Madam C. J. Walker to become the first black self-made millionaire, but she did it anyway!
5. *If only I were (fill in the blank)*
    What, taller? Thinner? Smarter? Please! You have all the tools to be whatever you desire. There have been sisters before you who had less

talent, fewer opportunities and definitely fewer resources, who made big splashes. Stop giving yourself permission to stay out of action. There's nothing to it but to do it. Ask Rosa Parks.

6. *But I don't have enough money.*

   Money, schmoney! Did Harriet Tubman fret over her financial deficiencies when she devised a brilliant plan to lead thousands of slaves to freedom? I doubt it. Stop shopping till you drop, and you'll have plenty of money to launch your business.

7. *But what if I don't make it?*

   You'll have plenty of company because there are a lot of sisters who've fallen into the "I'm too chicken to make it happen" syndrome. If you set out to do something you *will* make it. Progress is relative. If you don't reach your destination the first time, dust your little self off and go for it again!

8. *But it's still a man's world.*

   There's a notecard in my desk drawer that reads, **"It's MY world!"** I look at it every morning and smile. If you think it's a man's, white man's, blue woman's, skinny woman's world, you won't be motivated to go after all the riches and wonders available to you. When it's *your* world you not only go for it, you expect to get it!

9. *I'll lose friends and family if I become successful.*

   Sounds strange but there are black women who won't take flight because they think they'll forget who they are (whatever that means!) or where they came from (I never understood this either). I've discovered that black folks use these phrases whenever we want to knock people down a few notches or when we, ourselves, are afraid of success. Don't be afraid to leave the cotton fields. Trust me, entrepreneurship affords you more opportunity to help other black folks. Of all the things I've forgotten, who I am is not one of them.

10. *All good things must end.*

    Says who? All things must *change,* yes. But end? I don't think so. I have every intention of riding the crest of the entrepreneurial wave for a long, long time—how about you?

Choosing Your Own Belief System

You are ultimately responsible for your beliefs. You choose what you believe, period. Yes, our parents, siblings, friends and teachers have all given us tons of messages, some even conflicting. However, ultimately *you* decide what to believe. Why is developing a positive belief system so important? Because it determines whether you fly or fizzle. Plus, once you can steer your thoughts and beliefs in the direction of power and productivity, you are on your way to creating an incredibly successful business and life!

Take a look at this model and see if there's anything you can do about your current belief systems.

Experience ⇨ Thought ⇨ Validation ⇨ Belief ⇨ Habit ⇨ Life

Can you see where you fit into the model? Everything from the experiences you have right to the habits you form can be influenced by you. However, there are some things you have no control over. For instance, you can't stop someone from cutting you off on the highway, but you can definitely affect how you *respond* to the experience and the beliefs you form thereafter. Take this example of forming a negative belief.

Someone says that you are stupid. You think about it. What do I know about stupidity? It means that I'm not very smart. Well, I did make a D on my last exam, and I did forget to sign my check in the grocery store last week. Okay, I believe it. Now, since I'm stupid, I should probably act accordingly. I will now live my life as a stupid person.

An extreme example? Not really. This is exactly how we develop our belief systems. Can't you see how easy it is to control the variables in that equation?

Breaking Habits

While we're on the subject of habit breaking, what habits do you currently have that could possibly impede your entrepreneurial success? Right now, make a list of the bad habits you have (that you are aware of) that have caused you problems in the past or could possibly hurt your chances of excelling.

Habit   **How It Kills My Business**

1. _____   _____
2. _____   _____
3. _____   _____
4. _____   _____

Subconscious Reprogramming

Subconscious reprogramming is not a new concept. It's simply assessing your old thought patterns to see if they are capable of delivering the results you want for your life and, if they are not, then you must reprogram your old conditioning to net you more positive results. Also, understand that every thought you have creates a correlating response in your body. Since most of your foundational programming was done by the time you were six years old, it was more than likely programmed by someone other than yourself. You were given your earliest messages by your parents, siblings, teachers and friends. Since it's impossible to redo the past, the question you must ask is, "How can I leverage what happened to me as a child, now?" It doesn't matter how horrific your beginning, you can still have a successful life.

As a Sister Thinketh and Speaketh, So She Is

Okay, so I adapted the scripture a little but you get my point—if you think it and *act upon it as though it were true,* it becomes true for you. That's why we're going to check your language. Are you enrolled in SuccesSpeak or NegaSpeak? Your language, the words you use tell who you are. Are most of the words in your vocabulary empowering or disempowering? If you are filling your head with empowering thoughts, great, keep up the good work. If you're gassing up on words that ultimately tear you down, you should replace them with words that build you up and inspire greatness. Where are you on the SuccesSpeak scale of one to ten? Take the short quiz and see.

When someone compliments you, which is closest to how you'd probably respond?
(1) Thank you.
(2) Oh, this old thing, I haven't worn it in ages. I was too fat to get into it last year.

When you see or hear a successful person do you
(1) applaud them for their efforts in your thoughts or by your actions?
(2) find a way to discredit them by making a comment disguised as a joke (by the way, we don't think you're joking, we know you mean it)?
(3) say nothing, which in itself is a reaction?

When you make a mistake, do you
(1) berate yourself with words like "I'm so stupid" and "I'm such an idiot?"
(2) say, "I'll get it the next time?"

Physical Fitness

Any thought you hold hostage in your subconscious mind will manifest itself physically. Since your body is an important part of this journey, you can't afford to let it go. I'll remind you again. You are an athlete. Athletes treat their bodies as temples. You must commit to a fitness plan. That means take it easy on the hoagies, fajitas and burgers, they'll slow you down in the race. That means get your body up and out and get to the gym or the hike and bike trail or the track or whatever you do to get your heart rate up for at least forty-five minutes a day. I'm serious. You hurt your chances of winning this race when you come to the gym out of shape. Why do you need to get in shape? Because at first you will be working your tail off to get this business going, off the ground and into the air. All of that takes energy. Tons of energy. It takes time to run a business. At times you'll need to rise early and stay up late. You'll have to increase your productivity hours. Even starting out part-time requires good physical conditioning.

What happens when you're not in shape?

Black women have the highest rate of death before age fifty. We die more from hypertension than any other group. More than 50 percent of us are overweight. Wake up, girlfriends, it's time to get serious about our health and fitness plans, especially if you're considering entrepreneurship. You will never be the business success you can be unless you commit to get fit. Listen carefully, I'm admonishing that you get fit. Fit means in a physical condition that allows you to fully maximize your physical and emotional well-being. It means a combination of exercise, healthy food choices and a balanced lifestyle. Let's start with working out. You say, "I don't work out and I'm doing just fine." You probably are doing just fine. But are you winning? Are you putting your previous year's business sales to shame? Not if you're huffing and puffing after you climb that flight of stairs. You're lagging behind in the race, and your business is suffering. Plus, when you're out of shape you become tired and sick quicker than normal. The only person you're fooling is yourself, but let me tell you, you're not fooling your body. It's the first to know that you're stressed mentally. If you're in shape, it hangs in there with you. It goes the distance for you. If you're not physically fit, you'll have a difficult time handling the rigors of entrepreneurship.

While we're on the subject of eating: Most nutritionists recommend eating five to six meals a day, not three squares as we've been taught for ages. That does not mean five or six full-course, meat-and-trimmings meals. An apple is considered a meal. A glass of juice is too. It's possible to actually increase your calories and lose weight. I have a high-calorie shake every morning, a mid-morning snack, a salad or light lunch, another piece of fruit, a mid-afternoon snack and a light dinner. And I'm rarely hungry. I try to stay away from what nutritionists call empty calories—sweets and fat (although I do love creme-filled chocolate chip cookies!). The point is, you need the calories for the energy but the fat makes you seem as though you're running in sand. So, remember, eat low-fat, energy foods, and you'll have the fuel you need to win the race.

Your Spiritual and Psychological Well-Being

Most successful African American women attribute their success to a connection with a higher being, God, Allah and the like. Sometimes you'll need to tap into that spiritual reservoir for inspiration to run on. I recommend some form of meditation for anyone on the entrepreneurial trail. It helps to keep you focused and nourished emotionally. Yoga and tai chi are excellent choices if you like meditative and focus regimes. Running does the same for me.

> *If love is the answer, can you please rephrase the question?*
> —*Lily Tomlin*

Your Emotional Well-Being
It's time for some tough love. If you're carrying around some heavy emotional luggage—a malfunctioning, dysfunctioning or ill-functioning relationship—it's time to drop it. Drop kick it once and for all. I can't tell you how many sisters I meet who are lugging this trunk of old hurts and pains around with them! Can't you see what it's doing to you? You have no energy. You're moodier than normal. You're always negative. You know that you need to let it go but you don't. It's warm and fuzzy and, sometimes, cute. But it leaves its shorts in the middle of the floor constantly. To let it go means that you've failed, that you're less than, right? Wrong. To let it go means that you've triumphed, that you love yourself.

Black women have historically carried the emotional weight in relationships. Not just romantic ones either. When there's a problem in the family, how often do we hang out at home for periods of time, never getting out of bed, not eating and basically just quitting? How often do you see your brother lying awake at night, losing sleep over something that neither one of you can change anyway? You don't. How many times have you lost weight after a breakup or when things just weren't right? So, if there's something going on with you right now, please postpone starting your business. The last thing you need is the stress of running a business on top of your emotional distress.

Emotional issues don't have to center around relationships. If you're not feeling like *you're* your best, you can't possibly give your best to your business. If you've just gone on your thirtieth diet, you don't need the pressures of business weighing you down too. If you've just lost a good friend or loved one, you'll never have the focus to launch a successful enterprise. So, don't do it. Running a business requires confidence, savvy and persistence. If you don't feel good about who you are, your enterprise will reflect your emotional state. It will be a weak, anemic vessel in need of nourishment that you can't provide.

MORE MIND GAMES

I want you to go through this exercise I use in my consulting practice to show you just what you're considering getting yourself into. I want you to list all of the words, phrases and comments that *other* people use when they think of women. Do the same for black people.

What Other People Say About Women **About Blacks**

_____ _____
_____ _____
_____ _____
_____ _____

Now, look at your lists. Combine the two lists and you have the perception the general population has of you as the black female entrepreneur. What's your reaction? Disgust? Anger? Disbelief? Do you care? Your reaction is not as important as your understanding that people don't think you're cut out to do this, which is fine as long as *you* believe you're cut out for it. More important, the outside world—and some of the black world—may try everything to sabotage your efforts. Can you honestly say that you're up for that kind of opposition? Can you weather the storms of racism and sexism? Lookism, classism and other isms? Now, take the same exercise and add a different twist to it. How do *you* feel about women and black people?

What *I* think about women **What *I* think about black people**

_____ _____
_____ _____
_____ _____

Now, look at this list. What does it say about what you're doing to help your business enterprise? Do you have a positive or negative self-image? Do you have self-limiting beliefs about yourself and black people? Women? How different are your own beliefs from others' beliefs and perceptions of you? Have you bought into society's portrait of who you are? If so, how do you change those self-defeatist attitudes? Few of us have escaped the effects of racist and sexist remarks. Imagine how difficult it was for our ancestors to keep it together, to raise strong, vibrant children who felt good about who they are. Sadly, as we approach the twenty-first century, we are still trying to heal those wounds.

The Color of Success

The issue of skin color within the black race is the most notable, though hardly the only evidence that we haven't overcome. I am the daughter of a mother who was very vanilla, particularly when she was a young woman, and a father who is Dutch chocolate. My mother was a beautiful woman, and my father is still as handsome as the man who stood next to my mother on their wedding day. My mother's side of the family runs more in the butterscotch and caramel family, and my father's side, without question, cocoa and rich chocolate. In my family, I was never subjected to comments about being light-skinned and dark-skinned and the advantages or disadvantages of either. My mother called me her Chocolate Princess, so being milk chocolate (definitely Dutch in the summertime) was never a bad thing to me. So I don't identify with the madness that I sometimes hear from our sisters and brothers.

In fact, I had to put a couple of people in check in a recent conversation, in which the individuals said that they would never date a man or woman who was "black," "can't have no black man," this sister said. I just looked at her. "What? I don't have much to add to this conversation about self-hatred," I added. Of course all five or so people tried to convince me that it wasn't about self-hatred, and I maintained that it was. Otherwise, how can you say that you would deny a member of your lineage the opportunity to love and adore you? I reminded them that in all of us black folks there is someone, somewhere in our blood line who was as dark as the night, and we ought to be eternally grateful that he or she made the journey to America safely. I refuse to deny that that individual, along with my Native American and other ancestors, is a part of me. We ought to be honoring our people instead of buying into this old slavery nonsense about pigmentation. If you think that your entrepreneurial race will be made any better or worse because of your skin tone, think again. White America does not care where you fall on the color spectrum.

In business, it's important to feel good about who you are and what you look like. Understand that color is one of the most beautiful things about our people. Don't be naive enough to think that in business one shade is better than the other. I'm not naive enough to think that negative self-images are not impeding our progress as businesswomen.

The Power of Empowerment

Everything we've talked about so far has to do with how empowered you are. Empowerment is a critical element in business success. Let's do a survey on how empowered you feel today, this minute. Place the appropriate letter or letters next to the statement. SD = strongly disagree, D = disagree, A = agree, SA = strongly agree.

- You consider yourself self-reliant.
- You're comfortable making decisions without the help of friends and family.

- You believe that women's intellect equals or exceeds men's.
- You believe that light-skinned blacks are more attractive than brown-skinned blacks.
- You would go to a party, networking or business function alone.
- You would walk up to a superstar and introduce yourself.
- You believe that you control your destiny.
- You're a risk taker.

Now, score it: SD = 1, D = 2, A = 3, SA = 4.
If you scored between 8–12, you haven't yet tapped into your entrepreneurial powers.
If you scored between 13–18, you're starting to understand the power that you have.
If you scored between 19–24, you're in good shape—proceed.
If you scored between 25–32, you flow, girl!

I recently attended a women's meeting where the facilitator gave us a similar empowerment tool. We were supposed to discuss our scores with our group. The general sentiment among the women in my group was that if you scored too high on the positive side you were out of touch, not being honest. Why? Do women have so little esteem? Why do women tear other women down constantly? Why do women think a well-adjusted (not perfect), empowered sister is "out there?" It's simple. We don't hold ourselves in the highest esteem. We think we're *all* screwed up. Well, I'm here to tell you we're NOT! Thinking highly of yourself is always an asset so don't believe the hype.

The Night Time Used to Be the Right Time

We need to talk about your social life. Your night life is going to have to take a breather when you start this business. No more all nighters. No more staying out until 3:00 A.M. and sleeping until noon. No more calling in sick when you're actually just hungover. You're going to have to raise your standards and your social life may suffer in the short term. Believe me, it's well worth it.

When I was in my plush, safe Fortune 500 position, I played golf two, sometimes three times a week! I ate out whenever I wanted. I shopped until I dropped—dead! I traveled at least once every two months. Cruises, parties, you name it, I was doing it. Yes, it was a big adjustment to give up nearly all of that. I cut back, *way* back on my golf outings. I took one major trip last year. I bought *In the Kitchen with Rosie*. And I learned how to truly budget. Before I just *thought* I was budgeting. Heck, I even considered relaxing my own hair! (I decided that was probably going a bit too far.) I at least wanted to look good even if I was poor. Fortunately, I had enough clothes to never look at another catalog or go to a department store again. I didn't need to strap myself to *look* professional.

Am I making entrepreneurship attractive yet? Let's see. I've told you that you can't go out, you can't eat out and you've gotta work out. By now you're either thinking that your job is looking mo' better or you're fired up and ready for the challenge of being on your own.

Why Are You Doing This?

What in the world would possess you to do this? Didn't you know that one out of every two small businesses fail? Black women more than anyone else must learn to tell the story. Because you will be challenged by friends, family, bankers, investors and other critics. Over and over again you must tell yourself why this is the best thing for you. Sometimes you will be the only person in your corner, so you must be clear about your purpose.

> *Two frogs fell into a bucket of cream. One of them thought it was hopeless to get out because she couldn't reach the top by jumping. She gave up and drowned in the cream. The other frog, even though it felt uncomfortable and like she wasn't making any progress initially, kept jumping up and down in the cream. Pretty soon the cream turned to butter, which gave her the base from which to jump out of the bucket and save her life.*

Keep jumping, even if it feels awkward. Eventually you'll make it.

I had a frog experience about two years ago when I started playing golf. I would swing at the ball and totally miss it. For nearly three months I swung and only made contact with the air. I kept working on my swing, my footwork, my follow through. I knew one day I was going to send that baby out of the park (oh that's baseball—but you get my point). Finally, one fine day I teed up and connected with the ball. It was such a beautiful sight and an even more wonderful feeling. So keep swinging, you'll get a hit.

Is Your Family Ready for the Ride?

Deciding to go into business will affect everyone in your life, so your significant and insignificant others will need to be ready. Have you discussed your dreams with your spouse or mate? Do they seem enthusiastic and supportive or are they simply being negative and skeptical? Black women have always put themselves on the back burner when it came to business. If your friends, lovers and family members can't get behind you, get rid of them.

Yes, fire them—at least until you are up and running strong. Now, you may be thinking, yeah, right, is that what you did, Fran? Actually, yes.

I had to make some choices when I was training for the Olympics and one of them was to be emotionally available—to pour everything into this goal. Surprisingly, my close friends supported me 100 percent and showered me with care packages and letters while I was away training in Italy. So I know you can do it. Handling loved ones takes skill and care.

How do you explain to your girls that you can't do the happy-hour thing every single weekday, that you've got some research to do on your enterprise? One recommendation is to call all your folk together at one time if possible, perhaps in a press conference style. Announce your plans, explain how important this dream is to you and tell them that you would appreciate their support, but that if they are not going to provide positive reinforcement and constructive feedback then your interaction with them *must* be limited.

I told one friend who was just so negative that I could only afford to talk with her once a week in her current (negative) state. She laughed and thought I was joking, until I didn't call or return her call until a week later. She soon discovered how serious I was. Guess what? She was miraculously inspired to be more positive and we resumed our regular communication. Sound extreme? If it does, you may not be ready for this ride. Depending on your style, people are going to look at you one of two ways: (1) in complete disbelief or (2) in complete support. As crazy as I can be, my folks knew I was serious. They've seen me work on a project. I got 90 percent support, and the other 10 percent has slowly joined the bandwagon and are now staunch supporters.

You must be willing to be unpopular, even talked about. Are you willing to endure that kind of abuse? Yes, abuse. People may tell you that you will never make it and will give you a grocery list of reasons why you will fail. Can you hang under those conditions? If not, hold on to your nine-to-five blanket because entrepreneurship will eat you alive.

How Bad Do You Want It?

Remember in the movie *An Officer and a Gentleman* when Richard Gere's character, Mayo, had gotten caught cheating in basic training? What did Lou Gossett's character do? He taught Mayo a lesson—he challenged his commitment to the Corps. He hosed him with water, made him do a zillion pushups, and kept asking Mayo for his D.O.R. (dismissal on request). Mayo kept saying, "I ain't gonna quit, I ain't gonna quit," right? Each time Mayo said this, the sergeant kept saying, "I wantcha D.O.R. I wantcha D.O.R." The sergeant tried everything in his powers to break Mayo. He talked about the boy's mother (I loved how he said, "I know aboutcha Mama"), and his delinquent background. If you saw the movie, you know that Mayo endured all of the sergeant's lessons and was allowed to stay in the marines.

You have to be like Mayo. You must believe and want this business to succeed so badly that you're willing to endure any form of humiliation and pain. You must subscribe to a "no surrender" policy. Remember, the road blocks that you'll face are simply nature's way of asking you, "How badly do you want it?"

Wanna Get Rich Quick?

While I'm the last person to throw a wet blanket on literally any enthusiastic would-be black female entrepreneur, the simple fact is that not many people are overnight successes. The real truth is that most entrepreneurs barely make it during that first year. They're not in it for the immediate financial payoff because smart entrepreneurs understand that, with sound business ideas and with persistence, eventually they'll turn a big profit.

GEARING UP FOR BUSINESS

One way to decide which business to go in to is to do a self-evaluation inventory. What are your strengths, what do you enjoy doing? Through this next exercise you may discover that you could start two, maybe three, different businesses or one big business with several twists.

What's in a Name?

Mucho. In fact, if I were you, I'd think carefully about what you will call your business. Some people get real creative when they select their names, and that's fine. Remember, people like and respond to the simple—not ordinary—but simple. Then there's another school of thought that says the catchier the better. Some people go with their own names in the business name or children's names or combinations. It's really up to you.

Selecting Your Name

How about a little word association. Look at this list of names and make note of what comes to mind when you read them.

Alisa Communications Do you know what kind of company this is? It could be long distance services, speaking, training, writing or twenty other things.
>Advantages: If your name is Alisa it gets people to remember that. It tells you what general industry you're in.
>Disadvantages: It doesn't tell the consumer what you do specifically.

A-1 Lawn Service
    Advantages: It tells you what they do. A-1 connotes top service.
    Disadvantages: Too ordinary and easy to copy or make derivatives.

Tachikariani Inc.
    Advantages: I can't find any.
    Disadvantages: Difficult to pronounce and doesn't tell you what they
    do.

I think you get the point. You must decide how you want your business' image portrayed through its name.

What Makes You Tick?

Most of us have skills, talent and potential that we never use or tap into. Unfortunately, we wait until we are too UNmotivated to do something about them. The purpose of this exercise is to help you tap into the talents that hide in your garden. On a scale of 1–10, rate your skill level for each talent listed on the next page and total your points to the right. Let's evaluate the entrepreneurial potential of each.

Level of Interest

It sounds stupid to ask you if you're interested in something, but you wouldn't believe how many people are in business because (1) a family member got them involved, (2) it sounded like a good idea at the time or (3) because people need (fill in the blank). Perhaps the biggest reason to go into business is because *you're* interested in that field. Never, never, go into a business situation hoping that you'll eventually be interested in it.

Personal Strength

It wouldn't be a real good idea to go into a business situation unless you were good at something. No matter how much I love listening to jazz, I would never attempt to try to teach people to play the saxophone. What I *could* do is handle the marketing and selling of a "Learn How to Play the Saxophone" seminar, because marketing and sales are two of my strengths. I'd need to hire the teacher but producing the seminars would allow me to maximize my strengths with something that greatly interests me.

Entrepreneurial Inventory				
	Level of Interest	Personal Strength	Market Need	Total Points
Skills				
writing				
math				
cooking				
speaking				
languages				
other				
Writing				
word processing				
proofreading/editing				
poetry				
technical				
manuals				
books				
publishing				
newsletters				
other				
Artistic				
painting				
photography				
prints				
sculpture				
watercolors				
other				
Performing Arts				
acting				
dance				
film				
singing				
Repair Services				
furniture				
plumbing				
appliances				
auto				
mechanical				
electrical				
Retail				
clothes				
shoes				
furniture				

	Level of Interest	Personal Strength	Market Need	Total Points
Decorating walls painting carpeting wall art				
Planning conferences meetings events				
Personal Services house cleaning catering image consulting secretarial personal assistant baby-sitting				
Crafts ceramics needlework glass jewelry design				
Communication public speaking debating training seminars interpreting your ideas				

Scoring: Use the scoring grid below to give you the 411 on where you might consider starting a business. If the total points for one skill/talent is:

0–10	Don't even think about it.
11–15	Maybe, but think about it some more.
16–20	Worth looking into.
21–25	Probably a winner.
26 and higher	Go for it, girl!

This checklist should give you a good idea of the type of business best suited for you and why. If you've scored 26+ in several areas you must decide which potential business area you are *committed* to putting your best effort into. You don't want to be a jack of many trades and queen of none!

Market Need

This is the key. Why? Because if there's no market for what you're selling, how are you going to make money at it? You can actually love something to death but, unless there's a consumer need and want, you have no business. In fact, even though you may feel confident that there's a market for your product or service based on feedback from friends and relatives, it's always a good strategy to test your ideas.

How Do You Test Market Your Ideas?

Easy. An example of an effective test market for a chef who's considering starting a catering business may be to cook several entrees and invite several friends over for a smorgasbord. Rather than just letting everybody eat until they explode, the chef provides samples in a systematic fashion, asking each person for specific feedback on the dish. If people are ooohing and ahhhing over everything you give them, you probably have a viable business idea.

What Business Are You In?

> One day Hank Aaron stepped to the plate to bat. He got the bat ready to swing and just as he was gearing to send that baby outta the ballpark, a voice from behind said, "Turn the bat so that the brand is facing you." Hank never lost focus of the outfield, instead he calmly said, "Didn't come up here to read . . . came to hit."

Hank teaches us a valuable lesson about business. *Know what you came to do.* He teaches us that if you don't know what you've come to do, you can be easily distracted.

Do you know what business you're in? Is it selling gift baskets at Christmas or selling goodwill? Take some time answering this question, it is the most important one you'll ever answer.

Do Something Daring

Deciding to go into business is daring enough, but now let's add something real challenging. Think of three women in your community whom you don't know, but who might be interesting to talk to. Call and invite all three of them to lunch—not at one time—separately. Tell these women that you are going to start your own business and you would like to visit with them about it, and about what's going on in the business community and with their businesses. Please, please don't say, "let's do lunch" or "I just wanna pick your brain." These phrases are stale, overused, overdone, completely cliched, plus, they make you sound anything but fresh and original. So for your sake, don't use them.

SETTING UP YOUR BUSINESS

Now that you've decided you're going into business, your organizational structure is the next thing you must decide. Will you be a corporation, sole proprietor or partnership? Before you settle on a choice it's very important to understand the ins and outs of each structure as well as the legal issues.

Sole Proprietor

The sole proprietorship is defined as a business that is owned and operated by one person. To start a sole proprietorship, you only need to obtain a license or business certificate to begin operations.

Advantages
Easy to form. There are fewer legal restrictions associated with establishing a sole proprietorship. It needs little or no governmental intervention and is usually less expensive than a corporation or partnership.

Disadvantages
Unlimited liability. The individual proprietor is responsible for the full amount of business debt, which may exceed the proprietor's total investment. This liability extends to all the proprietor's assets, such as your house and car. Additional liability problems, including physical loss or personal injury, may be lessened by obtaining proper insurance coverage. If you die or become disabled, your enterprise may be terminated.

Potential Financing or Investors
As a sole proprietor you generally have less access to long-term financing. Once you begin as a sole proprietor can you change? Absolutely. Sometimes people choose this structure to start out and as they grow, they change.

The Partnership

A partnership is an association of two or more persons to carry on as co-owners of a business for profit.

The *silent partner* is inactive in the business dealings but has usually made a financial contribution to the company.

The *active partner* is involved in the business on some level, perhaps in management decisions.

Advantages
Compared to a corporation, it's easy to form. There are few legal formalities.

Disadvantages
Liability Unlimited liability of at least one partner. Insurance considerations, such as those mentioned in the proprietorship section, may be necessary.

Uncertainty Elimination of a partner constitutes automatic dissolution of partnership. However, operation of business can continue based on the right of the survivorship and possible creation of a new partnership.

Financing It could be difficult to get financing. However, by using individual partners' assets, opportunities are greater than in sole proprietorship.

Corporation

The corporation is by far the most complex of the three business structures. For our purposes we shall discuss only the general characteristics of the corporation, not all of its intricacies.

A corporation is usually formed under the authority of a state government. Corporations that do business in more than one state must comply with the federal government.

Advantages
Limitations of stockholders' liability to a fixed amount of investment. Ownership is transferable.

Stability If you die, the corporation continues to do business.

Financing It's easier to secure money from banks and investors as a corporation. You can take advantage of corporate assets and personal assets of stockholders and principals of guarantors.

Disadvantages
It costs several hundred dollars to start a corporation, including attorney's fees—meetings, phone calls, etc.

PART TWO

❖ ❖ ❖

Get Ready

Leslie's Story

Sisters,

I can still hear my mother's reaction—"You're going to quit your job and start a consulting business? Can't you just get another job?" So in 1988 I started my journey—one that would require two paths. One, to convince my mother I had not lost my marbles and a second path to chart a successful business.

To say it's been quite a journey is putting things mildly. I spent my first year in business attempting to decide what areas to specialize in. Since my background was in academia, human resources and management, I decided to tackle a little bit of each area. Three times a month I coordinated job fairs for companies. On Tuesday and Thursday evenings, I taught a class on communication skills. Career counseling and career workshops were scheduled on Mondays and Fridays. I spent three to four evenings a week forwarding marketing materials to solicit business from government agencies and private sector proposals. I felt busy! I looked busy! Yet my bank account was not busy! As a result, I continuously turned to part-time employment to make ends meet.

An analysis of my first year in business revealed that I had:

- worked 208 days of fourteen-to-sixteen hour days
- received 355 rejections for my services
- attended 117 networking breakfasts, lunches and dinners
- maintained 300 days of bank balances below $100
- consumed 233 meals of tuna casserole
- earned $140.

After all of my good intentions, I was broke, disillusioned, frustrated, disappointed and ready for a REAL JOB! I gave myself ninety days to regroup, refocus and redirect. I closed my office (which I was never in), turned off the telephone, returned borrowed furniture and hid from creditors. I'd decided to start from scratch and found my way to a conference on starting a business.

One of the seminar speakers was a former classmate of mine from Howard University. Ron, who was always candid, told me in one breath how bad I looked and that he was sure he could help me. I didn't know whether to smack him or hug him. I did neither. Ron, with all of his candor, has become an expert on helping small businesses survive. I walked away from that conference knowing I was going to see Ron again!

Thanks to Ron, my business resurrected as Career Tailors, Career and Employment Specialists. My first major contact came ninety days after Ron and I made contact. Alas! My journey was not going to come to a dead end! My advice to you? Listen to the Rons of the world and be ready to take two steps backwards in order to take two steps forward. And most important, work Sister, work!

Leslie Shields, President
Coauthor, Work, Sister, Work!

UNLOCKING YOUR PASSION

Yes, being in business for yourself is sexy but, for now, let's move from the bedroom into the boardroom! Passion about your work is a beautiful thing to see and feel. How does one have passion? First you must love, absolutely love, your business. Someone once said of me that "she does a great job, she just doesn't seem passionate about the work." He was right, I wasn't passionate about selling toothpaste and it showed. Yes, it is possible to do good work when you aren't passionate, but the quality of output is far superior when you have passion for your work.

CLEAN UP YOUR LANGUAGE, WOMAN!

I'm not talking about those choice words you may use sometimes, although it probably wouldn't kill you to give up a few of those. I'm talking about our internal and external conversations. This is the first step you must take toward successful entrepreneurship. Your self-talk—the conversations you have with yourself on a daily, minute-by-minute basis—must be overwhelmingly positive and empowering. First there are four words you must erase from your vocabulary.

If

When your subconscious hears *if* remember what happens? It immediately creates a psychosomatic response. *If* means that there's doubt in your mind that something will happen. If you doubt it, you don't put it into the universe with the force essential to making it happen. *If* doesn't exist (*if* I lose my job, *if* I get AIDS, *if* I ever get in a good relationship). All of these things are not real and you can only deal with what is real today, right now. Remember also that if we want to train the subconscious mind to think a certain way we must replace the previous thought with another one. Your replacement word in this case is *when*. *When* I win the lottery (and I have gotten five of six correct in a $22 million pot!) I am going to take about five cruises! *When* signals the subconscious mind that you are doing something, that you are in motion.

Try

The next word to totally erase from your vocabulary is *try*. I heard a speaker say once that there's no such thing as trying, you're either doing it or you're not. People say, "I'm trying to quit smoking." Boloney! You're not trying to quit smoking, you're smoking! The other one is "I'm trying to lose weight." No you're not, you're either making healthy food selections, which is resulting in a positive change in your weight or you're not.

Can't

Can't is the third largest killer of would-be black women entrepreneurs. *Can't* means that you want to do something but you don't know how. When my sister asks her daughter to do something that seems too challenging, Miki says, "I cannnnn't" when what she really means is that she's not willing to do it. If you don't know how to do something and that lack of skill or experience prevents you from doing it, that doesn't mean you *can't*. What you need to do is get the necessary skills *or* courage to do it.

Hope

The fourth largest killer phrase is I *hope*. Cousins of it include *hopeful* and *hopefully*. *Hopeful* shows insecurity rather than optimism as we'd like to believe. We say, "I *hope* I get a raise" or "I *hope* this relationship works out." When we say this, we subconsciously put our fate into someone else's hands; we behave as though we have nothing to do with how it turns out. If you want a raise, blow your previous numbers out of the water. If you want your relationship to pan out, select a suitable mate and then invest in open, honest communication. Those things won't guarantee a successful relationship; however, they do put you in a position to at least get the information you need to make an intelligent decision.

Let's test your internal conversation patterns right now.

When you're faced with a challenge that seems impossible, say, making it home by 5:15 P.M. when you're stuck in traffic on the freeway, what are you most likely to say or do?

a. (Choice word)! I'm never going to get home by 5:15.
b. Smile and put your favorite music in the deck and relax until the traffic dies down.
c. Panic, swerve and curve to try to get somewhere and then get frustrated because the lane from which you moved started to make significant progress.

If you chose a or c, you need to fine-tune your internal dialogue, because it's probably immobilizing you. Black women in particular have been feeding themselves and other black women negative conversations for centuries, and it's time to bring it to a screeching halt. We are literally committing personal and professional suicide with our *own voices*.

CREATING A HEALTHY INTERNAL CONVERSATION ABOUT OTHER BLACK WOMEN

Don't hate me because I'm beautiful or tall or cute or smart or fit or outgoing or savvy or sassy or ambitious or risky or successful or thin or fine or determined or shapely or confident or light-complexioned or brown-complexioned or unflappable or gorgeous or whatever. You get the picture. We've shown so much hate and contempt for our sisters who, well, have something we want or wish we had. There's no other way to slice it. You're jealous of the sister about whom you seem to always have a comment. We deny up and down that we're jealous. So just what are you saying when you say things such as "she's so stuck up" or "she thinks she's all that" or "she's too skinny" or as a friend told me when we were on our way to work out, "why don't you put on some clothes, you're just showing off your body." My reply? "You're damn right! Sometimes it's my best work, don't you like to show off your best work?"

Let's start building each other up and stop tearing each other down. There are enough forces out there on *that* job. Positive energy is a magnificent power source, yet most black women I know are filled with self-condemning comments and attitudes, not only about themselves, but other black women as well. You see, it's impossible to have healthy, positive, esteeming thoughts about another black woman when you don't have those sentiments about yourself. We are all the same. If I make a negative comment about someone, 99 percent of the time I am having some negative, internal struggle or I'm not feeling as though I'm the best me at the time. You know what? When I'm feeling on top of the world, I see everything in a more positive light. I've spent the last thirteen years of my life understanding and practicing this thing called empowerment. The good news is that it works! The other good news is that it keeps getting better. I believe there's plenty of room to grow. This journey just keeps on getting better.

EMPOWERMENT . . . WHAT'S ALL THE FUSS ABOUT?

Black empowerment actually started when our people first came over. Since that fateful day a great majority of blacks have searched and found ways to keep improving the quality of our lives. It's not difficult to trace our roots of self-empowerment. Our most recent examples are the political activism of the 60s and the consciousness-raising efforts our people spearheaded in the 70s. We continue to find ways to further define who we are and what it means to be black women in this country. So, yes, I'm a huge fan of self-development, thus self-empowerment. Some people fight the term self-improvement because it implies something's wrong with the way we are. Call it whatever suits you. Self-enhancement has a 90s flavor, feel free to borrow it. Black women must be about something that makes us get off our behinds to look in the mirror and not only commit to making ourselves stronger, viable humans but also make the world a better place for those we love and those yet to come. That's what self-empowerment can do. Inspire nations. Breed greatness. Change attitudes.

THE POWER OF POSITIVE JUICES

Everything is energy. Reading this book produces an energy. When you're driving your car, you're emitting energy. When you're arguing with a sibling or friend, you're throwing out energy. More and more we realize that this journey we call life is more of a spiritual journey than a human one. We encounter all kinds of spirits throughout our daily lives. The spirit of love. Hate. Joy and pain. Sadness and gladness. Theologists continue to argue about which forces, spirits are more powerful. I believe that the forces of good always prevail. Naive? Hardly. I've never seen evil prevail—in the long term. We've seen the effects of negative energy in our sororities, families, relationships and at work. Why do these people appear to be winning? Because sometimes the positive folks are too quiet. Sometimes, not always. Sometimes we just let things take their course. When what we should do is exhibit the good, good spirits that exist in all of us, every last one of us.

As black women, it's sometimes easy to lose control and allow our negative emotions and reactions to dominate our personalities. True, the world has been cruel to us. Eurocentric values passed on through our ancestors have made some of us second guess our intelligence and our beauty. We need to recognize that feeding ourselves positive messages will help us achieve incredible personal and professional wealth.

Would you believe me if I said that everything I touch turns into something good? It's true. This is not about egoism. Not at all. It's the strongest testament to the power of positive energy I have. When I set a goal, I'm completely confident that no matter how high the goal may seem, I will achieve it. Plus the instant that I set the specific goal, I also picture the desired outcome. I'll give you an example.

I started a new wellness and fitness program in which I wanted a certain percentage of lean muscle mass and body fat. I closed my eyes and pictured what my body would look like—inside and out—when I reached my goal. Inside I saw clean blood and healthy organs. I saw my heart pumping vigorously, my brain working like an enterprising factory. Outside I was buffed! Or chiseled, as my little brother would say. My abs were strong, which meant that my back was too. I no longer shifted all of my weight to the right side of my body to compensate for an old injury to my left knee. I had strengthened that left knee and it was as strong as my right. My dream was real. Tangible. I could feel it. See it. I had dreamed in color. It was a very vivid and vibrant portrait of a healthy body. This has been a truly effective way of having the life I want. When you set goals, be positive that you will achieve them. I ask you, are you empowering yourself or disempowering yourself? Check out this list and put a dot beside the statements that are closest to things that you are currently saying either to yourself or other people.

Empowering	**Disempowering**
I will have a great week at work!	What's going to go wrong this week?

I'm pleased with my fitness program.	I'm too fat—I need to work out more.
Carol, you sure look great!	That's a nice dress—a little short . . .
I'm going to land this account, I know it!	They won't give it to a sister.
I appreciate your feedback on my presentation.	Who asked for your opinion?
I will.	I can't.
Even if this situation is challenging, I'll give it a shot.	It's too hard, I'll never make it.
You can do it—I know you can!	I don't know why you're trying that.
Let me know how I can help.	I don't know everything, but I'll try.

I think you get the picture. There's a distinct communication pattern for empowered and disempowered black women. We haven't been trained to rattle off the left column so we have to retrain ourselves to be more positive with ourselves and other black women. When we emit positive energy everyone wins. If I feel good about me, I'm more inclined to have good feelings about you and what you're trying to accomplish.

I have a friend who was so miserable with her life that all she had was negative energy. She was not empowered, so I don't care how exciting my news was, she wasn't that excited about it. At first, I was really hurt by her response, and then I realized why she was so negative and unresponsive to all the good things I would share about my life. Her life was the dumps! Her job was completely draining her. Don't ever downplay the effect of a bad job situation. Think about it. We spend more than a third of our day involved in some way with our jobs. Anyway, I took this friend aside and had a little talk about her energy and offered some friendly suggestions for having the life she wanted. It started with her making a conscious effort to be more positive.

Don't always think the worst. I don't care how many people have died on you, how many lovers have abandoned you, how many times you've been fired, how many times you've been told you aren't attractive or smart, how many times people have insulted or ignored you. You can still be positive. At first it may seem corny or weird. Hang with it, it gets better and, more important, you start to see how different you feel as a result of it. Positive energy not only changes you, it changes those around you.

Remember my friend who was a big ball of negative mush? Well, today, I'm so proud of her, she's planning to leave her job to start her own enterprise. She is not the same woman I told to stop being so negative eighteen months ago. She's well on her way to creating her own empire, and it's because she changed her internal conversations. Yes!

Okay, you've made the decision for sure. Now what? Black women, we must take time to create a company image. This is one of the most important conversations you'll have with yourself. Image. Just what is it? Why is it so important? It's important because it's what people will think of when they think of you. It's important because black people have historically and generally not taken care in developing a solid image.

THE BUCK STARTS WITH YOU

First, I ask you to do another exercise called "Imagine Your Image." If you were looking at you what would you think of you? Tough question, I know. But think of some of the comments or remarks people have made about you. Do people say that you're unapproachable, moody, witty or personable? You do have an image. Unfortunately, sometimes as black women we're not as in tuned with our images as we need to be. We often say, "Child, I don't care what people think of me." Well, you'd better. Your business depends on it. Now, that doesn't mean that you should go around *worrying* about what people are saying about you. You simply need to take a personal inventory to assess your strengths and development areas. Answer the following questions.

- When you meet strangers are you the first to initiate contact or introduce yourself?
- When you leave a function, do you say good-bye to acquaintances and friends or do you just leave?
- In your current situation, has anyone ever told you that you're hard to get to know or that you always seem to have on your "poker face"?
- In arguments with friends or lovers, are you more interested in having your say or getting to a solution that is good for all parties?
- When you make a mistake, do you say, "I'm sorry" or just figure the other person knows you're sorry or will eventually get over it?
- When you encounter someone whom you've met before, yet he or she has obviously forgotten your name, are you appalled that they can't remember you?
- Do you always tell people that you're an MBA, Ph.D., JD or CPA?
- Do you finish people's sentences?

I ask these eight questions because they reflect some of the comments white and black people have made regarding black women. Let's look at a few of them individually.

When you attend a function, you keep to yourself, don't mingle or initiate meeting people.

Perception: You think you're all that and quite a bit more.
Recommendation: Extend yourself, you will seem like a warm down-to-earth, confident person. Your warm reputation will precede you. People will say how wonderful you are to other people. Your business will increase.

Black women feel that it's not necessary to check out with people before they leave. Besides, what's the point?
Perception: You're unpolished and socially inept.
Recommendation: If you're at a business function you need to let a few people know that you're leaving. Not because you're checking in, it's simply a gesture of courtesy, particularly to the hosts.

You're aloof, hard to get to know.
This is a biggie. Sometimes I can appear distant and aloof. I am aware of this and I've improved. Have you ever said, "they don't need to know me."
Perception: You're potentially difficult to work with and probably to work for!
Recommendation: Relax, girlfriend. Nobody's going to hurt you. It won't kill you to let people at least get in the same room with you. People need to know that they can connect with you. Extend yourself, don't make people always come to you.

Finishing other people's sentences leaves them with the feeling that they're incompetent or stupid. It makes you look like an egohead who only likes to hear herself talk.
Perception: You think you know it all.
Recommendation: Shut up! What the other person has to say is important. Just listen. Even if you think you have the answer.

Yes, I'm an MBA and a Ph.D.
Big deal! Nobody cares. Black women are proud of their accomplishments and we should be, we've made tremendous strides. But spouting off acronyms is annoying, not impressive. If someone wants to know about your scholastic background they'll ask.
Perception: You're arrogant, self-absorbed. It will make people avoid you like the plague. The cost of doing business with you will be too great—you'll be dropped like a hot bowl of soup.
Recommendation: Just chill out. Save your MBA and Ph.D. spiel for your obituary—or your bestselling autobiography.

I know I goofed . . .
Saying you're sorry puts you in a position of power, not weakness. Don't ever pass up the opportunity to admit your mistakes. Just say you goofed and move on, don't dwell on it.

Perception: When you don't say you're sorry, people have a difficult time respecting you.

Recommendation: Understand that you're not perfect. It's okay to mess up. It's not okay to not acknowledge it. People see you as human, someone they can talk to and identify with. They'll want to do business with you because they'll feel they can trust you to hold yourself accountable.

Obviously you may not be faced with each of these challenges. However, thinking about them could help prepare you for what's ahead.

SO WHAT'S YOUR BIG IDEA?

You have a winning idea, right? Let's see if you know just how big your idea is. Explain, in five words or less, the business you're going into.

_____

Good, now explain in ten words or less why I would choose to buy your service or product over one of your competitors. (And because I'm cute or a sister is not going to get it.)

_____

Who would buy your product or service? Remember, be very specific.

_____

How much money will you need to start and operate your business for six months, assuming no one buys your service or product?

_____

Where will you get the money? Savings? Investors? Family? Retirement fund?

_____

Today's date_____   Your start-up date goal_____

Now copy this page out of this book and put it in a place where you'll have to see it everyday. Frame it if you have to. Don't let it collect dust or you'll never see your dream realized.

DO WHAT YOU LOVE AND BUMP THE NAYSAYERS

You're a remarkable woman. Not only because you're starting your own business but because you're doing so in spite of those thousands of people out there who want and expect you to fail. You say everyone's on your side? Boloney! In fact, if I were you, I'd count on one person—you! Sound cynical? Good. You're getting my point. You may be fortunate (I don't believe in luck) as I was when I started out on the E-journey. My family was and has always supported me, totally and completely. If they didn't, I never heard about it. My family consists of seven people including my mother, who died fifteen years ago.

Who do you think your support system is? Family? Lover? Spouse? Friends? It's important to understand who will be available and in what capacity they can help you. Be realistic. Don't count on people whom you know through experience have never been there for you. Don't set yourself up to be disappointed. Don't expect people to perform beyond their usual capacity. If you know that your sister won't remember to pick up a package from a client, why are you asking her to do it? Do you really believe that because this is an important pickup that could mean $1 million for you, your sister will be any more motivated to follow through? Don't you believe it. Know your people.

One of the most important things you can commit to as an entrepreneur is to know your people. What does this mean? I played basketball so it was critical for me to know the players on the court with me. There were players whose role was to stand underneath the basket, catch the ball and shoot. No more, no less. They were even told not to venture beyond four feet of the basket. When those players ran to the outside (where players like Michael Jordan play), I knew better than to pass them the ball. Why? Because they were not in a place where they were going to be their best; passing the ball would have created a bad situation for all of us. In your team, know how to assign roles. Give important jobs to people who have shown they are responsible and reliable.

SUPPORT IS BEAUTIFUL

Everyone needs support. And support comes in various flavors. When I started out I needed people around me who were not afraid. I appreciated sentiments of "you can do it," but I didn't need those words. I needed people to show their support by *not* saying, "are you sure you want to leave a $65,000 salary, company car and benefits for the uncertainty of full-time entrepreneurship?" I had plenty of people making those kinds of statements. So many that I could have thrown up. Fear is rampant, particularly among black women. We are so afraid. And I'm not sure if it's of failure or success. It really doesn't matter because fear in any form immobilizes. It keeps us out of action. So check out your support system. What are your expectations for the people in your life? Write the names of a few key people whom you believe will be instrumental in your success. I'll give you a few of my examples.

Who Can I Count On?

Person	Role	Limitations
Sister, Debra	Intellect, wit and spiritual connection	She lives in Florida
Brother, Chris	Humor, male perspective, savvy	Twenty years old/little business experience

You fill in the blanks for your situation.

_____	_____	_____
_____	_____	_____
_____	_____	_____

Once you've completed this exercise, review it. Look at what those people give you and be aware of their limitations. I wouldn't call my twenty-year-old brother about a business problem involving invoicing a client, because he would be ill-equipped to help me. I would and I do call Chris when I need to have a male or young person's point of view. He represents the market I'm trying to attract sometimes, so he's a great test market for ideas. He has a great sense of humor and his contribution to my empire is as appreciated as my sister's business experience. Who are the players on your team? Let them know what they give you and ask if it's okay to call upon them if you need them.

Always feed your mind—empowering thoughts, positive energy. Read books or listen to tapes constantly. I pass along anything empowering I get—a book, a tape, an article—and guess what happens? As a result, people start looking for things to empower themselves and get in the habit of snipping and sending, not only to me, but also to everyone around them!

Expect to make a million dollars overnight. I know this may shock you, because everyone tries to tell us to aim low. Most people say *don't* expect to make a million dollars overnight. Planning to make a million dollars is more important than actually doing it (in case you fall a few dollars short the first time!).

Everything I Need to Know about Entrepreneurship I Learned from Mother

❖ ❖ ❖

My mother started her own business two years before she made her transition from this life. Before that she was full-time mother to my four siblings and me and wife to the only man she ever loved, my father. Like many black women her age, she had cleaned the homes of white people off and on when my brothers and sister were young. But her entrepreneur race didn't begin until around 1979. I was fourteen years old, living with a woman who was trying to come into her own in the face of a troubled marriage. Mom had given birth to my precocious little brother, Chris, four years earlier. She was in for a big challenge. She had always done hair, as we like to say. And she was very good at it. But doing hair in the cozy confines of our kitchen got to be a bit boring for Mom. She was not going to sit on her butt all day, listening to the stories and cooking red beans. She wanted something besides us to call her very own. One day she learned of a nearby cosmetology school and decided to enroll, of course, under tremendous resistance from my father. She did it anyway.

My mother, whom my sister and brothers all knew was a strong-willed, determined woman was taking flight. For a year or so, I watched my mother get up before the crack of dawn, study for her class, practice on her mannequin heads and sometimes mine. She would get my little brother dressed for day care and we'd be off to school, all three of us. Mom, to beauty school, me to high school and Chris to nursery. As I reflect, it was beautiful and absolutely remarkable. During her last years, my mother was her happiest and her saddest. Happy because she was finally fulfilled, sad because she still needed a strong support system to help her know that she was going to make it, that the clients would come and that she would no longer have to depend on a man—my father—who was no longer living with us.

When she died in 1981, she had instilled in me all of the qualities and beliefs that made her the most incredible woman I know. For the first time, I share those creeds with you, my sisters. I trust that you too will find success by implementing them in your life. I sure have.

YOUR OPINION OF YOU IS IMPORTANT

When I was nine years old my mother and I went shopping. I tried on a dress and I walked out and asked my mother if she liked it. She looked me over and asked, "do you like it?" I answered yes. Without changing her expression she said, "then that's all that matters." I will never forget that day. I learned that my own self-image would be a driving force in my success. I learned to never fall prey to someone else's opinion of me—to respect others' viewpoints but to never allow those alone to guide my life. As black women, we will always be second-guessed. Be strong in your convictions. If you believe in your idea and it makes good business sense, then do it.

TREAT PEOPLE RIGHT

Sounds simple but it works. My mother used to say, "I don't wanna be a part of no mess," and I feel the same way. People struggle with treating people the same. It's impossible to treat people the same because people are different. My mother said that you can always treat people fairly.

IF YOU'LL LIE, YOU'LL STEAL

My mother was unmerciful with lying. She would always say as she was beating my behind, "if you'll lie, you'll steal." I never quite understood what that meant. All I knew is that she wanted me to hold honesty in the highest regard. I'd never stolen anything in my life, so I was puzzled about why "if you'll lie" was always followed by "you'll steal." She explained that she didn't think I was a thief. She explained that dishonesty is rarely limited to one arena—it's a mind set, she said. In business, if you discover that you've been lied to or have not been dealt with ethically in one area, it's important to break ties with that individual because they're probably headed for bigger offenses.

YOU DON'T HAVE ANY FRIENDS

Sounds like cynical advice to give a ten-year-old, but this is what my mother told her children. It boggled our minds for decades. I think we all understood that mother wasn't saying that we would be friendless for life. She was warning us of wolves in sheep's clothing. Particularly in business, black women must be good at telling the sheep from the wolves. Be a good judge of character. Mother said that friends show themselves to be friends and don't need to march around telling you that they're your friends.

FINISH YOUR HOMEWORK BEFORE YOU GO OUT TO PLAY

You've probably heard this one from your mom. It was strictly enforced at my house. As business owners you obviously have the flexibility to work and play when you please. As black women, we must remember that our work is a result of how good we've been at doing our homework. If we are committed to practice, our work will reflect this commitment. If you want to enjoy your time in the sun or on vacation, finish your work and then play.

STRIVE FOR EXCELLENCE, NOT PERFECTION

My mother knew what I was capable of. When I brought my report card home, she expected As. If I had anything other than that, we'd have a discussion about it. My mother never said to me, "Don't bring anything home except an A." Instead she always said, "I'm proud of you, do your best, that's all Mama asks." Perfection is something the insecure strive for. Otherwise why wouldn't your best be good enough?

I'M HARD ON YOU BECAUSE I LOVE YOU

What a crock! Or so I thought as a teenager. When I would disobey my mother, she'd punish me and say, "I'm doing this because I love you." As an entrepreneur you must be hard on yourself, hold yourself accountable. If you love this business idea enforce rigid and reachable goals. Reward yourself for good work and slap your wrist when you've been naughty.

READ A BOOK

My mother read to me constantly. Once I could read, she bought me every book I asked for. Reading is a great way to expand our knowledge centers and develop professionally. Always keep a book in the car and in your briefcase or backpack. Reading helps you become better writers and communicators. Mom obviously knew this before I did.

DON'T WATCH SO MUCH TELEVISION

When I wasn't reading, I sure wasn't watching television. My mother didn't really care what I was watching. She just thought watching television all the time was a waste of time. Find more productive pasttimes—writing, puzzles, games and, of course, reading.

BUY GOOD CLOTHES, NOT A LOT OF CLOTHES

Mother believed that good clothes were a better investment than tons of clothes. She wouldn't let me buy the latest trendy articles if they couldn't be found at a quality clothier. She helped me develop my own style this way. Today's smart black businesswoman dresses for success by buying good, quality clothes that will stand the test of time. If you've got to have the latest craze, save it for the night on the town or the concert, not for business.

PART THREE

❖ ❖ ❖

GO!

Creating Your Company Culture

❖ ❖ ❖

This is actually where everyone who ever starts a business should begin. What will your business stand for? When people think of your company what will they think of? How will your clients and future employees feel when they work or visit your space? These are all important questions for us. Part of creating your mission statement means that you'll need to have some idea where you are now and where you want to be in the future. What do you stand for? What are you striving for? All of these questions will help you create your company culture.

I polled seven black women business-owners who all admitted to never giving their company cultures any thought. Surprised? Sometimes we just take off in the race without a clear vision of where we're going. Let's brainstorm or, as I call it, mindschlepp. When people think of you and your products or services, what words would you like to come to their minds?

_____

_____

_____

_____

_____

Now, flip the coin. What *don't* you want people to think of when they think of you and your business?

_____

_____

_____

_____

_____

Now that you know what you want and don't want said about you, let's create your company culture—even if you haven't yet started your business.

HOW DOES ONE CREATE CULTURE?

Like you, the entrepreneur, your company has an image to uphold. It needs makeup and attention. Let me share a good example of creating culture. A friend of mine has a successful marketing company in downtown Austin. When you walk into her conference room you see four walls—all a different color. What would you think? Creative? Artsy? It's a bright place with sectionals instead of traditional offices with doors. The only doors that can be closed are hers and her partner's, and they are rarely closed.

You walk into her receiving area and a man or woman is sitting there working on a computer. They turn to me and say, "Hi Fran, Cecilia (not her real name) is just about out of her meeting, can I get you something to drink—coffee, water, juice?" Then they escort me to a conference room with multicolored walls, black Scandinavian chairs and a marble meeting table. Are you getting a picture of what this place feels like? My beverage arrives (with a smile, of course), and a couple of people come out of their cubicles to speak. We chat and laugh, then they offer to refreshen my drink. Moments later, my business friend walks out in a pair of khaki slacks, silk and cotton-blend shirt, tweed blazer, white socks and loafers. She gives me a hug and offers to refreshen my drink again. Her employees say good-bye and shut the door on their way out. We have our meeting, she escorts me to the door and gives me her latest advertising specialty item, a stress ball with her company's name on it.

Now, what perception do you have of this company? Read the story again and see if you can tell what image and culture my friend is trying to cultivate.

Now let's give you another example. On a recent weekend trip I walked into a black bookstore to see if they had a book I'd been looking for for several weeks. I walked through the door around 10:30 A.M. and about five seconds later, a sister emerged from a doorway. She said good morning in a dry, I-just-got-out-of-bed tone. The place itself was clean and seemed to be well-organized, with nothing striking or particularly unique about the layout. I walked around looking for my book. This sister, who looked like she had just hit the snooze five minutes before I walked in, didn't ask me if I needed any help, how I was doing or if I'd read Maya Angelou's latest work. Nothing. She was wearing a pair of wrinkled blue slacks and her hair was barely combed. The feeling I got when I walked into this place was low energy and no enthusiasm. Her culture has been created and it is dead. If it sounds like I'm giving her a hard time, I am. You say, "Fran, you didn't go there to be entertained," and I say "you're right." If you had an option of going somewhere where they shower you with attention, good products and professional niceties, wouldn't you choose that establishment over one that gave you the distinct feeling that you'd just walked into a morgue?

Now, I don't know if this was a typical or atypical day for this sister and I don't really care. I just know that I'll probably go get my books at another black bookstore when I visit this city again. My point is that you may only get one shot at someone's business and if your culture reeks indifference or even boredom, you may not get the chance at that customer's business again or at least for a while.

What Message Will Your Company Send?

Take a step back and decide what your image and your company's image will be. Create a day when someone walks into your place of business: What will they see and, most important, what will they feel? I'll be your first customer. Write everything I will see and experience from the time I walk up to the door until the time I leave.

_____

_____

_____

_____

_____

_____

_____

_____

_____

_____

How did that feel? Good? Can you see your company? Can you feel the energy of making things happen? Can't you hear all the positive comments from customers and clients who absolutely adore you, your product or service?

I know when I started out I wanted people to think of professionalism, quality, class and humor when they thought of me or my company. Sometimes things don't run smoothly because sometimes we aren't where we need to be when we start our companies. I know one black woman who wanted people to think of professionalism when they thought of her consulting firm, yet when you called her office, her receptionist was rude. You can't have those kinds of inconsistencies flowing through your company. If there's something or someone who's throwing your system off, you must fix them or fire them.

IT'S AN IMAGE THANG!

"Girl, you don't wanna cross that sister, she needs an attitude adjustment."

"But isn't she the owner of that successful print shop on the corner?"

"Yep, but her employees are rude and she seems to be exactly like them."

"Oooh, then I'll be sure to buy my paper somewhere else."

True story? Of course, we all know a sister who needs to refine her image. We black women, especially, should be mindful of what message we send. People are always taking inventory of us—how we dress, talk, walk and conduct business. Whether you know it or not, you have a reputation. If you wanna know what it is, just ask someone.

Perception Versus Reality

The old axiom "perception is reality" is a bit simple for my taste. No, perception isn't reality, but people's perception of you is how they see you, that's all it is—it may not necessarily be completely accurate. Since perception isn't reality, does that mean you shouldn't care what people think of you? I didn't say that. What black women must understand is that everyone's perception of anything is a function of three things: (1) what we see, (2) how we interpret what we see (which is a result of our own personal coding methods and how we've been trained to respond to the world) and (3) what we know to be true about the person or thing through interaction with them.

Sometimes we black women are given a bad rap because people don't understand us. When I worked in corporate America, my reputation included many positive adjectives—professional, sharp and witty. I also heard that I was aloof and difficult to get to know. Do I think that these perceptions of me accurately portrayed me? Yes, to some degree. I wasn't as open with some of my white counterparts as I probably should have been. Yet, it's interesting to note that all of these non-positive comments came from people who were not black, which led me to think that it was more of a cultural thing.

Sometimes people of other cultures don't understand that we are sometimes protecting ourselves when we appear to be distant and detached. We understand why we give this impression but, because others know very little about our history, they shrug it off as aloofness or lack of commitment to the team. I've heard similar comments made about sisters in other corporations and organizations.

Selling Out or Selling Strong?

As black female entrepreneurs who desire to capture the business of both blacks and nonblacks, we must work to break down gender, racial and/or cultural barriers. Does this mean more work for you? Yes, but it's easy work. All of us have endearing qualities, and it's important to just let people see those. Don't be so protective, let people get to know you a little bit—it will help your business tremendously.

HIRING PEOPLE

Finding good people is tough. Finding those who will fit into your culture is even tougher. I heard one businesswoman say that she hires the right *people* and trains them. To some degree, this means that if you have two candidates and candidate one has superior skills but won't fit in with the team, and candidate two has good skills and fits nicely into your system does that mean that you chose candidate two? Whom do you hire? Depends on your needs. If you need someone to go out and make you money immediately, you might want to take a chance on candidate one and hope that they will eventually fit in. By contrast, if your business can survive short term while this budding star gains experience then doesn't it make sense to take a chance on candidate two?

When I was coaching basketball one of my responsibilities was to recruit players for our team. Sometimes I would come across girls who were awesome basketball players and tremendous athletes. However, some of their attitudes put a skunk to shame. While all the other schools were courting these superstars, I had my eye on the little girl who worked hard, got the job done and seemed to be respected by her teammates. Occasionally, we'd take a chance on a kid who was a super player but who didn't seem to get along with her teammates. Guess what? Our guts were right 100 percent of the time. Those players always ended up destroying the team's culture. Our high hopes of them eventually fitting in never came to fruition, and we spent years shaking our heads at how stupid we'd been.

Hiring Family

In a few words—proceed with caution. Your family loves you but they can also sometimes disrupt business and drive you insane. In 1995, I decided to bring my brother on board in one of my companies because he's interested in sports management. He's twenty years old—which, though not a bad thing, certainly brings with it a unique set of issues. I was willing to deal with it. After all, he is the love of my life.

So far, it's working out. But there are days when I could stare a hole right through him. He has all of the basics in place—he's honest, hard working and willing to learn. But sometimes his lack of attention to detail means rework for me.

Here's what to consider if you're going to hire family.

- Do you *like* the person? Love is one thing, like is a whole different ball game.
- Are they interested in building your business because they like the industry? Don't bring *anyone* into your company if s/he doesn't want to be there.
- Are they hard workers, honest and coachable? Starting out means that everyone must be committed to working hard. Family members sometimes feel like they can be slackers—don't hire people who have a hard time rolling out of bed each morning.
- Have they ever been arrested or convicted of a crime? Dishonesty is dishonesty. If a family member has an obvious disregard for authority or the law, what makes you think you can straighten him or her out?
- Do they or could they portray the image your company needs? I'm all for diversity, but sometimes people simply don't send the message you want delivered.
- Are they the kind to take advantage of a good thing? If your family member is slow to pay back a loan from you, he or she will more than likely take advantage of you by taking long lunches or using your phone to make long distance calls.
- Are you going to be able to be hard on her/him? If you can't put your foot down, you don't need to hire a family member, period.

Follow Your Gut, Not Your Heart

Our hearts make us do some crazy things. We want to hire women and blacks, but are they always the best people for the job? In other words, feeling sorry or wanting to improve someone's plight are not bad reasons, but they can't be the sole reason for hiring someone. Additionally, hiring someone because of some unfortunate life circumstance is not smart. A friend's brother was a recovering drug addict, so she decided to try to help build him back up by giving him a job in her store. Hold on, that's not a bad decision yet. Her mistake was in putting him in a situation where he could destroy her business.

One day they were the only two people in the store. She got a call for lunch and decided to take off, said she'd be back in a few minutes. She thought, my brother loves me, he'd never do anything to hurt me! When she got back, he'd not only cleared out her register, he'd stolen a few customers' credit card numbers from invoices. A classic case of following your heart and not your gut. Her gut told her not to leave, to have her friend come over or try to have dinner. But her loving heart said, "this is your brother, he wouldn't do this to you." Follow your gut. If something doesn't set right in your stomach, then it'll probably give you indigestion.

The First Time Is the Right Time

How many times have you said, "I wish I had . . . ?" I bet if I gave you a hundred dollars for every time you've said it you wouldn't need to start a business because you'd be set for life, right? Many times we have all or at least most of the information we need to make good decisions even though we don't. I've done it more than I care to admit. And I hate redoing anything. Yet that's exactly what happens when you don't commit to doing it right the first time.

Take your time when hiring anyone, inside or outside of your family. Mistakes always cost us—maybe not financially but, in some way, we suffer when we make them.

GETTING OFF TO A GOOD START

Face it, black women sometimes get a bad rap when it comes to perception and image. Face it, black women sometimes deserve just what they get!

How do we avoid getting off on the wrong foot when it comes to our images? First, we need to understand the perceptions currently out there. Do you fit into any of these stereotypes?

The Angry Black Woman

We've heard it all too often: "You don't wanna mess with an angry black woman" or "there's nothing worse than an angry black woman." I tend to agree. I've seen them and on occasion, I am one. What she doesn't realize is that this is the most suicidal state she can be in.

What does she look like? Her countenance says "get out of my way or get run over." She rarely smiles or has a discussion without it leading to an argument that climaxes with words like, "we've been taking this (expletive) too long, you're messing with the wrong (expletive) or I'm sick and tired of this (expletive)."

How people respond to her? They avoid her. They only deal with her when they have to. They send other people to talk to her because she usually has a select group of people who can deal with her. She's invited to functions, not because people want her there, but rather because it's polite.

Disadvantage of being her: missed business opportunities.

Miss Armani Beverly Hills

We all know these sisters, too. They don't mind telling you where they bought their car, clothes and jewelry and how much they paid for it. They have designer toilet tissue (that they call bathroom tissue).

She's the well-dressed sister in the meeting who's putting a price tag on everyone in the room. She can leave a business meeting and tell you what everyone was wearing but nothing about the business meat.

How do people respond to her? They notice her clothes more than they do her. When they speak of her, they talk about what a sharp dresser she is but never say anything about her business acumen.

Disadvantage of being her: not viewed as a serious player.

The Cubic Zirconium

These sisters think they are diamonds who've got it going on and on. The sad part is that they're the only ones who think it.

What does she look like? She's the sister in the corner with the gorgeous black dress on who has accessorized to the point of obscenity. She wants to impress but she's not quite sure how to do it. Rather than get a womentor, she keeps making etiquette blunders that make her look unpolished and uncouth.

How do people respond to her? They smile in her face and laugh behind her back.

Disadvantages of being her: not included in circles with the movers and the shakers. Perceived as unrefined, so not given opportunities for major contracts.

Holy Roller

What does she look like? Every religious sect has one of these sisters. She's put her religion on the front burner in a business meeting. She finds a way to testify.

How do people respond to her? People are turned off by her, not because of her religious convictions, but because of her obvious disregard for other people's choices and affiliations.

Disadvantage of being her: not included in major deals because people think she will use it as a platform for her religion.

Sweet and Tender Wallflower

What does she look like? Not to be confused with wildflower, this sister fades into the decor at business meetings. She doesn't know how to draw attention to her smarts and savvy. She goes to networking meetings and talks to no one.

How do people respond to her? They don't, they don't see her.

Disadvantage of being her: no one knows she exists.

The Bull Horn

What does she look like? This sister never needs a megaphone to be heard. She's loud and tacky. Gets down and dirty with the boys and doesn't mind offending the girls. Class and her name would never go in the same sentence.

How do people respond to her? They say, "Oh, here comes old loud mouth." They gripe and grin while she's standing there and comb their hair back in place when she leaves.

Disadvantage of being her: seen as unprofessional even when quite competent.

The Wonder Years

What does she look like? This sister truly believes that just because bell bottoms are back that the actual clothes she wore twenty years ago are back too. You look at her and even if you aren't shallow, you can't help but laugh. She doesn't get it.

How do people respond to her? They can't figure it out. She's smart, so she has to know. But then if she knew, surely she'd improve her image.

Disadvantages of being her: People are hesitant to refer strong clients her way. People warn people about her. They say, "disregard her clothes, she's really sharp."

WHAT STATEMENT ARE YOU MAKING?

After looking at these profiles, what do you think about the message you're sending? Are you prepared to sharpen your image for the sake of your business? Your image consists of everything about you—how you dress, speak and conduct business. Here's a list of the most important image factors.

Personal Grooming

Is your face acne prone? Are your teeth clean? Is your breath offensive? Does your hair look like you've been in a windstorm? Do you have chipped, unmanicured nails? Believe it or not, these are all areas that people have cited for not doing business with black women. People make assumptions about how you do business based on how you look. If you are neat and well manicured, they'll be more likely to think your business is conducted in a like manner.

Wardrobe

You don't have to spend a small fortune on clothes to look good. The important thing is to buy quality clothes that flatter you. Make sure you're wearing the shades that make you look dynamic, not dull. Always buy good shoes, it's one of the first things people look at. Don't over-accessorize, it makes you look unpolished and gaudy.

Physical Presentation

Did you know your posture is a result of how you feel about yourself? My mother used to tell me to quit walking like a saddled horse. I didn't know at nine years old that being tall was a good thing. When I realized it, I stuck my chest out and straightened up my back. Straighten up, girl, and feel good about yourself. People will take note!

Yep, you've also got to get in shape. Make sure your height and weight are in proportion. It may not be correct in some circles to talk about weight; however, as your tour guide I must tell you that when you feel good about how you look, you relate to people in a completely different manner. So get your physique in order, and your customers and clients will feel your enthusiasm and confidence.

Speech

Don't talk too fast or too slow. If you don't know whether you're a fast or slow talker, take out your Dictaphone or recorder and talk. If you're having trouble listening to yourself because you keep falling asleep, or if you have difficulty understanding yourself because you sound like you're running from a bandit, make the necessary changes. Also, don't overuse your hands when talking, they're distracting.

Brace yourself, some people have said that there are certain sounds Black Americans have had trouble saying. In general, we don't finish words, we don't enunciate, we deaden the "th" sound and we don't work hard at grammar. Obviously, this is not true for all of us. Just be sure you enunciate and speak clearly.

A word about slang. I try to stay abreast of the latest slang because I speak to kids all the time, and sometimes I have to speak their language. In business I would never say in a serious meeting, "yo, peep this fly promo tip I put together, would you?" Although my twenty-year-old brother would be proud that I even know these words, I don't recommend that you use them in the business environment. They'll get you big points with your homies and kids, but they'll get a door slammed in deals.

Etiquette

This is such a biggie there's a whole chapter on it. Knowing what to do, in what proportion and when is a challenge we've all faced. Brush up on your etiquette. Composure and detail can help you impress the best.

Style

How do you relate to the world and people? Some people have incredible style and flair. Susan Taylor, though I've never met her, strikes me as a person of tremendous style. Alfre Woodard is another—she appears comfortable with her beauty and intelligence. Also realize that your style is a combination of your walk, talk and physical presence.

WHAT CAN YOU DO TO IMPROVE YOUR IMAGE?

First, you need to find out what you need to work on. Many black women haven't a clue about what image means and how they contribute to the overall perception people have of them. Our self-image plays a critical role in the message we send the public. If you lack confidence it shows up in how you dress, walk, talk, act and speak. How do you refine your image so that it helps you in your business?

Ask for Feedback

I know we're not always comfortable putting ourselves in the firing line, still it's important. Select four people— two who know you well plus two casual acquaintances. Ask both duos the following questions: What do you think of when you think of me? What area do you think I should develop to improve my image? The reason you're asking friends and acquaintances is to make sure you get balanced feedback. Sometimes friends aren't as honest as we need for them to be. Acquaintances will be honored that you asked for their opinions and will give great feedback. Both are valuable. Be sure to write down all responses for your review later.

Note: This is an important step in your business success. If you can't accept this kind of feedback, then don't start a business. Be in a good mood when you ask for this feedback because you don't want your friends to think they're going to be in trouble if they tell you something unflattering or even negative. If anything, this should strengthen your relationships.

Get a Professional Opinion

A session with an image consultant is a worthwhile investment. These people can assist you with developing the look that's you. We already have so many things working against us, we need to control as many factors as possible. Image consulting is one of the fastest growing industries in the 90s. Look in the phone book under Image Consulting or call BeautiControl. They are well known for their image-consulting services. They can do a color analysis as well as make recommendations for clothing choices.

Learn What's Appropriate for Your Industry

I never recommend dressing like everyone else—you'll never stand out this way. I do advise people to dress like the people they want as clients. If these are snazzy, smart dressers, emulate this style while incorporating your own spices.

When I'm pitching corporate sponsors, I wear clothes that people will remember—positively. Sometimes this means a well-tailored, stunning pants suit, sometimes it's slacks and a funky tie. I am well aware that people respond differently to women wearing ties, but I am willing to risk wearing them because ties are a part of my personal style (I always get rave reviews from men who want to know where I buy my neckwear!). Just remember to be yourself without being too offensive.

Make Up, Not Make Over

If you decide to skip the image consultant, at least learn how to properly apply makeup. Makeup should enhance your features not make you look like Bozo the clown. Image consultants say that black women have a tendency to wear too much or too little makeup—leaning more toward not enough or what I call misplaced makeup.

Eyes We have beautiful eyes, although we don't always know how to accentuate them. We tend to put on too much eyeliner and not enough eye shadow. Or worse, we put the same amount of eyeliner on top as below, when the top should have more. If you run out of eyeliner, run out putting it on top, the bottom will be okay if you put nothing down there.

Cheeks I have the high cheekbones of my Native American ancestors, so blush, when applied correctly, really accentuates this feature. Sometimes black women still think that a round circle or long streak of blush from the center of your cheek through your hair line looks good. It doesn't! A make-up artist once told me that once you've applied the line of blush on your cheek you should follow with an applicator on the southern line so that it doesn't look like you've drawn a line on your face.

Eye shadow The sky blue eye shadow that was near and dear to Diana and the Supremes doesn't work in the 90s. The perfect eye shadow can make you look like a million bucks; the wrong shade can cost you about as much in missed business! Discover the correct shades for everyday, daytime and nighttime.

Lips We have beautiful, voluptuous lips. Again, coloring is so critical. Find a shade that you can wear with jeans and different shades for your evening wear—these aren't usually the same color. Use lip liners; they really accentuate color and contour. I own at least twenty shades of lip colors—entirely overboard, I admit. Image consultants say that five, even three shades are adequate, because you can mix to find the shades you need.

Foundation As many companies as there are trying to get our business these days, there's no excuse for not finding a good foundation. It's important to find your color—not too dark and certainly not too light. There are some scary-looking sisters out there because their foundations are way off. Foundation is where it starts, and a bad color can make you look like a ghost or ghoul, take your pick. Foundations help even out your skin tone—it's going to look funny if you have a copper face and a milk chocolate neck—so choose carefully!

If You Don't Make Up

I'm not a slave to makeup, and most days I don't even wear it. I don't panic when I don't have lipstick with me. I do, however, recognize how radiant I look when I do wear it. And I recognize how people respond to me when I'm "made up." I use makeup to accentuate my beauty. Understand that while you may be a beautiful woman, makeup makes you look even better. If you don't like makeup, fine. However, people don't just see the work, they see the face in front of the work first. At least highlight your eyes with a little eyeliner and mascara and your lips with a bit of color. Heck, most men could stand a little makeup!

CULTIVATING A WINNING IMAGE

Building a good image takes more time than money. If you're not sure what looks good, ask someone or read magazines. Here are a few hints for face-lifting your image starting from head to toe.

- Get an attractive, non-busy hairdo.
- Keep your hair well groomed—wash it and avoid having dandruff on your clothes.
- Get a grown-up hairdo. Avoid big bows, ponytails, ribbons and barrettes, or people may see you as a little girl.
- Be careful pulling your hair back (Sade-like). It works for some people, but it's certainly not for everybody.
- Avoid changing your hair color or style frequently.
- Take care of acne if it's a problem for you. Most dermatologists can prescribe things to help your condition—a special cleanser or soap.
- Wear tasteful makeup. Don't mix incompatible colors on your face (pink eye shadow and a red-based lip color). Bad girl! It throws off your colors.
- Avoid wearing several earrings in one ear. Even if you have several holes, use the primary one and save the centipede effect for the parties.
- Wear earrings for the occasion. Diamonds and pearls, believe it or not, are not everyday wear. So, although you're proud of your 2-carat Valentine's Day gift, they just aren't appropriate with everything you wear. Diamonds are literally for evening wear. If you're determined to wear diamonds during the day, buy a smaller pair.
- Don't wear earrings that are too large or too small.
- Be conscientious about cleaning your nose. Most people will not tell you when you have something in your nose. You don't want to be in an important meeting with something hanging from your nostrils.
- Wear lip color even if it's a natural shade. It will highlight your face and make you look better groomed overall.
- Be a teeth freak. Carry floss, toothbrush and paste in your car. Bad breath is offensive, and yellow teeth turn people off.
- Wear one necklace and make sure it's suitable for the occasion. Pearls don't go with blue jeans—in any country! If you look like Run-D.M.C., you won't get the attention of serious business people.
- Don't show your breasts. If you're sporting a low-cut suit, wear a camisole—it adds taste and elegance.
- Don't show your stomach. Unless you're at a swimming party, no one needs to see your abs.
- Be mindful of female hygiene. Change your tampon/pad frequently.
- Wear skirts of appropriate length. If you have long legs, you should probably avoid long, flowing, pleated skirts.
- Don't wear skirts that are too tight.
- Wear tasteful, runless panty hose. Avoid color and designer hose if you're serious about business (keep an extra pair of full length and knee highs in your car).
- Buy quality shoes.

- Buy a nice leather purse. Your friends may be impressed with your Vuitton or Dooney, but serious businesspeople recognize quality over name brand.
- Buy a nice attaché or briefcase.
- Buy a quality, simple coat, like a London Fog or a solid color wool one.
- Wear a maximum of two rings on your fingers—one on each hand.
- Keep your nails manicured whether you polish them or not.
- Wear a maximum of one bracelet.
- Buy a nice watch.
- Buy a nice pen and pencil set.
- If you use a pager, use the vibrating setting over the beeper sound.

Final Image Note

When you walk into a room does everyone takes note? Has anyone said lately, "Where do you shop?" Or "You're such a dynamo!" If no one has made a similar comment to you, there's a good chance you're missing the mark with your image. Of course, your worth is certainly not tied up in what other people think of you but figure this: If you never got a letter or comment from a client saying something positive about your business or product, wouldn't you wonder if you were doing a good job?

Penny's Story

I was a copywriter and worked in advertising for about fifteen years before I started my first business. Of course, I have always enjoyed baking. I have a very large family—many women in my family are great cooks and bakers. In addition to home baking and cooking, my mother worked in large-scale baking/cooking facilities, so I was exposed to wonderful products being turned out professionally as I grew up. Throughout my life baking has been a consistent and somewhat expensive hobby. I have collected over the years hundreds of cookbooks, and have enjoyed countless classes—most of them centering around pastry. But it wasn't until Christmas 1983 that I really started to think seriously about a career in baking.

My father is a diabetic and I wanted to make something special for him for Christmas. I created a whole grain, naturally sweetened cake with a pretty clear glaze finish. It was very popular with my family and friends. Everyone kept saying how good it was and that I should try selling the cake. So, I thought to myself, hmm, maybe I'll give this a try. We sold hundreds of these cakes, baked in my home kitchen with the help of my mother and sisters. After the holiday, we went on to add additional products to the line—most were whole grain, naturally sweetened pastries. I wholesaled these products to day cares, farmer's markets around the D.C. area and did real well—plus I was having great fun!

Anyway I did that for a year and a half and then found this really great place in Reston, Virginia for a small retail bakery. My husband and I did the remodeling and turned this tiny space into a wonderful, quaint little bakery. It was really cute—Laura Ashley wallpapering, little wooden bakery cases and tons of baskets to hold all the cookies and brownies. We also brought in beautiful loaves of bread from another small woman-owned business in the area. I worked long hours, loving every minute of it. I was also rewarded for my effort—the bakery was a huge success. A few years after opening the bakery, we sold it and moved to Austin, Texas.

When I got to Austin, I wasn't sure what to do with myself so I took several jobs in local bakeries. The last bakery I worked in, I was actually fired. It's a long story, but suffice it to say, I was devastated.

So there I was, at home, depressed. So, what do I start doing? Baking, of course. A friend, who owned a coffeehouse called to say she was going to pay me a visit. By the time she got to my house, I had baked over a hundred cookies! We talked, she loved my hand-decorated cookies—so much so that she wanted to sell them in her shop. I ended up giving her most of them to sell.

That was around Christmas '91. By February '92, I was separated from my husband, had young twin boys and had a major financial decision to make. How was I going to support us? I started thinking about starting Penny's Pastries again, but this time as a wholesale bakery specializing in cookies and brownies. While thinking about this new venture, I decided to go to a career counseling center hoping they could provide some much needed clarity. A woman there, Maydell Fasion truly inspired me. I told her my little pathetic story and she looked at me and said, "Penny, you should do it . . . what do you have to lose?" And so with a little fear and very little money, I was back in business again.

Last year, we had sales of $116,000—almost three times what we did in our first year. We've self-stabilized a line of our casual cookies (chocolate chip, oatmeal raisin walnut, etc.), which, believe me, was a big deal for our little bakery. Anyway, since we have this line available now, we've been able to land a deal with Southwest Airlines and we've moved the bakery into a wonderful new facility. We're working hard and suffering through loads of "learning experiences" but I wouldn't change a thing about this experience. I am exactly where I was meant to be.

Our motto at Penny's Pastries is "changing the world one bite at a time," which really summarizes where I am. I am really involved in our community and I'm passionate about contributing to the change and empowerment of East Austin.

Best advice given to me: Comes from two very important sources. One from Wilbert Alix, one of my "life teachers." He tells us we create our own reality. We have the divine power to create our lives. This simple statement has had a profound impact on my life. I live it everyday.

I have a sign in my production kitchen that says "The only failure is the failure to participate." I don't know if this would be considered "advice" but it comes to me from another teacher. I believe in it, I do it—full-tilt participation in my life every day.

My advice to you: There is a big gap between dreams and making them reality. If you want something, you must develop something called "sustained motivation." If you're learning and growing and going after what you want oftentimes life can become challenging. Know that what keeps you going, what keeps the finish line in view is something you feel in your gut. I call it motivation. Develop it and enjoy the journey.

Penny McConnell, 42
Penny's Pastries: Brownies, Cookies and Shortbread
Austin, Texas

The Business Plan

❖ ❖ ❖

TALENT + MOTIVATION + EFFECTIVE PLAN = SUCCESS.

I used to think that to be successful you only needed to be talented and have the motivation to work to make it happen. I've since added another factor to the success equation, a solid business plan. When I started my business, believe it or not, I had people telling me that I didn't need a business plan to start my business. Looking back, I wonder what those people had in store for me, success or failure. I don't know many black-owned businesses—man- or woman-owned, with business plans—good ones. Those who have them are riding the waves of success like you wouldn't believe. Those who lack them—some of them—are just barely hanging on.

Sure, there are businesses such as salons and lawn services who really don't see the value of a business plan. After all, they're grossing $60,000 or $70,000 a year, so they don't see the point. The point is this. Imagine how much more business they could bring in if they just understood how to better allocate their marketing/advertising dollars and how to double their customer count! If black women are to create strong, vibrant businesses we must commit to accurate projecting and forecasting.

When those poor souls told me that I didn't need a business plan to start my sports and event marketing company, I didn't listen. I knew that as a black woman—a young, black, female athlete—my ducks not only had to be in a row, they had to have their heels on the line and toes straight ahead. No, I didn't need a business plan, but I knew that having one would put me at least twenty yards ahead of any competitor. While a business plan will never guarantee you success, it can help navigate the trip.

So, black women, I will say it for the fiftieth time—*we must do it the right way* and *we must do it well.* You will never hear me tell someone to start a business without a business plan, especially not a sister. If you'll review the reasons for the failure of black-owned businesses you'll remember that lack of a plan is top on the list. Now, if that doesn't move you to get on the business-plan bandwagon, you're just stubborn and the other "st" word.

DEVELOPING THE PLAN

Although a business plan doesn't have to be a hundred-page document, it must be written. A business plan is the result of you simply thinking about every aspect of your business and committing those thoughts to paper. It will remind you who your customer is and why you're in business. Let's start with the obvious question, your mission.

What is your mission, what is the higher calling of your business? Think for a second. Are you interested in helping people? Providing the absolute best service to your customers? Would you like to help empower the black community? Let's examine a sample business plan, then you can develop your own plan.

There are three kinds of business plans: (1) an introductory plan that addresses each section, though not in great, intricate details; and (2) a more explicit plan including financial forecasts. I'm sharing it to show you what a solid plan should resemble. This business plan can also easily be used as an investment proposal.

Before we build your business plan let's go over what a good plan is, what it's intended to do and why you need it.

What Is It and What Does It Do?

A business plan:

- is a written document that tells the story of your business, how it grows and becomes profitable.
- is an accurate, concise and ever-changing document.
- clearly outlines the operational characteristics of your business.
- outlines how your enterprise will be managed.
- serves as a prospectus for potential investors and lenders.

Why Do You Need It?

You need a business plan:

- because black women must do it better, faster and more effectively.
- because the process of gathering and writing this plan forces you to take a microscopic look at your business.
- because once finished it can help you communicate your ideas and goals to bankers, financial folks and potential investors.

How Will You Use It?

Once you've finished writing your business plan, you will use it:

- to make critical business decisions—expansion and development.
- to reel in investors.
- to measure operational progress.
- to project capital requirements.

Now, do you see why I harp on the business plan? Having a solid plan can take your business to new levels of excitement and growth.

Let's start with the mission statement. This one or two sentence statement tells you and your customers who you are and how you do what you do. Try putting into words your company's mission. A mission statement answers the question, why am I in business? Use the space below.

Sample: At Company XYZ, our mission is to provide our customers with the best training services at the most reasonable prices.
Yours: _____

_____

What do you need to get started? Determining how much money you need goes into the business plan development. Let's take a sample business start-up model. Mo Better Graphic Design is owned by who else? Mo Better. Mo designs newsletters, brochures and such for small companies. This is what she thinks she'll need to get her enterprise off the ground. She's working out of her home.

Start-up Estimates

DBA Certificate (doing business as)	$ 25
computer and printer (new)	3,000

computer and printer (used)	2,000
paper supplies	250
software	300
business telephone	200
business cards/letterhead	200
misc. office supplies	150
insurance	150
unanticipated expenses	150
Total start-up costs	$6,075

It's not enough to just know what you need to get going, you must also know what it will take to keep you afloat at least for six months. That's where the cash flow analysis and profit and loss statements come in. We're going to continue to use Mo Better as an example.

SAMPLE BUSINESS PLAN

Below is the first step toward putting together a business plan for Mo Better.

Executive Summary

The Company
Mo Better Designs was started in June 1995 to provide graphic design and layout services for a profit. In September 1995, it was incorporated and expanded into writing and creative services for a diverse client base including for profit and non-profit organizations.

The Business
In analyzing recent economic trends, Mo Better, President of Mo Better Designs, has discovered that the need for graphic and creative services in the corporate sector has increased tremendously in the last ten years. Mo Better Designs meets a need currently unmet in Wherever, When area.

The Market
The local market for MB Designs consists of approximately 500 profit and non-profit businesses. Of these, only ten have an in-house graphic design department, the other 490 have used outside consultants or companies to meet this need.

Management
Mo Better Designs is managed by the President, Mo Better, a twenty-year veteran in the graphic design industry. Mo spent the last ten years of her life

as the Creative Juices Director of Company X. She is responsible for new business development as well as the production of all designs. An artist since age five, Mo has a wealth of computer and freehand experience and has won more than thirty-five awards for her work including Outstanding Artist of the Decade, an honor bestowed upon the city's best artist every ten years.

Business Philosophy

Mo Better's motto is "Mo Better Makes It Mo Better," which epitomizes her approach to her clients. She is committed to providing a unique flavor that involves unusual usage of color and shapes. She has never used a design twice, giving each client the individual flair it deserves.

Where Is Mo Better Going?

Currently Mo Better clients include 20 percent of the city's non-profit organizations and 50 percent of the largest companies in Wherever. The company's goal is to capture an additional 20 percent of the non-profit business within six months.

This is definitely a simplified business plan, but just because it's simple doesn't mean it's ineffective. It is a good stab at addressing some key issues. With the exception of missing forecasts, this is actually a great start for a business plan. It addresses, in a top-line fashion, who Mo Better Graphics is, which customer base it serves and where it would like to go. This condensed version could easily be a seventy-five-page document and, in fact, it should get longer as the business diversifies and grows. Later, I'll share a longer, yet still condensed business plan version of my company, Nouveau.

For now, let's review the components of a business plan, and later you'll get to develop your own.

The Executive Summary: This part of the business plan is a mini, scaled-down version of the big plan. It is usually placed at the beginning of your business plan. Sometimes, an executive summary is given separately to someone who perhaps wants to invest in your company or to a banker who shows a little interest in financing your enterprise. It's a teaser—it gives your reader just enough information so that they understand the basic nature of your business, and it gives them an introduction to you and your background. It is not intended to get into the intricacies of your day-to-day operations, only to provide introductory information. Once someone reads your executive summary, then they may ask for a full-blown business plan complete with forecasts and other financials.

The Company: This section gives information on your company, its name, when it started and its location.

The Business: What business are you in? In this section, you should address the type of business and what makes it unique.

The Market: Who uses your product or service and is this market growing? Although you want to touch on the specifics of your consumer, you will not get into your customer's in-depth profile until later in the business plan.

The Management: What qualifies you to run this business? This section tells who you are and any relevant background to this business. You'll get to tell the whole wonderful story later.

Business Philosophy: Why do you do business the way you do? This is your philosophy and it's what governs how you do business.

Where are you going/company vision? You should have some idea of where you want to go. Any ideas you have on growth and expansion should be touched on here.

Now let's take a look at a full-blown business plan for my company, Nouveau. This plan incorporates real and fictional information for the purpose of helping you develop your own plan. I used a long version of this plan to attract investors for expansion plans. (*The numbers in the plan are completely fictitious.*)

SAMPLE BUSINESS PLAN FOR NOUVEAU, INC.

Confidential

This Business Plan does not constitute an offer to sell nor a solicitation of an offer to buy any security. The material is being delivered by Nouveau, Inc. to a limited number of parties who may be interested in Nouveau, Inc. The sole purpose of these materials is to assist the recipient in deciding whether to proceed with a further investigation of Nouveau, Inc. This document does not purport to be fully inclusive or to contain all the information that a prospective party may desire in investigating Nouveau.

By accepting this material, the recipient agrees to keep confidential the information contained herein or made available in connection with any further investigation of all or part of Nouveau. The recipient by receipt of the Business Plan acknowledges that the recipient may not copy, use, disclose or distribute to others the information contained herein as well as other information provided. Upon request, the recipient will promptly return all material received from Nouveau (including these materials) without retaining any copies thereof.

The materials have been prepared only for information purposes relating to the recipient's investigation and upon the express understanding that they will be used only for the purpose of determining recipient's interest in Nouveau. In this regard, Nouveau makes no express or implied representation or warranty as to the accuracy or completeness of the information contained herein.

Acceptance of the material constitutes an acknowledgment by the recipient that Nouveau expressly disclaims, and will not be subject to, any liability based on such information, errors therein or omissions therefrom, whether or not Nouveau knows or should have known of any such errors or omission, or was responsible for or participated in its inclusion or omission from these materials.

To the extent that representations and warranties are made to the recipient of information by Nouveau in any legal and final agreement, the recipient shall be entitled to rely solely therein. In furnishing this material, Nouveau undertakes no obligation to provide the recipient with access to any additional information. This material shall not be deemed an indication of the state of affairs of Nouveau, nor shall it constitute an indication that there has been no change in the business or affair of Nouveau, or a part thereof, since the date hereof. All questions regarding theses materials and Nouveau should be addressed to Fran Harris, President; Nouveau, Inc.; 1615 West Sixth St.; Austin, Texas 78703. Telephone: (512) 555-7465; Facsimile: (512) 555-7466.

Given to _____

on_____ Number_____

Nouveau, Inc. Confidential Proprietary

Table of Contents

Executive Summary

The Company

Nouveau was started in April 1988 to produce sporting events, camps and clinics. The owner organized and produced three summer basketball camps, as well as consulted high school coaches on conducting successful clinics. In February 1994, Nouveau, Inc. was incorporated and expanded into major event and sports marketing, including its flagship event, Bump It Up, an amateur volleyball tournament.

Sports Marketing

Nouveau produces events for the purpose of promoting teamwork and competitive fun. Participants pay an entry fee to compete with players of similar ages, skill level and experience. In 1995, Nouveau will produce a diverse line of sporting events including four Bump It Up volleyball tournaments, The Women's Games, ExecuSport, two golf tournaments, two basketball camps and Austin's first Corporate Tennis Cup in association with the National Tennis Directors Association.

Events Marketing

In 1995 Nouveau will produce five special events focusing primarily on professional development, entrepreneurship and empowerment such as business conferences and recognition galas. This area of Nouveau is an extension of the owner's organizational development experience in a Fortune 500 company.

A Little Volleyball History

The Federation International de Volleyball reports that more than **800 million** people play indoor and outdoor volleyball worldwide. With more than 50 million players in the United States in 1993, volleyball popularity continues to incline as we approach the twenty-first century. Considered a minor sport for most of the 80s, volleyball has emerged as one of the fastest growing sports in the country, with courts popping up on church grounds, parks and apartment complexes all over the United States. Beach volleyball, in particular, has seen tremendous growth (4 million participants in 1992) and has experienced phenomenal national exposure, becoming an official sport in the 1996 Olympics.

Professional Development

Most people would agree that, along with the information age, our society has become tremendously interested in professional development and empowerment. This area of Nouveau will benefit from the owner's eight years in event production coupled with a successful career in organizational development. Every major company has a Human Resources department that focuses on the development and empowerment of the company's employees, thus affording Nouveau the opportunity to capitalize on another booming industry.

The Business

In analyzing recent economic trends, Fran Harris, Nouveau's President, has discovered that amateur sporting events and professional development series have catapulted to new heights in the last ten years. Nouveau has created Bump It Up, an amateur volleyball competition for participants ages ten and up, to allow them to compete locally, nationally and potentially, internationally, in a double-elimination tournament played over the weekend. Nouveau's special events will tap areas that focus specifically on empowerment, entrepreneurial development and small businesses.

The Market

The worldwide market for Bump It Up is estimated to be approximately 800 million, most of whom are ages twelve to thirty-four. Within the volleyball market there are at least three segments: indoor, outdoor and sand players. Additionally, within those three categories are four primary segments: two-, three-, four-, and six-player formats. The two-player teams represent the highest, most skilled level of volleyball players. These players generally play exclusively in the sand. The remaining player formats represent a majority of the indoor competition.

Specifically, potential primary Bump It Up players are junior high, high school, college, former college and recreational players. In 1992 there were 300,000 girls and 23,586 boy players in the U.S.

Professional Development

The number of individuals who attended professional development seminars and conferences in 1994 exceeded 10 million. It is safe to assume that in this age of corporate down-sizing and entrepreneurship this number will continue to increase.

Marketing

Bump It Up players are solicited by direct mail promotions and through an aggressive direct response radio campaign. Nouveau's strategy for marketing Bump It Up is simple: Use the success of local tournaments to expand statewide in 1995, nationally by 1996 and internationally by 1997. Currently, Nouveau is scheduling tournaments for the 1995 tour, which already includes two Austin events, Killeen and San Antonio, Texas.

Special Events

Participants for the professional conferences and special events are attracted through direct mail and print advertising in business publications and newspapers.

Management

Nouveau, Inc. is managed by Fran Harris, President, who also founded Bump It Up in 1994. Fran has been an entrepreneur since she started her first business enterprise at age nine. She brings sixteen years of sports marketing, publicity and promotions experience to Nouveau. She has spent the last ten years in sales and marketing, including a successful sales management and training and development career with consumer products giant, Procter & Gamble. Additionally, she is an author, whose second book, *About My Sister's Business,* will be published by Simon & Schuster in 1996.

She is a syndicated columnist who has been featured in numerous national publications and was recently nominated for *Inc.*'s Entrepreneur of the Year. She was an All American basketball player at the University of Texas, which she led to a perfect season and national championship in 1986. She has played professionally in Europe and was an alternate on the 1988 U.S. Olympic team.

The Investment Opportunity

Nouveau has secured $100,000 in capital and is now seeking $250,000 to continue funding its next phase of operating, development and expansion of Bump It Up volleyball tournaments and professional development conferences. Common stock is priced at twenty-five cents ($0.25) per share. Any investment in Nouveau, given it is in the early stages of existence, would be highly speculative and would involve a high degree of risk.

Opportunity, Philosophy and Strategy

It is estimated that at least 95 percent of the U.S. population has seen or participated in a sporting event. Little league participation has skyrocketed over the last five years and collegiate sports are expanding into sports such as soccer, rugby and water volleyball. With the popularity of amateur sports, Nouveau is primed to capitalize on this excitement by producing an amateur event, Bump It Up, that allows participants to compete for cash and other prizes.

It is further estimated that more than 65 percent of the professional population has heard a lecture, attended a seminar or workshop or bought a professional development audio or video cassette within the last six months.

Nouveau Business Philosophy

Nouveau was founded to provide teamwork and competitive opportunities for individuals of diverse backgrounds. It is one of two companies currently providing this service through major amateur sporting events. Nouveau strives to capture a market untapped by competition, the junior, twelve-to-seventeen-year-old market. Because Bump It Up's market covers a wide spectrum of ages, Nouveau's marketing strategy must be diverse in nature.

Nouveau will break into an area that is virtually untapped—entrepreneurship and small business development—in a conference setting. These conferences will provide participants the opportunity to gain knowledge in areas including securing capital, maximizing a small advertising budget and expanding or starting a business.

Nouveau's Business Strategy

Nouveau is committed to bringing amateurs from different locations together to compete in Bump It Up. Nouveau's strategy is to take advantage of the opportunities available at the grassroots level by capitalizing on the steady growth of volleyball, subsequently tapping into other amateur sports. Nouveau will partner with companies that allow Nouveau's events to be different than the competition from an aesthetic perspective. For example, a pending partnership with SportCourt, a flooring manufacturer, would allow Nouveau to produce any event as an outdoor *or* indoor event, regardless of the season.

Nouveau's approach to professional development conferences, a somewhat saturated industry, is to utilize unconventional thinking and focus on untapped markets, such as gay and lesbian professional development and recognition events, ethnic and diverse markets, as well as women and youth entrepreneurship.

Nouveau Is Committed to the Community

A portion of Bump It Up's proceeds go to a carefully selected charitable organization. Nouveau has taken a special approach to selecting that organization. Rather than going after the often-used, sometimes overexposed charities, Nouveau will strive to educate through its selection of charities. The 1995 charity will be FAITH Home for babies who are HIV+ or who have AIDS. By partnering with a charity, Nouveau not only has the opportunity to give back to the community, it also allows the charitable organization to capitalize on substantial publicity and advertising.

Fran Harris has spent her entire life in the area of self-empowerment and helping to move people forward. The development of Nouveau's special events is a result of that commitment. In September of 1995, Nouveau will bring the first of four national speakers to Austin. Terrie Williams, author of *The Personal Touch* and president of The Terrie Williams Agency in New York, will speak to professionals on the business of people.

The Business

Nouveau is developing Bump It Up as the premier amateur volleyball tournament in the world. The first Bump It Up tournament was done in Austin, Texas in June of 1994. That pilot three-on-three tourney drew more than thirty teams. In 1995, Nouveau plans to tour a minimum of three Texas cities in 1995, ten U.S. cities in 1996 and will go international by 1997.

One unique aspect of Bump It Up is Nouveau's approach to customer service. Nouveau is the only company that provides special surfaces for the physically challenged participants. Another unique element of the Nouveau system is that it seeks to provide employment, womentoring and networking opportunities for young entrepreneurs and community volunteers.

Has It Been Done Before?

Bump It Up's pilot tournament was launched June 1994, a month after its prime competitor, Spike It Up, a production of Streetball Partners, was done in Dallas, Texas. This organization is also the creator of Hoop It Up, the world's largest three-on-three basketball tournament. Hoop It Up began in one city in 1986 and grew to more than fifty in eight years, including an international format. Nouveau will duplicate the success of an already proven concept: Amateur sports participation is increasing at an alarmingly fast pace. The second annual Austin Bump It Up was a huge success. Results are below.

	June 1994	May 1995
Teams	30	90
Players	90	450
Spectators	50	250
Local sponsors	3	8
National sponsors	0	3

Current Year Plans

The 1995 Texas Bump It Up Tour

Austin	May 27, 28
Georgetown	July 4
Austin-Aquafest	August 22–31
San Antonio	September 2, 3
Killeen	October

1995 Special Events Tour

1st ExecuNet Conference	September 15	Austin
2nd ExecuNet Conference	October 21	Austin
3rd ExecuNet Conference	November	Houston
4th ExecuNet Conference	November	Dallas
5th ExecuNet Conference	December	San Antonio

As Bump It Up and ExecuNet gain more credibility and popularity, Nouveau will be able to secure more and larger sponsorships by offering them the opportunity to capture a captive target audience. The 1995 BIU schedule represents a strong volleyball community with more than 30,000 players in Austin, San Antonio and Killeen combined. The special events tour taps into the strongest professional communities in Texas, with plans to expand nationally in 1996.

Funds Sought

Nouveau has secured more than $100,000 in capital and is seeking $250,000 to continue funding its next phase of operating and expanding. Common stock is priced at twenty-five cents ($0.25) per share.

Investment Letter

All shareholders in Nouveau are required to sign an investment letter stating, among other things, that the shareholder has been provided with all requested financial and other information, that that shareholder understands that an investment in a start-up company involved in the events production industry is highly speculative and involves a substantial degree of risk, and that the shareholder has sufficient resources so that a loss of the entire investment in Nouveau will not produce economic hardship. A sample of this investment letter is attached as Exhibit 1.

Management

The success of Nouveau will largely depend on the contribution of its key management, Fran Harris, and its ability to attract and retain highly skilled management, sales and marketing personnel.

Fran Harris, President

Fran Harris, a marketing and sales executive, is responsible for the overall development of Bump It Up. Her responsibilities include securing corporate sponsorships, supervising tournament operations, staffing all events and soliciting a suitable charity. An Olympic athlete with more than twenty years experience as an entrepreneur and a successful career as a sales and training executive for consumer products giant, Procter & Gamble, Fran makes an exceptional leader for Nouveau Sports Marketing. She has a wealth of hands-on knowledge and familiarity with sports management and marketing events. She has also spent her career utilizing her creative talents; she is an author, small business consultant and motivational speaker.

Marketing

Nouveau's market is literally anyone who likes or plays volleyball. Bump It Up tournaments are structured such that there is a division for every player, regardless of skill, experience or age. Bump It Up will be marketed differently depending on the site. However, the basic strategy is to utilize a data base of more than 10,000 volleyball players, and tap into school systems, volleyball clubs, parks, recreation leagues and leisure formats.

The key to growth is saturation and penetration. Bump It Up's main marketing vehicle is, again, direct mail and radio. Radio sponsorships typically cost $3,000 to $5,000 in exchange for $10,000 of media buys. Bump It Up offers participants the convenience of registering for events by phone, fax or mail. Participants may also pay with Mastercard, Visa, American Express and Discover.

Market penetration is critical to Bump It Up's success. Nouveau will saturate the market by utilizing many distribution points for Bump It Up entry forms such as local retail outlets, restaurants, parks, recreation centers and sporting goods stores.

Corporate Sponsorships

Critical to the success of Bump It Up and any Nouveau event is the securing of corporate moneys. In exchange for their dollars businesses receive substantial advertising and publicity, increased awareness through sampling, signage and banners. Corporate sponsorships typically range between $500 and $15,000 per event, per city. In exchange, sponsors receive benefits that include sampling, prominence in media and on advertising specialties and banners/signage during events.

Nouveau is negotiating future sponsorship deals with several national sponsors including Spalding, the ball manufacturer of the Pro Beach circuit; Music Television (MTV) and Pepsi. Additionally, local sponsorships will be solicited for individual tournaments.

Risk Factors

As a start-up company, investment into Nouveau involves a high degree of risk and prospective investors should consider the risk factors involved with a venture such as Nouveau. These factors include, but are not limited to, the following:

(1) Insufficient Support for Future Capital Needs

Nouveau expects that the net proceeds in the development of its first full year with tournament formats will be only sufficient to satisfy its capital requirements for the first months of its operations. Additional capital must be secured. Nouveau's capital requirements up to and beyond the time for product market introduction will depend on many factors including the rate at which corporations and businesses support by contributing their marketing dollars as well as the rate of market acceptance.

(2) Development of Alternative Products by Competitor

Even if Nouveau's Bump It Up gains rapid market acceptance from players, our success is still dependent on being sufficiently capitalized until we gain momentum with sponsors. Since it will take time to penetrate the specific segments within the volleyball market, our success will depend heavily on being sufficiently capitalized to do direct mail and all forms of advertising.

(3) Market Acceptance

Nouveau is at an early stage of development and is subject to all of the risks inherent in the establishment of a new business enterprise. Foremost among those risks is the response of the market to the products and services offered. No assurances can be made quantitatively or qualitatively of a positive market response. As mentioned in a previous section, the results of the second annual Bump It Up indicate that once Nouveau and Bump It Up establish credible name recognition, additional player formats and suitable playing surfaces the market will respond positively.

Management of Growth

Nouveau has already received twenty requests to produce events in other states for 1996. Nouveau intends to meet this challenge by examining which markets present a clear immediate opportunity—from a participant, community and sponsor perspective. This growth could place a significant strain on the current Nouveau management, operational and financial resources if the company is not sufficiently capitalized. Nouveau's failure to manage growth and stay proactive in its expansion plans would have an adverse effect on Nouveau's results and its ability to execute and implement its business strategy.

CONFIDENTIAL

FRAN HARRIS
709 OAKLAND AVENUE
AUSTIN, TEXAS 78703
(512) 472-7465

MARKETING MANAGER

Product & Account Management • Business Development • Marketing Programs • Marketing Research • Sales Management • Training Programs

---

SUMMARY

A resourceful, results-oriented marketing manager with a record of generating significant revenues through effective product and account management for a Fortune 500 consumer products distribution company and several multimillion-dollar wholesale and retail customers. Demonstrated ability to identify potential marketing opportunities, then develop and implement comprehensive action plans that achieve corporate objectives. Strong closer.

PROFESSIONAL ACCOMPLISHMENTS

- As the account executive for a multibillion-dollar consumer products distribution company, responsible for sales through a large retail customer; successfully planned and directed introduction of a new health-care product in two major Texas markets—including all shelving, merchandising and pricing initiatives—with initial results exceeding retail sales objectives by about 17 percent.
- Directed a seven-member team which became the top-performing group in the district, generating a 35 percent sales increase over the same six-month period the previous year on annualized sales approaching a half-million dollars.
- Managed the allocation of $1.3 million to part-time contractors across multiple brands.
- Identified for a multistore account additional annual sales potential of about $1 million through improved inventory management; then presented results to company executives, store manager and sales force. Assisted in developing new performance incentives and tracked results, including store volume, sales revenues and customer satisfaction; ultimately generated an average 25 percent improvement in sales across all categories.
- Successfully implemented new merchandising concepts with a large retail customer, exceeding sales objectives for a 13-store district despite a 50 percent reduction in available space—effectively doubling display productivity.
- Established a business relationship with a difficult yet potentially important account, ultimately facilitating faster introduction of new products—including the use of pre-assembled display units which saved the customer nearly $700,000 annually—development of more effective display and merchandising programs and the implementation of more aggressive pricing initiatives.
- As part of a comprehensive business development effort, successfully developed more vice president and other senior-level business contacts in six months as a unit manager than had been established in the preceding two-and-a-half years.
- Directed marketing presentations at an important customer-sponsored trade show, generating product sales 16 percent greater than the previous year.

- As a training and development specialist and recruiting coordinator for one company, successfully directed the new sales representative training school "Fast Start," developed a training module and evaluation program for new sales hires and account managers and served as a moderator for implementation of a new sales organization.
- Designed and trademarked a team-building program presented within the multibillion-dollar consumer products company and subsequently to other Fortune 500 corporations.

EMPLOYMENT HISTORY

An Account Executive in Austin, TX, *Procter & Gamble Distributing Company*, Cincinnati, OH. Previously employed as a Unit Manager, Market Field Representative and a Sales Representative, also with Procter & Gamble. Also a public relations assistant, Grissom, Webb & Webb, Austin.

EDUCATION

Master's degree in Journalism, minoring in Business Administration, University of Texas, Austin, TX.
Bachelor's degree in Journalism, University of Texas

AFFILIATIONS

Numerous civic, charitable and athletic organizations and events.

PERSONAL

Olympic Basketball Team (1988)
Captain of University of Texas' NCAA national champion women's basketball team (1986)
Author, *About My Sister's Business* (Simon & Schuster, 1996)

References available upon establishment of a strong mutual interest

Appendix A: Articles and Media Kit

This appendix contains articles or clippings that discuss Nouveau, Fran Harris, professional development, volleyball or other industry topics.

NOUVEAU SPORTS & EVENT MARKETING INC.
1615 WEST SIXTH
AUSTIN, TEXAS 78703

Balance Sheet
May 1995

Assets

Cash On Hand			
Checking Account I	$17,544.49		
Total Cash On Hand		$17,544.49	
Computer		4,702.81	
Software		80.98	
Office Furniture		597.19	
Total Assets			**$22,925.47**

Liabilities

Equity

Capital			
Owner			
Owner Investment	$38,338.06		
Total Owner		$36,338.06	
Investors			
Max Griffin & Associates	$66,680.00		
Total Investors		$66,680.00	
Total Capital		$103,018.06	
Current Year Earnings		(40,209.22)	
Retained Earnings		(39,883.37)	
Total Equity			$22,925.47

Total Liability & Equity   **$22,925.47**

NOUVEAU SPORTS & EVENT MARKETING INC.
1615 WEST SIXTH
AUSTIN, TEXAS 78703

Profit & Loss Statement
May 1995

Income

Expenses

Credit Card Equipment	$ 115.90
Postage & Delivery	213.79
Telephone	526.19
Tournament Operations	3,172.91
Printing	182.35
Advertising	81.00
Office Expense	253.60
Professional Memberships	138.26
Consulting FH	4,200.00
Advertising BIUA	1,388.00
Equipment BIUA	2,783.01
Total Expenses	$13,055.01

Net Profit/(Loss)	($13,055.01)

NOUVEAU SPORTS & EVENT MARKETING INC.
1615 WEST SIXTH
AUSTIN, TEXAS 78703

Profit & Loss Statement
May 1995

	Selected Period	Budgeted	$ Difference	% Difference
Income				
Expenses				
Credit Card Equipment	$ 115.90	$ 0.00	$ 115.90	NA
Postage & Delivery	213.79	0.00	213.79	NA
Telephone	526.19	0.00	526.19	NA
Tournament Operations	3,172.91	0.00	3,172.91	NA
Printing	182.35	100.00	82.35	82.3%
Advertising	81.00	4,500.00	(4,419.00)	(98.2%)
Office Expense	253.60	250.00	3.60	1.4%
Professional Memberships	138.26	0.00	138.26	NA
Consulting FH	4,200.00	0.00	4,200.00	NA
Park Deposits	0.00	3,000.00	(3,000.00)	(100.0%)
Advertising BIUA	1,388.00	0.00	1,388.00	NA
Equipment BIUA	2,783.01	0.00	2,783.01	NA
Total Expenses	13,055.01	7,850.00	5,205.01	66.3%
Net Profit/(Loss)	($13,055.01)	($7,850.00)	($5,205.01)	66.3%

NOUVEAU SPORTS & EVENT MARKETING INC.
1615 WEST SIXTH
AUSTIN, TEXAS 78703

Accounts List (Detail)

Account	Type	Header/Detail	Level	Chkg	Balance
Assets	Asset	Header	1	N	$ 13,708.23
Cash On Hand	Asset	Header	2	N	8,327.25
Checking Account 1	Asset	Detail	3	Y	8,327.25
Checking Account 2	Asset	Detail	3	Y	0.00
Accounts Receivable	Asset	Detail	2	N	0.00
Office Equipment	Asset	Header	2	N	0.00
Office Original Cost	Asset	Detail	3	N	0.00
Office Accum. Depreciation	Asset	Detail	3	N	0.00
Automobiles	Asset	Header	2	N	0.00
Auto Original Cost	Asse	Detail	3	N	0.00
Auto Accum. Depreciation	Asset	Detail	3	N	0.00
Leasehold Improvements	Asset	Header	2	N	0.00
Improvements Original Cost	Asset	Detail	3	N	0.00
Improvements Amortization	Asset	Detail	3	N	0.00
Pre-paid Insurance	Asset	Detail	2	N	0.00
Deposits Paid	Asset	Detail	2	N	0.00
Computer	Asset	Detail	2	N	4,702.81
Checks Cashed	Asset	Detail	2	N	0.00
Software	Asset	Detail	2	N	80.98

Account	Type	Header/Detail	Level	Chkg	Balance
Office Furniture	Asset	Detail	2	N	597.19
Liabilities	Liability	Header	1	N	0.00
Credit Cards	Liability	Header	2	N	0.00
American Express	Liability	Detail	3	Y	0.00
MasterCard	Liability	Detail	3	Y	0.00
Visa	Liability	Detail	3	Y	0.00
Accounts Payable	Liability	Detail	2	N	0.00
Sales Tax Payable	Liability	Detail	2	N	0.00
Accrued Payroll Taxes	Liability	Header	2	N	0.00
Federal Taxes Payable	Liability	Detail	3	N	0.00
State Taxes Payable	Liability	Detail	3	N	0.00
FICA Taxes Payable	Liability	Detail	3	N	0.00
Unemployment Taxes Payable	Liability	Detail	3	N	0.00
Bank Loans	Liability	Detail	2	N	0.00
Client Deposits	Liability	Detail	2	N	0.00
Notes Payable	Liability	Detail	2	N	0.00
Equity	Equity	Header	1	N	13,708.23
Capital	Equity	Header	2	N	103,018.06
Owner	Equity	Header	3	N	36,338.06
Owner Investment	Equity	Detail	4	N	36,338.06
Partner A Withdrawal	Equity	Detail	4	N	0.00
Investors	Equity	Header	3	N	66,680.00
Max Griffin & Associates	Equity	Detail	4	N	66,680.00
Partner B Withdrawal	Equity	Detail	4	N	0.00
Current Year Earnings	Equity	Detail	2	N	(49,426.46)

Account	Type	Header/Detail	Level	Chkg	Balance
Retained Earnings	Equity	Detail	2	N	(39,883.37)
Historical Balancing	Equity	Detail	2	N	0.00
Income	Income	Header	1	N	5,172.87
Media Billings	Income	Detail	2	N	0.00
Copywriting Income	Income	Detail	2	N	0.00
Consulting	Income	Detail	2	N	500.00
Creative Income	Income	Detail	2	N	0.00
Production Income	Income	Detail	2	N	0.00
Delivery Fees Collected	Income	Detail	2	N	0.00
Late Fees Collected	Income	Detail	2	N	0.00
Other Income	Income	Detail	2	N	0.00
BIU-Austin	Income	Detail	2	N	4,471.35
Vendors-BIU-Austin	Income	Detail	2	N	201.52
Expenses	Expense	Header	1	N	54,599.33
Purchases	Expense	Detail	2	N	0.00
Commissions Paid	Expense	Detail	2	N	0.00
Depreciation Expense	Expense	Detail	2	N	0.00
Contract Services	Expense	Header	2	N	0.00
Art Production	Expense	Detail	3	N	0.00
Copywriting Expenses	Expense	Detail	3	N	0.00
Production Expenses	Expense	Detail	3	N	0.00
Creative Expenses	Expense	Detail	3	N	0.00
Photography	Expense	Detail	3	N	0.00
Discounts	Expense	Header	2	N	0.00
Discounts Given	Expense	Detail	3	N	0.00
Discounts Taken	Expense	Detail	3	N	0.00

Account	Type	Header/Detail	Level	Chkg	Balance
Dues & Subscriptions	Expense	Detail	2	N	0.00
Credit Card Equipment	Expense	Detail	2	N	677.01
Insurance	Expense	Detail	2	N	0.00
Interest	Expense	Detail	2	N	0.00
Late Fees Paid	Expense	Detail	2	N	0.00
Leasehold Improvement Expense	Expense	Detail	2	N	0.00
License Fees	Expense	Detail	2	N	0.00
Maintenance & Repairs	Expense	Detail	2	N	0.00
Media Bookings	Expense	Detail	2	N	0.00
Office Supplies	Expense	Detail	2	N	654.47
Payroll Taxes	Expense	Detail	2	N	0.00
Postage & Delivery	Expense	Detail	2	N	2,250.51
Rent	Expense	Detail	2	N	0.00
Salaries	Expense	Header	2	N	0.00
Salary, Partner A	Expense	Detail	3	N	0.00
Salary, Partner B	Expense	Detail	3	N	0.00
Salaries, Administrative	Expense	Detail	3	N	0.00
Salaries, Creative	Expense	Detail	3	N	0.00
Telephone	Expense	Detail	2	N	2,309.78
Travel & Entertainment	Expense	Detail	2	N	1,104.85
Utilities	Expense	Detail	2	N	0.00
Other Expenses	Expense	Detail	2	N	0.00
Bank Charges	Expense	Detail	2	N	9.58
Credit Card Charges	Expense	Detail	2	N	102.36
Taxes	Expense	Detail	2	N	0.00
Marketing Consulting	Expense	Detail	2	N	290.04

Account	Type	Header/Detail	Level	Chkg	Balance
Tournament Operations	Expense	Detail	2	N	3,243.38
Graphic Artist	Expense	Detail	2	N	379.62
Charity	Expense	Detail	2	N	814.99
Trade Shows	Expense	Detail	2	N	650.00
Printing	Expense	Detail	2	N	5,423.90
Advertising	Expense	Detail	2	N	1,343.93
Parking	Expense	Detail	2	N	0.00
Direct Mail	Expense	Detail	2	N	602.77
Storage	Expense	Detail	2	N	225.00
Hotel	Expense	Detail	2	N	0.00
Professional Resources	Expense	Detail	2	N	23.92
Legal & Accounting	Expense	Detail	2	N	989.95
Office Expense	Expense	Detail	2	N	2,520.46
Professional Services	Expense	Detail	2	N	626.50
Professional Memberships	Expense	Detail	2	N	363.26
Media Kit	Expense	Detail	2	N	0.00
Consulting FH	Expense	Detail	2	N	14,700.00
Chargebacks	Expense	Detail	2	N	175.00
Park Deposits	Expense	Detail	2	N	2,400.00
Press Conference	Expense	Detail	2	N	33.12
Advertising BIUA	Expense	Detail	2	N	5,084.80
Equipment BIUA	Expense	Detail	2	N	2,880.73
T-shirts BIUA	Expense	Detail	2	N	2,672.00
Printing BIUSA	Expense	Detail	2	N	1,905.00
Printing BIUAq	Expense	Detail	2	N	130.45
America Online	Expense	Detail	2	N	11.95

Financing Your Business

❖ ❖ ❖

GETTING IN SHAPE TO RAISE MONEY

If it seems as though I'm always on the "in shape" soap box, I am. It's because I believe so fervently in being ready for everything. And raising money is no different. Raising money is a time-consuming endeavor. It wears on your mind and body, so they both must be ready. Ready to land millions of dollars. Ready to be rejected hundreds of times.

RELATIONSHIPS ARE EVERYTHING

Before you open your mouth to ask anyone for anything, let me tell you something that's vital to landing money. *Getting money, getting clients and building a successful business will depend on your ability to build solid business relationships.* I've heard some strange (but not so strange) reasons for why people are able to build good relationships with investors and subsequently get money from them:

1. They are fraternity or sorority siblings.
2. Their children attend the same school or college.
3. Their kids are teammates in sports, dance or theater.
4. They belong to the same civic, social or country club.
5. They share the same political views.

WHAT ARE YOUR OPTIONS?

You can borrow money from just about anybody. However, here are a few conventional places to find money.

> Private financial institutions
> Venture capitalists
> Small Business Investment Companies (SBIC)
> Small investment banks
> Finance companies
> Federal or state agencies
> Small business administration
> State development agencies
> Public financial institutions
> Banks
> Private investors
> Family
> Friends
> Private Financial Institutions

Before you ask anybody for money, make sure you know three things:

(1) how much you need;
(2) what you're going to use it for; and
(3) where you're going to get the rest of it if the investor gives you only a portion of what you need.

Unfortunately, seed money, or the money you need to literally get your business off the ground, usually comes from your personal funds plus friends and family. Many start-up businesses fail in the start-up stage, not because they are incompetent idiots, but rather they failed to come up with the clear, concise terms of what cash they need. You, the new entrepreneur, need to determine exactly how much money you'll need, not only to get your business going today, but also how much you'll need to sustain you for at least twelve months.

Let's go through an exercise to help you figure out how much you need to launch your enterprise. Let's say that I lived in Florida, so my snow cone business is not subject to real fluctuations from the weather. I can run it from January to December. To get it going, I need to determine what I need to sell one snow cone. I don't really need an office but, for practical purposes, let's say I need an office to meet vendors and suppliers.

The upcoming chart shows how money will flow in and out of my busi-

Monthly Financing Chart			
	Jan.	**Feb.**	**Mar.**
Sales	500	600	600
Less Collections/Returns			
Total Sales	500	600	600
Cash Expenses			
Payroll	20	20	20
Operating Expenses			
Snow Cone Flavors	25	25	25
Cups	10	10	10
Spoons	10	10	10
Napkins	5	5	5
Cooler	100	0	0
Ice	30	30	30
Scooper	25	0	0
Pump for Flavors	15	10	10
Rent	100	100	100
Telephone	25	25	25
Advertising	10	10	10
Office Supplies	10	10	10
Total Expenses	385	350	350
Monthly Profit or Loss	115	250	250

ness on a monthly basis. It shows how much money I will need to finance this stage of my business as well as expected sales. This is an extremely simple example that can be tailored to meet your needs, and it's easy to set up for your particular business. The important thing is to try to include every single item you need to run your business effectively.

BE THRIFTY

Remember, your business needs your money and your smarts. Be frugal at the beginning. You don't need that $500 phone system that pages you when you're on the line and another call comes in, serves you exotic coffees and biscotti and returns your calls for you. Go with the simple and efficient model that will save you bucks. A common mistake we, black folks, black women business owners make is to overspend unnecessarily. This behavior will kill your business. So, go slow. Spend money only on what you need.

FORECASTING

The exercise you went through regarding your capital needs is important for a number of reasons. First, effective forecasting is a smart business practice. Those forecasts should guide you and help you understand where you are on a monthly basis and what you can expect from your business. Second, it takes the guesswork out of your business. Third, it shows prospective businesses that you mean business and that you're not here today, gone tomorrow. Let your forecasts be your business bible and it will be difficult for you to go wrong. Remember also that forecasts can be changed. If economic trends change, you gather new data. When changes occur simply revisit your forecasts and make the necessary adjustments, plus jot a note explaining why your numbers changed.

Example: The number of teams entering one of my tournaments changes from 500 to 250 because volleyball players are on strike.

HOW RISKY OF AN INVESTMENT ARE YOU?

When you approach someone for money, they may run a risk analysis of you. Most of the time this is just a study of your business situation; they ask themselves the following questions: Does the product or service you're offering fill a need or meet a market or demand? Do people want it, and what are they willing to pay for it? Does this person have enough personal savings to take care of personal expenses while the business is developing?

Does Your Service or Product Meet a Market Demand?

Many people rant and rave about their business enterprises because they think it's the best thing since pot liquor. But unless you plan to be your only customer, you don't have a business.

Do People Want It?

Let's say you have a product that the black community needs but, unless they know that they need it, they're not going to buy it. I tested one of my businesses by placing an ad in a national publication. My product was geared toward African American professionals. I saw the field wide open and wondered why there weren't more of us capitalizing on, what appeared to me, a phenomenal business opportunity and something our people so desperately needed. Was there no market for these products? Were black professionals not interested in self-empowerment and personal development? I believed there was a market and that we were ready for them. Anyway, I took out an ad in *Black Enterprise,* the ad ran and my suspicions were confirmed. I received an overwhelming response to a business card-size ad that offered blacks help in improving our personal and professional lives.

Do You Have Funds to Live on While Your Business Is Growing?

This is a biggie for investors. They want to make sure you're not using their money to live on. To some degree, investors want to make sure the entrepreneur has given much thought to this question. If you answer, "I'll make it, I've always made it," you are dead in the water. Don't say it. You won't get my money saying this and I believe in you. The answer, "I think I'll probably get help from my spouse, parents, homeless sister, crackhead friend," is another killer. This sentence is filled with too many uncertainties. Tell an investor that you *think* you'll be able to get some money to pay your rent and they will toss your business plan in Thursday's trash. Have a definite plan for how you will live or don't ask anyone for money.

VENTURE CAPITAL FIRMS

What is a venture capitalist? A venture capitalist can be an individual, but it's usually a company that invests, usually at the start-up stages of a business. Most venture capitalists invest capital in exchange for equity in your company. In other words, if I were a venture capitalist and you wanted me to invest $10,000 dollars into your company, I'd want to know what percentage of your company would a $10,000 investment represent. Twenty? Forty? Venture capitalists generally look for a range of returns to fall between the 25 to 40 percent per year. Obviously this in itself is a weeding out process because not many small, new companies can afford to dish out those kinds of returns. Venture capital firms come in all sizes and shapes, colors and hues. Some have $50,000 to invest, others have billions.

FEDERAL AND STATE AGENCIES

You've probably heard of the SBA or Small Business Administration. It's probably the best known federal agency for helping start-up companies. Every major city has an SBA office, and the application process is generally painless. The SBA offers basically two types of assistance: direct loans and guarantees for bank loans. Said another way, you can get your money directly from the SBA or from the bank because the SBA guarantees it. Here's the trick. In order to get an SBA loan, you must be turned down by at least two commercial banks.

SBA Low Doc Loan

This is a one-page application for entrepreneurs seeking $100,000 or less. If you have 100 or fewer employees and your average annual sales for the preceding three years do not exceed $5 million, you qualify. Low Doc focuses on your credit history, your character and your business experience, and banks love 'em! Plus the approval process is said to take only three days!

Microloan Programs

Recently, the SBA has placed more than 101 economic groups around the country with as much as $2.5 million each. Their goal is to provide technical assistance and make loans of up to $25,000 to companies in inner cities and rural areas—a big proportion of these run by women and minorities. The average microloan is approximately $10,000, compared to more than $150,000 for traditional SBA programs.

The Women's Prequalification Pilot Loan Program

The SBA is attempting to increase the number of SBA-guaranteed loans that go to women. Last June, they introduced the Women's Pre-Equal program, which is geared toward helping women business owners qualify for loans of $250,000 or less. Under this program a woman business owner can receive preapproval from the SBA for a loan guarantee before going to a bank. Since its inception in 1994, the program, which is piloted in sixteen sites, has approved more than 350 loans, totaling $33 million. For more information call the Office of Women's Business Ownership (202-205-6673).

COMMERCIAL BANKS

Commercial Banks are one of the less expensive sources of borrowing as a small company. According to *Money* magazine, in 1994, U.S. banks handed out $646.4 billion in commercial loans, up from 10.1 percent in 1993. Commercial lenders typically charge interest rates of just one to two percentage points above prime for small business loans. Currently, small business loans are around 9 percent.

What do you need to do before applying for a loan? Get to know your banker or investor. Invite him or her to lunch to discuss the city's economic vitality, sports and, of course, your business. Getting financing is just like courting a client. You need to get to know each other to feel good about doing business together. Would you buy a car without a test drive? Probably not. Well, you're the car, and your investor needs to know that you can handle the road, if you hug the curves and how many miles you get per gallon.

Borrow money when you don't need it. Sound weird? It's not. A bank needs to see how you pay your bills. If you plan to start a business, take out a small loan ($3,000 to $5,000) six months before you start your business. Be sure to pay off the loan before you apply for your big (real) loan. Doing this helps you establish a lender/debtor relationship and gives the banker confidence that you'll fulfill your obligations.

Volunteer your financial statements. Having sound financial statements shows the banker that you mean business and that you understand the importance of financial statements. If your business is brand new, offer your personal financial statements. At the end of the chapter are sample income statements, cash flow statements and balance sheets.

Get letters of recommendation to attach to your application. You can never have enough nice words said on your behalf. Get your accountant, attorney or another banker or financial person to write a short note saying what a wonderfully responsible individual you are.

Clean up your personal finances. Remember, bank officers want to know that you're going to pay back the loan. When they check to see if you have a good credit history be sure that your house is in order. It's a good idea to see what your credit report shows. You can order your credit report from one of the three major companies: Equinox (800-685-1111), Trans Union (610-690-4909) or TRW (800-682-7654).

First-Stage Financing

There are generally several factors that go into an investor's decision to give you money: personal history, business experience, financial status and reference letters. Are either of these more important than others? Yes. All are important and a negative in one can sink your ship.

A banker's decision to accept or reject a loan application for first-stage financing is primarily based on the following things:

- relationship between the bank and the applicant
- management ability of the business owner
- references from other banks
- credit history
- amount of equity capital
- collateral to secure the loan
- your ability to repay the loan.

Management Ability

Without a track record, you are all the bank or investor has to go on. If you are well-packaged, the lender or investor feels better. How you present yourself could make or break the deal. Remember, the banker doesn't know you, he or she doesn't know what a brilliant problem-solver you are or how hard you work. All s/he can go on is what s/he sees. A banker/investor must go on the perception of how well you will manage your business and turn a profit.

Personal Data

Like it or not, the banking community still harbors traditional racial and gender-based misconceptions that must be attacked head on if you want to secure financing. This means that your application is subject to your banker's biases and prejudices regarding your skills as a black businesswoman. Some feel that a single woman in her early twenties has no business applying for a start-up loan. Others feel that a black woman past the age of 55 won't be around long enough to pay the loan off. Still others maintain that young applicants lack the necessary business skills and experience to make the enterprise prosper.

Business Experience

Investors also want to know what qualifies you, a black woman, to operate a business. Investors look at experience from two perspectives, management experience and technical experience. Can you manage the business' growth? In other words, what unique talents qualify you to run this business successfully? The answers to these questions must be clear and concise in your mind *before* you approach any investor. Don't expect an investor to understand all of the intricacies of your business. In fact, you're lucky to find one who does. The first three of my nine investment meetings were spent explaining my business. I thought it was a fairly simple and straightforward business, but that's probably because I've done it for more than ten years. If I told you that I was in the sports marketing industry what thoughts would come to mind? Sneakers and tennis racquets? Team uniforms and professional athletes? Actually it's the marketing, the production of sporting and special events.

If a banker can't be convinced that you can handle both the managerial and technical aspects of your new business, it's virtually impossible to get the loan.

Equity Capital

The bank wants to know how much money you're anteing up. Years ago, this wasn't a big deal, but now it is. Today most commercial banks lend a maximum of three times the amount of capital in a business. So, if you want to borrow $30,000 from your bank, you must have contributed at least $10,000 of your own personal cash and assets to the business. The more you put into your business, the more favorably a bank looks on your application. An investor believes that if the entrepreneur has a substantial stake in the business s/he will be less likely to head for the hills when trouble arises.

Cash Flow

How do funds flow through your company? My sports/events marketing doesn't have a daily, steady stream of cash flowing through it. Money comes through it when I produce an event, which might be three or four times a month. One of the reasons I couldn't get conventional financing is that I have a unique business, one that has seasonal cash flow. Even though the bank will have liens on all of the business' assets, it wants to feel comfortable that enough free cash exists to repay the loan and interest when due. The banker refers to free cash as the amount of cash remaining in your company's bank account after all expenses and obligations are paid.

Credit History

Unless you've filed personal or commercial bankruptcy, credit history plays second fiddle to the other factors. This doesn't mean that because you defaulted on your Sears account the bank will forgive and forget—they won't. It simply means that if everything is in order, you shouldn't be turned down for your loan.

Economic Trends

The final bank criteria are current and near-term projected economic conditions. Are we heading for a recession or a boom? If the economy has a clean bill of health, bankers are usually eager to lend money to a good candidate. Are you entering an industry that is growing or declining? I would think that someone whose business venture was building a new computer would have a difficult time getting conventional financing. But wait, isn't the computer industry booming? Of course, that's the problem. The problem is that it's saturated and, unless you have the most revolutionary product, banks will not believe that you can compete with the Apples and IBMs of the world. By the same token, if you are cracking into an area, say, computerized landscaping, where there's tremendous growth opportunity, you may get a banker to listen to you.

Second-Stage Financing

As your company grows into its second stage, a clean record of loan payments causes banks to shift how they see you and your business. They place more weight on the business and less on your personal aptitude and integrity. Personal assets and individual financial standing remain important, but by this time banks expect the business to generate enough cash to repay the loan and look to you only as a fall-back source.

Investors Want to Know Where You're Going
Your business, that is. What are your objectives for the next five, ten or fifteen years? Discussing these objectives clearly reflects your commitment to the business. Bankers only need to see forecasts for new businesses, say, for the first eighteen months—be prepared, however, to discuss your longer term plans.

Questions Bankers/Investors Ask:

1. How will you pay the loan back?
2. When will you pay the loan back?
3. What assurances can you give that you will pay it back on time?
4. What evidence can you give that you know how to run the business?
5. Who is your competition, and what are they doing in the market?
6. Why is your business better than the others?
7. How much money can you put in?
8. Will you sign a personal guarantee?
9. What collateral can you provide?
10. If you are undercollateralized, can you get a cosigner?
11. What are your plans for building your business in the next three, five and ten years?

Don't Take It So Personally
Why is it that some people respond so strongly to being told no? Because we like to have our way, right? I don't know anyone who enjoys rejection. However, we can all learn from it and develop strategies for handling it better. Being turned down for anything can cause you some anxiety but look at it this way. If someone says no to a great idea it means that they need more information. Once they get that information, they may be closer to saying yes. We break out in hives when someone rejects us because we equate being told no to "there's something wrong with me." Think about it—when someone initiates a relationship breakup, we immediately think that somehow, some way, we've fallen short of this person's expectations, when in many cases it's not even about us. It's the same with seeking investors. You must train yourself to handle rejection in a healthier manner. *Remember, when a bankers tells you no, it means that they need more information.*

No Really Means Maybe
A rejection may not mean that you were subpar; it may mean that the banks don't have any money to invest right now. It may also mean that I'm scared

or that I have a low-risk tolerance. Then again it *could* have something to do with you. It could mean that you had a shoddy business plan, and the investors don't feel good about investing in you because they don't think you're capable of building a successful business enterprise.

Investors Invest in People

It doesn't matter how wonderful your idea is, investors invest in people, not ideas. If they feel good about you, you're more likely to get further in the investment process. In fact, investors will even help people they like and feel good about develop stronger business plans by offering advice and counsel on how to strengthen it. Sometimes entrepreneurs, particularly black women, don't understand the personal aspect of seeking money. It behooves you to build rapport with people in the financial community who can vouch for your personal character and integrity.

Breaking Down Barriers

Unless you're well connected in the African American money circle, it's a sure bet that you'll be asking someone who's not black for money. When this happens, *you* must break down the racial and cultural barriers that might exist between you and your potential investor—do not expect the investor to do it. Is this really necessary? Completely and absolutely.

SOURCES OF CAPITAL

Here are a few conventional sources of capital. You decide which is best for you.

Banks

All of the hype and propaganda out there tells you that the banks will hand over their money because you're a black business woman. And I'm sure you've heard or seen all of the Small Business Administration information saying it's upgrading its percentage of moneys to minorities. Don't be fooled by all of this propaganda. Getting money from any conventional financial institution is T-O-U-G-H, period. Tough, not impossible. There are black women who get money from the SBA. I've read about them in *Inc., Entrepreneur, Success* and *Black Enterprise* magazines.

What people *don't* tell you is that the process is sometimes a lengthy, grueling one. Sometimes you'll go through the whole ordeal only to be denied. So don't get your feelings hurt over that rejection letter from the bank president who's told you for 363 days to come see him when you need some money. Instead, get your business plan and investment package together and let's start tapping into other funding opportunities.

Financial Institutions

First, I believe that we should all approach banks for money—if only for the experience. The first time I approached a banker about one of my businesses, she seemed genuinely interested. What ensued, though, told me the true story. I made an appointment with her to explain my business idea and why it was the best thing since Green Apple Now & Laters. She listened intently, nodded and said all the right things. So, of course I thought I was in there! Until she asked for my financial statements. I had put together what I thought were sound financials. She went over them and several days later, explained that they couldn't do the loan. At the time, I had two accounts at that particular bank.

The next week, I closed my accounts and went bank shopping. I was offended and a little angry. Okay, very angry. What did this bank think they were doing, turning down Fran Harris, entrepreneur extraordinaire? When I settled down, I reassessed the whole process. Maybe my financials were weak. I sought advice and learned that they were weak! I also learned that banks luuuuvvv impeccable financial statements! In fact, I learned that what I thought were sound financial statements were amateur at best. Boy, I wouldn't have given me a $50,000 loan either!

Still, I had a good, no, great business idea and I wasn't about to let this lil' ol' bank stop me. I left that situation knowing two things: (1) I still needed the money and (2) my financials needed to be seriously upgraded. I bought a few books on forecasting and financial statements, reworked my numbers and went off to another bank. Same hymn, second stanza. Only this time, I stayed with this bank because they worked with me a little more than the first. Finally, I said forget the banks and I started just talking about my business to professional acquaintances.

This time my self-assessment took a bit longer. Why was I being rejected? I talked to several business and personal acquaintances and, within a week, I had the answer. Financial statements and collateral. I was severely anemic when it came to collateral. I'd driven a company car for almost four years, so I didn't own a car. I was living in an apartment and to my knowledge, my great-grandfather hadn't left me any lake property. No wonder banks wouldn't touch me. Banks need to know that if you fail they can come and get some of your stuff. If you have no stuff, you're an even bigger risk.

Is there hope for you if you have no collateral? Sure, but I wouldn't bank on getting conventional financing. I courted and presented my business plan to one group of potential investors on the average of once a week for at least two months. Finally, they said yes. Yessss! I was so fired up! I had the money to put my dream in motion the way I wanted to and, more important, I learned some valuable business skills along the way. And guess what, I'm going to share it all with you. I don't want you to have the same frustrations I had trying to finance my enterprise. It certainly doesn't make a whole lot of sense to make the same mistakes that I did. So, clue in for the next few pages. If you are intimidated by financial statements and the language of numbers, I say get thee over it. I did. This is one of the most crucial components of building a strong, profitable enterprise.

Can I make another promise? If you will commit to your forecasts and start having a love affair with the numbers around your business, you'll have at least a fifty-yard advantage over other beginning entrepreneurs. I want you to think for a second about where you could get money for your venture. Don't limit yourself. Think of all the possibilities there are out there. You know people with money. Write your thoughts below.

1. _____
2. _____
3. _____
4. _____

I bet you came up with savings, spouse, family and friends. If you did that's great, it's a good start. We will examine the benefits of getting money from these sources and also take a look at alternative sources of funding for your enterprise. First, let's look at the people closest to you.

Family

When it comes to green, blood can seem pretty thin. Family can be good when they're good, but ooooh when they're bad, they're badddddd. The mistake most of us make is not being a sound judge of character. What makes you think that the person in your family who has never been able to keep a dollar in her pocket for a second is going to give you the money she keeps saying she has. Don't expect miracles. And don't take money from family members whose nicknames are Squeakers and Thrifty-Tyrone.

Friends

Sometimes friends are our best source of funds. They're close but not too close. But friends can be just like family in many instances. Let's hope that you've been good when it comes to reliability and handling money, because if you haven't you've already got one strike against you. Our friends know us. Although your friends love you , they also know about your money management skills.

Extended Family

There have been various stages of my business planning where I've considered asking aunts, cousins and uncles to be investors. I did some investigation and discovered there were people in my family who had defaulted on loans (some to me), fallen short on payback promises and certainly not handled their own finances properly. I decided against this option because they were not good prospective investors. For my emotional well-being I decided to pass on extended family members.

WHO ARE GOOD PROSPECTIVE INVESTORS?

Some people truly believe that any money is good money, and I say BEWARE—that philosophy is dangerous! It's erroneous and can cause you much mental anguish. All three of my businesses are in industries that are booming, so I can almost always get a potential investor's attention. The problem is that sometimes I get interest from people whom I would never recruit for my team. Just as investors have a certain criteria for potential entrepreneurs, you too should develop a profile for prospective investors.

What to Look for in Prospective Investors

I don't know about you but I tend to gravitate to people with whom I share certain—not all—characteristics. I like people who are unconventional thinkers, hard smart workers and who have what I call healthy relationships with money, competition and success. If certain qualities are in place, I usually have solid relationships with these people even if we have varying opinions about religion and politics.

Believe me, I have encountered many moneybags who were dying to give me money but who I wouldn't touch with a fifty-foot pole! Why? For various reasons, but mainly because they were either control freaks or egomaniacs, or they were suffering from the I-got-all-the-answers syndrome. No thank you. I'd rather have five small investors with the right attitude than one big one who's certain to try make my life a nightmare. When you're out there looking for money consider the following profile of a good investor.

A good investor has money to spare. You may find someone with money but does s/he have it to give to you? I once had a woman friend who wanted to invest in my company. I was thrilled until she told me that this was her retirement money. I got out of there as soon as I could. I didn't need her golden-years money hanging over my head.

A good investor has money to spare and doesn't mind parting with it. You don't want an investor who's holding on to her money so tightly that she squeaks. If she can't let it go, you don't need it.

A good investor has money to spare and doesn't mind parting with it and is willing to negotiate the terms of repayment. Sharpen your negotiation skills, you'll need them to be in tip-top shape when you're looking for money. No matter what anyone tells you, everything's negotiable. If you find someone who's willing to loan you money, make sure you negotiate terms that you can live with. Don't agree to accept a $10,000 loan at 25 percent interest payable in eighteen months if you don't feel good about those terms.

Before Seeking Investors

❖ Be ready to make your life and your habits an open book. Investors will want to know all of this and more.
❖ Be prepared to tell how much money you're accustomed to earning.
❖ Be prepared to share your plan for how you're going to make money during your lean years.
❖ Do you have a supportive spouse?
❖ How have you paid your bills in the past?
❖ Have you ever been to jail and why?

Impatience Is a Virtue

The investment process is a tedious one. It only took me a week to raise some expansion money, but remember, it took me at least a month to land my initial start-up money. I'm not a patient person, so I won't tell you to be patient. In fact, being *impatient* in this area might help you get your money sooner. Go out there and knock down doors. Remember, our motto: *Expect the best, prepare for the worst.*

Keeping Investors Happy

Remember, getting the money is only half the chore. Once you get it, you must keep your investors feeling good about giving you all of that money. This is so important for us as black women. Remember, no one thinks black women should have access to large sums of money, let alone be running businesses. Instead of being defensive about this fact, just take care of business. This means setting up regular meetings (quarterly, biquarterly) and discussing the progress of your business, complete with financial statements and any other information pertinent to your business. I actually have a bi-monthly meeting with my investors. One of those meetings is to discuss strategies for my business, the other meeting is to review financial statements. Both of these meetings are usually very beneficial and, if there's nothing to discuss, I simply call them and recommend that we skip the meeting. I find that investors are quite responsive when we keep the communication lines open.

The Roles of Investor and Entrepreneur

Just because someone gives you money doesn't mean that they should run your business. *Just because someone gives you money doesn't mean that they should run your business.* JUST BECAUSE SOMEONE GIVES YOU MONEY DOESN'T MEAN THAT THEY SHOULD RUN YOUR BUSINESS. I mean it. When you find an investor, be careful not to relinquish too much of your company's stock (ownership), especially early on. In fact, I would avoid entering a relationship with someone who has always wanted to be in your line of business. This is an early sign of potential danger. I've had a few people who fit into this category whom I had to gently tell that I didn't want their money. They were good people with intentions that could possibly hurt my business down the road. No matter how much you need the money, *never* take money from someone who wants to control your business—you are asking for trouble on top of trouble if you do.

Your job as the entrepreneur is to build a successful business; the role of the investor is to provide financial and often professional advice and assistance. Investors may want to give their input on where to purchase materials or how to go about hiring people, but the ultimate decision is still yours. It's important to learn how to effectively and tactfully deliver this message. Sometimes (often) investors don't know your business as well as you, so you may need to cut them some slack, listen and humor them. Understand also that they want your business to be successful because they have a substantial financial investment at stake. Remember: It's your dream and your business, and no one will love it and nurture it better than you.

Marketing, Public Relations and Advertising, Oh My!

❖ ❖ ❖

THE DYNAMIC TRIO

Some people argue that public relations, marketing and advertising should be separate and unequal. Others maintain that the three should never be separated. While I definitely agree with the latter, you must understand that they all play distinct roles in helping your business succeed. Understanding how they work independently and together will put you on the fast track to business success.

Creating synergy between marketing, advertising and public relations is critical to your business success. When done effectively, it is beautiful to see and the results are amazing. A solid marketing plan incorporates effective advertising, marketing and public relations strategies. To develop this plan, you must define and address each of them separately and then as a team. They *are* a team. In this chapter we'll see how to create a linear relationship between the three components that will result in huge wins for your venture. Let's start with marketing.

WHAT IS MARKETING?

Marketing identifies customer needs and develops strategies to meet them. It researches and discovers what makes your customers tick, finds out what consumers are buying and how they're buying it. Marketing assumes that consumers are just waiting to be told what to do—you just have to figure out the best way to talk to them.

Start-Up Marketing Strategies

Before you can begin to map out a strategy for marketing your service or product, you need to do a mini business review. A business review provides a quantitative and qualitative decision-making basis for the marketing plan you will develop for your company. It helps you understand your history as well as the future of your company. The best thing to do is do the business review twice, once now and then after you've absorbed all of the incredible information in this book! The business review process will better prepare you for starting or running your business more successfully. First you need to know about SWOT.

SWOT

You may have heard of SWOT or some other business tool like it. It's designed to help you analyze the current situation of your business as well as opportunities for growth. In fact, that's what SWOT stands for: Strengths, Weaknesses, Opportunities and Threats.

Strengths What are you good at? What advantage does or will your business have over the competition?

Weaknesses What areas aren't as developed as they need to be, for you personally as well as your business?

Opportunities Is there a market out there to be captured? If so, how will your business strategically gain acceptance in that segment of the market?

Threats Is there a person across town opening at the same time as your business? Does an existing competitor have more money/resources than you? Can they move on something before you?

You, the entrepreneur, must examine SWOT for your enterprise on a regular basis. The most effective way to maximize the SWOT model is through business strategy sessions. Solicit the time of friends and acquaintances who are interested in your business. Buy them pizza and spend four to five hours on your SWOT. Using a flip chart, gather all of the data and compile it. From this session you should have an objective look at your business, its future and potential impediments.

Components of a Business Review

Company and Product Review

You must understand who your company is and what product or service you sell. Here you develop your company mission and write a description of your company's overall business philosophy as it relates to marketing, growth and business success.

Questions: What are my long- and short-term goals and objectives? What are my company's sales goals for the next six months? A year?

Target Market Analysis

Do you have a clear picture of who your consumers are? What are their purchasing habits? Have they bought the type of product you sell?

Questions: How would I describe my consumer in terms of age, sex, income, occupation, education and marital status?

Product Attributes

In this section you get a clear understanding of your product, its benefits and features. You should know why someone would even consider purchasing your product.

Questions: How is my product or service used? How often would a consumer need my product/service?

Distribution/Penetration

Distribution is the method of delivering the product to the consumer. Your role is to determine which methods of distribution are used most successfully in your industry. Penetration refers to the percentage of consumers who use a certain product/service. For example, toothpaste has a 95 percent share in U.S. homes, which means that 9.5 of every 10 homes in America have toothpaste in it.

Questions: Where do consumers purchase your particular product/service? Have trends changed recently—are people buying their greeting cards through catalogs or are people still going to the card shop?

Sales and Market Share Analysis

This section looks at how your industry is doing and how it's done in the past. Have the sales tripled in this field in the last five years and if so, why? Also, which companies are getting all of the business (market share) and why?

Questions: What's driving sales in this category? For example, the fitness industry has experienced tremendous growth lately. Why? Because we seem to be interested in getting and staying in shape.

Pricing

How much will you charge for your product/service? First, you need to find out what people are paying for it currently. Depending on the image you're striving for, you'll want to meet or beat market price. I always go higher—

I'm in a business where people are not extremely price sensitive. I also heard someone once say that if you build a superior product using only the best materials and parts that there's no amount of money that people won't pay for it.

Competition
Yes, you need to know what the comp's doing. The worst thing you can do is ignore your competition—they are a valuable source of information about the industry, consumers and market information.

Questions: How much market share does my competitor have? Are they growing or fading? How is their pricing?

Demand Analysis
This is a biggie. If no one **wants/is demanding** your product/service you don't have any business going into business. The only way to find out whether there's a demand for your product/service is to research and test market.

Questions: How many if any people want my product or service? Where are they?

The Marketing Plan

The following questions are designed to get you to give serious thought to every aspect of your marketing plan. Once you've answered these questions (even if not completely) you will have a clearer understanding of how to develop your business—the dominant goal of marketing. Take your time and don't worry if you don't have the full answer today and if something doesn't pertain to your particular type of business just skip it. The important thing is to touch each question by making it real and alive for your current or prospective business idea.

The Company _____

What is your company's mission?
What business are you in? Be specific and clear.
What are the short-term and long-term goals and objectives of your company?

Long-Term Plans
Are there existing sales goals, profit goals, marketing objectives?
What is the operating budget for your company?
What are the margins, and what are the planned profit contributions of each product?

Is there a corporate philosophy on how to do business?

Is there a plan for how you do business?

What are the principles of the business in regard to working with customers, developing and selling product and internal management?

What is the history of your company?

Why was it started, how did it grow and why has it been successful?

What products does your company sell?

What is the makeup of your products?

Product Competition

What advantages do your products have over the competition?

What is the history of your products?

Have they always been successful?

Over the years, how have your products changed? How has your industry changed?

What is the sales volume, margin and profitability of each product or product line?

What product categories are most important to the company?

What plans are there for growth and expansion among existing product or categories?

New products?

More geographical markets?

New product users?

Are you the first to market the new products?

What single thing does your company want to be known for?

Marketing Advantage

What are you best at? What's the trademark of your company?

Why do consumers purchase from you?

Where has your company succeeded or failed? Why?

To what degree is your company committed to marketing?

Do you have enough resources to develop, execute and analyze results?

Where does marketing fit into your overall organizational structure?

Is your company operations-driven, finance-driven, merchandise-driven, product-driven, sales-driven or marketing-driven?

In other words, what area is most responsible for company's success?

Target Market

What is the national consumer demographic profile of the product category?

What is the profile of the individual who consumes or purchases the most from a volume standpoint?

Do some demographic categories have a higher concentration of purchasers?

What is *your* specific, local customer demographic profile?

How would you describe them in terms of age, sex, income, occupation, education, number of children, marital status, geographic residence, ownership of home and cars?

What are your customers' attitudes, interests and activities?

Are they different, in terms of demographic and lifestyle characteristics, from the national product category consumer profile?

Product Usage

How is your product used?

Why is your product purchased?

What are the benefits inherent in your product that encourage purchase from consumers?

If there are multiple uses of your product, are there consumers who use the product for one type of use or benefit but not another? Are there multiple, independent user groups?

Are the users of the products also the purchasers?

If not, who has the most influence over the purchaser's decision?

Does your target market account for approximately 50 percent of the sales volume, or are you going to specialize against a very narrow segment?

Is the target market growing, stable or shrinking?

Are there distinct secondary target markets for your product that have common characteristics apart from your primary market?

Are there opportunities to tap additional markets? Which ones?

Sales

Is the overall product category strong?

Is it growing or declining? What have industry sales been for the past five years?

What is the percentage of increase over that period?

What are the total company sales and profit levels for the past five years?

What is the growth rate compared to the industry, compared to key competitors?

Are market sales likely to expand or shrink in the next two, five or ten years?

How will this affect your company?

Market Share

What is the market share of your total company sales within your industry over the past five years?

Are you gaining or losing market share? Why?

What is the market share for each of your company's products relative to the national product category or relative to key competitor's products over the past five years? Are you losing or gaining market share?

Which competitors have gained or lost the most market share? Why?

What are the store-for-store sales over the past years?

What's your break-even point?

Seasonality of Sales

What products sell during what time of the year?

Does demand vary by season, business conditions, location, weather? Trading Area?

What is the trading area for your product?

How far do they have to travel to purchase your product?

Brand Loyalty

How loyal are customers to brands?

Do you carry the major brands?

Do you carry a high cost, low cost and medium cost?

Do you know the demographics of customers who buy each?

Buying Habits

What factors are important to the purchaser's decision-making process?

What is the purchase decision sequence a consumer makes when purchasing your product?

How can you positively affect this?

How frequently are purchases made?

What is the purchase cycle for your product?

What is the size and quantity of each purchase?

What is the purchase ratio? What percent of customers make purchases when they visit with you?

Do you follow up with every customer regardless of purchase?

Do customers usually pay with cash/check or do they finance? Do you have demographics of each of these groups?

Pricing

How are your prices compared to local competitors? National competitors?

Does raising or lowering prices affect demand?

Why is your pricing where it is?

Distribution

Does your company use the same distribution channel as your competitors?

What are the strengths and weaknesses of your distribution methods versus your competitors?

How long does it take for a customer to purchase and receive product?

Promotion and Advertising

What are you currently doing to promote your business? Be specific.

What are your plans for attracting customers this year?

What were the results of your company's promotions last year? Your competitors?

What was successful or not?

How do your promotions differ from competitors?

Advertising Message

What kind of advertising have you done?

Which were most effective and how do you know?

What forms of advertising does your competition use?

How does your message differ from your competition?

What are the strengths of your advertising?

What is the amount spent on each media category and the total spent on all media for your company and your competitors?

Do you dominate any one medium?

Where are your competitors the strongest?

Customer Service

What are your company's customer service policies?

Do they differ from the competition? How?

Public Relations

Do you have an active publicity program? Public relations plan?

Does your competitor?

Merchandising

What is the merchandising philosophy?

Does your merchandising help to communicate your position?

PUBLIC RELATIONS: THE MEASUREMENT AND INFLUENCING OF OPINION

Public relations or PR as it's sometimes called is not an exact science. Sometimes viewed as nebulous, it falls in that forbidden gray area of marketing.

Public relations not only influences *opinion,* it also influences *reaction.* Said another way, how you or your company handles any situation—a new product or a crisis—can determine how your public perceives you and your company. Would you believe it if I told you that PR is one of the most critical components to your company's and your personal success? As misunderstood as PR is, you owe it to yourself and your business to learn as much as you can about it.

PR History

Old school public relations used to be the stepchild to marketing and advertising, but not any more. Used to be that PR was reactive and sedentary in nature. Not any more. Contemporary public relations is progressive and innovative. Companies, large and small, are starting to realize the power of public relations. It can be as basic as oatmeal or as sophisticated as what Procter & Gamble had to do when women started to get skin irritations from its new Oil of Olay product in 1995.

Your Personal PR Campaign

Let's talk about your PR for a second. Before you go out to conquer the world (and I know you will), I want to be sure you understand where PR fits into all of our lives as African American female entrepreneurs. It would be nice if we lived in a world that judged our performance and not our skin color and gender for just one day! But face it, that's not our reality right now. So getting your ducks in a row becomes paramount, because everything you do and everything about you as a black female will be dissected. Not fair, huh? I agree, but it's life. So roll with it.

Your personal PR is the best place to start. Everything you do or don't do, for that matter, is a part of your PR campaign. If you're rude to a client, that message will get back to the public so fast that all kinds of relations could be ruined. Don't return your phone calls, and again you've influenced the public's relations with you and your company. I realize that we are all busy superwomen, but you've got to return your phone calls. As African American women, our image is always under scrutiny. I'm not whining. I don't whine. I'm being honest. Our work, our appearances are always under the microscope. So it's important to dot your *i*s and *j*s and cross your *t*s and *f*s. I don't see this as pressure; I want to be seen as an expert, a credible person in whatever I do. So I advise you to pride yourself in being good and don't worry about the outcome. If you play hard, you always win.

It goes back to your company culture. How do you want people to view your company. Don't forget that *you* are a part of that.

Publicity is Advertising

When I left Procter & Gamble in September 1994 to pursue my business full time, I had already made big entrepreneurial plans. One of them was to appear in two national publications by the end of the year. By November, the *Essence* article had run, and I had been quoted in *USA Today*'s Money section. Mission accomplished. When I set my publicity plans for 1995, I wanted to make aggressive goals. Finally, I had it. The goal had to be realistic yet a stretch—appearing in five national publications. By June 1, I'd reached 50 percent of my goal—*Emerge, Today's Black Woman* and *USA Today*. These plans were part of my personal/professional PR campaign. I wanted to be visible, get my name out there and gain exposure.

A friend and I were standing in Barnes & Noble when she picked up a magazine that listed black-owned businesses and asked, "Why aren't you in here?" Before I could answer the question, she said, "because you didn't *know* about it (the magazine)?" We both laughed. My friend knows how much energy I put into publicity and self promotion. Is there a difference between the two? Not where my business is concerned. I don't have a ten-person marketing department. I have a publicist who knows me well and is a sassy and savvy businesswoman. Before I hired her, I *was* my marketing department for the first six years of my business. When you are your own publicist and advertising and marketing departments, you learn quickly how to be creative in your efforts.

Enhance Your Image

Someone once called my office, which incidentally is equipped with all kinds of phone enhancements and mailboxes, and said, "When I call your office it sounds like you have about thirty people working in your organization." Bingo! Sometimes people may be skeptical about working with a new business, particularly a woman or a black woman. So enhancing the appearance of your business can only benefit you.

Mostly everyone has a voice mailbox these days. Be sure your system allows the caller to hear clearly. If you don't have a good speaking voice, get someone to record your message for you. If you have several businesses in one office, it's a good idea to separate them, say, use box 1 for one business and box 2 for the second. This way callers won't get confused about whom they're calling and what they can expect—plus you seem super organized.

How to Get Free Publicity

Yes there's free and paid publicity. Free publicity is what you get when you don't pay money for it! Everything is paid for—in some fashion. The free publicity I'm speaking of is that which doesn't put you into debt. Seriously, free publicity can come in many forms. When you send a press release to the newspaper and they run it, that's free publicity. When someone asks you to speak on your expertise at a brown-bag luncheon, you're getting free publicity. When someone likes your product and runs and tells everyone they know, that's free publicity!

If you're like me when I started out, you don't have a $20,000 advertising budget. Free publicity made me salivate to the point of embarrassment. I knew that in order to be successful, people needed to know that I was in business. Since I didn't have $20,000, I just started telling everybody about me and my business. How? You name it, I did it.

Press Releases

A press or news release is a document that tells a brief story. Its function is to inform of a special event—to announce a sale or the introduction of a new product. It can be sent to anyone from newspaper or magazine editors to organizations and businesses. A press release is your opportunity to tell the story exactly as you wish for it to be told. You are the author, you tell the story. If you want your grand opening to appear to be as large as the Janet Jackson concert, then make the story sound like that.

Press Release

Ex-Longhorn Basketball Star Fran Better Scores with Volleyball

*Second Annual Austin Bump It Up Set
for Memorial Day Weekend*

For Immediate Release	**Contact: Fran Harris**
May 1, 1995	**(512) 472-7485**

Austin, TX—The Second Annual Bump It Up volleyball tournament will be held Memorial Day Weekend, May 27 & 28 at Zilker Park.

Fran Harris, former Longhorn basketball standout, is founder of Bump It Up and President of Nouveau Sports & Event Marketing. Nouveau produced the pilot Bump It Up last June and drew nearly 50 teams despite utilizing only the 3-on-3 format.

"The purpose of the pilot was to get a feel for the volleyball community's pulse. I got great feedback for producing the BIU sequel," she said. Harris's hunch appears to be right on track. Austin has approximately 10,000 volleyball players and in 1994 junior volleyball events pumped in an estimated $54 million into the Austin economy.

"Volleyball has experienced phenomenal growth in the last five years," said Better. "In 96, sand volleyball will be introduced as an Olympic sport, I think that says it right there." The 2nd Annual Bump It Up will use the 2, 4 and 6-player formats—the 2s are arguably the highest level of amateur competition. "There are so many segments within the volleyball community. What will be unique about Bump It Up is that it allows all levels of volleyball enthusiasts the opportunity to participate," she said.

Austin sponsors include The Drew Pearson Company, All Sport, Whataburger, TexStyle, *Austin Monthly*, Zeal Marketing, Caremark Physical Therapy and Sports Medicine, The Greater Austin Sports Foundation and KNACK radio. The Austin charity is FAITH Home for AIDS Babies. Although Harris is still seeking a title sponsor she says she is optimistic about her chances. "Hopefully, the success of Hoop It Up will show potential sponsors just how big amateur sports in this country are," Harris said.

Registration deadline for the Austin tournament is May 24. Participants may call (512) 472-7485 to register or for more information. The 1995 Bump It Up Tour includes Austin, Aquafest, San Antonio on Labor Day weekend and tentatively Houston and Killeen tournaments. Other 95 Nouveau events include The Mo Better Golf Challenge, Hoop Fest and a 3-on-3 basketball tournament.

This release was sent to approximately fifty local and national media two weeks before the event. Of those fifty newspapers, ten ran a portion or the entire release verbatim and three ran features. That's a pretty good return on a twenty-five dollar investment—copying and postage expenses. Seventy-five percent of the features that have been run on me or my company were the result of, you guessed it, a press release from my office. Not many people realize that publicity is an ongoing process. Many people don't realize that writing an effective release could mean thousands of dollars in business or tons of exposure to potential customers. Think of how many advertising dollars I saved by getting all of this free publicity.

My volleyball story ran because it was interesting, timely and complete—I'd done all the work for the newspaper. It gave them enough information to round out a small story. Sometimes editors have space to kill, so they are dying to get interesting stories to run. However, if they have to work too hard to run your story, they probably won't. In other words, if information is missing and they can't get you on the phone on the first try, they are likely to go to the next story. So be sure you are thorough in preparing your press release. Essentially your release should answer the 5 Ws—who, what, when, where and why.

Who? Who is this story about? Is it about your new clothing store? If so be sure to include the pertinent information—name, location and age.

What? What exactly is the purpose of this release? Is it to announce new products, a grand opening or some other unique happening?

When? Is there some special date attached to this story? Are you introducing a new line of products or services and, if so, when can your public expect to see them and subsequently purchase them?

Where? Where is this story taking place? If you are holding a special event, be sure to give landmarks when providing an address (1231 Law Dr., across the street from McDonald's).

Why? What makes you or your product so special? Are you the first black woman to open this kind of business in your state/city? Have you discovered a revolutionary way to do something? Your release should explain (preferably in your headline) why your story is newsworthy.

Now reread that release. Does it answer most of these questions? If not, write in the margins what additional information you would need.

Those are just the basics of press releases. A good release should also be:

Newsworthy I always say if I get a press release and after reading it I can say, "And?" then it's not newsworthy or you've left something out. What makes something newsworthy?

Relevant Imagine this. You live in a small town of 10,000 people. The closest place to get a video is thirty-two miles away. You are a newspaper editor, and a press release with this headline comes across your desk:

Blockbuster Video to Open Labor Day

Do you run this story? Yes, Ma'am! Why? Because it's big news to a town that has to drive a half an hour to rent a video.

Interesting Take the same scenario. Do you think the townspeople would be interested in hearing about the tens of thousands of videos that will be right at their doors within two weeks? Of course they would.

Brief yet meaty Just because I stress brevity doesn't mean that your release should be boring and empty. In fact, it should be just the opposite. Fewer words to more words is my motto. If you can't describe your product, service or special event in a page, it's probably too complicated anyway.

Readable Use the correct format and make it aesthetically pleasing. Don't use a font that's too small or difficult to read. Don't use all caps for more than two words. Use proper line spacing so that there's adequate white space on the page.

Simple You've heard the old KISS rule, right? Keep It Simple, Sister. Releases are read by folks who have about as much time as you and I. If your release means that they have to go to the library to do some research, it's not simple.

Creative Innovation sells and it'll get you more publicity than a boring sheet of paper full of words. Don't be afraid to toss a graphic on your release. Remember, there are at least 1,000 people trying to get the same editor's attention—so be sure yours is eye-catching.

You can't just write up a release and expect to get publicity. You have to have something interesting or controversial to say. Once you discover that you indeed have something to say, you must be good at saying it. If you aren't a good writer, buy a book on writing or have someone write a release for you.

Part of landing publicity is knowing how to package it so that it is well received. If someone told you that they had a diamond ring to give you and then proceeded to hand you a brown paper bag with the ring in it, would you be completely unimpressed with the presentation? (Sure, you'd take it, but would you like the manner in which it was given?) Sometimes we black folks have great ideas, yet we don't know how to package ourselves.

A fellow sister entrepreneur once called and said she needed some marketing advice. She gave me her address and I went over one day after work. A funny thing happened. I couldn't find her shop even though I knew the area quite well. I drove around for fifteen minutes and finally just decided to walk from one end of the block to the other. When I got about half way to the end, she popped out of her shop and said, "where are you going?" "Where's your sign?" I said. "Right there," she said, pointing up as if I should have seen it. I looked around and there it was. A pitiful—no, pathetic—little sign that looked like something I brought home from art class in the second grade. It was ugly, and it was not visual. It was about a 24" × 40" blue wooden sign with small white lettering. It didn't use colors well, and it was too small. I told my friend that part of the reason her business wasn't growing was because no one could find her! Once I got inside, her issues became even more serious. Her place was dirty, messy and completely unorganized. Her *packaging* stunk! I told my friend that if she wanted to stay in business and eventually grow her business she would have to work on her presentation. I told her that everything about her physical business operation looked like she was a poor, starving, country black woman.

Although what I said to her as her consultant may have offended her in the short run, in the long run she knew that I was telling her this because I didn't want her to fail.

Although you'll probably be sending multiple releases out at one time, you'll want to be frugal in your choice of paper. The best bet is a 24-lb. bond sheet of cotton/recycled paper. There are other paper options out there—linen, laid (pinstripes) and colors are all nice, but they send your expenses through the ceiling. Be creative with your actual writing presentation and save money when buying paper. After all, once you catch their eye, your release will be going in the trash or recycle bin in a matter of days.

Since you will have already bought your letterhead, there's not much to say about the actual envelope. The message on the envelope, though, is important. First, be sure you have the person's name—don't send a release to the "Sports Editor." You won't get too far. Here's what it should resemble.

> *The Texas Register*
> *456 Rotten Egg Way*
> *Dallas, Texas 75222*
> *Attn: Betty Yolk, Sports Editor*

This tells the people in the mailroom exactly who to deliver your fabulous release to. A few other tricks for your envelopes include words such as stamping, "Time Sensitive Information," "The Information You Requested" or "News Release Enclosed." Simple, yet proven effective tools to get your release read and written up in the morning's paper.

Sending a photo will increase your chances of getting publicity by at least 50 percent. Don't send that Polaroid your friend took the other day. Have professional black and white, glossy pictures taken to accompany your release. Send a good, black-and-white glossy picture. If you wouldn't want your picture to appear on the cover of the paper, don't send it because it just might.

Once you've written your release, proof it at least five times yourself, then have at least one other person read it twice for spelling, grammar and clarity. Ask this person if they feel as though they've been given adequate information. If not, ask them to tell you what else they need to know.

More Publicity Strategies

There are many other ways to get publicity in addition to press releases. Don't forget to be creative, the idea is to get the world buzzing about you and your business. Here are a few recommendations for getting started.

Public Service Announcements (PSA)

A PSA is an advertisement that the media runs free of charge. PSAs are not, in the truest sense, publicity because you do not control when or how much your advertisement runs. You do, however, participate in the development of the message. The number of PSAs your company will get will depend on a medium's time or space. In other words, if there's some free air time, they'll insert your ad.

Write an Article

Being published is one of the most effective ways to get publicity. Look around and see if your town newspaper could benefit from your unique talent. If so, write a query letter to the editor of your specific department and offer to write a column or story on your topic.

Speaking

Speaking engagements are also another way to increase your exposure. Let people know that you have a particular interest and expertise and that you are interested in speaking. Also sharpen your speaking skills, and you may find incremental income on the side.

Press Conferences

A press conference, sometimes referred to as a news conference, is a gathering to share information on an event, person, product, company or other newsworthy entity. Press conferences can be excellent at generating publicity. They are relatively inexpensive to organize and are usually held at hotels, convention centers, conference centers and restaurants.

Press Parties

They are fine and they are fun. If you decide to throw one, make it first class. No Ruffles and bean dip. Although there's nothing wrong with potato chips and dip, having them at a first-rate press party sends a different message than, say, a light buffet of assorted vegetables, cheeses, fruits and wines.

Whenever you're organizing an event such as a press conference be sure you:

Have a newsworthy event. If you're going to hold a news conference, you'd better have something special to highlight—a new product, an exciting event or controversial issue.

Announce the press conference. Your press release is your invitation to the event. It should be timely and thorough. Don't have media wondering how to get to your conference. Include a contact name and phone number as well as the pertinent information (if any celebrities will be present, time, date and directions).

Select a suitable location. Rent or reserve a room that is located conveniently for the media and one that is friendly and accepting of all people. Stay away from any place that tends to be elitist in nature.

Have an effective room setup. The best way to arrange the chairs is classroom style with a dais in front. Make sure there's good light and space for television and radio people.

Have food and drinks. Since this is a news conference, go easy on the food. In fact, if you can swing coffee, tea, sodas and snacks, great. Don't create a party atmosphere at your press conference, or the attendees may forget about your story. If you want to throw a media party, that's fine—just do it separately from your conference.

Have optimum time. This is the most important factor. You want to have a well-attended event. A mid-morning news conference is what I recommend. Your story has a better chance of making the evening news, and it lets reporters write their stories for the next day.

Have rehearsals. It's better to find out that your microphone doesn't work twenty-four hours before your event than the morning of, right? Do a run through to make sure everything is working properly—lights, mikes and visuals.

Your conference and party will be reviewed in much the same way as a new movie. You're the director, make sure everything's in place, or people may not come back and watch your flick.

Has *Essence* Called Yet?

Did I ever think I'd be featured in *Essence* magazine? Of course I did. So can you if that's what you want. When we're starting out sometimes we think that no one big is interested in the work we do. Nothing could be further from the truth. I was selected to be featured in *Essence* because of networking contacts. I was featured in *Emerge* because I had a newsworthy story and sent them a press release.

Remember, you are your own publicist. If you want publicity you have to go out and get it. I dedicate a certain number of hours per week to promotion of me and my company. I send out press releases at least twice a month to a variety of media contacts. Why so often? Because repetition makes the heart grow fonder. If an editor sees a release roll across her/his desk twice a month from the same company or individual, pretty soon s/he is going to say, "Let me call this woman, she seems to be doing something every time I turn around."

The African American Media Queen

How many times have you watched a black person during an interview and thought, good grief, woman! or said "what?" after the interview? I'm not going to lie, I have felt everything from proud to sorry to embarrassment when we don't shine in interviews. As an entrepreneur, the way you present yourself is critical. You never know when you'll be given the chance to be interviewed. Whenever we've fumbled through an interview it's because we're not prepared, not because we're inarticulate or stupid as the media would have us believe. Being good in interviews, whether you're black, white or red, takes practice and skills.

Barriers to Black Women in Interviews

Inexperience on camera Face it, unless you do something frequently, you'll appear to be a novice when you're thrown into a situation.

Poor self image How you feel about yourself influences the words and phrases you use. When you don't have a positive self image, you don't deliver the best you.

Limited experience talking to other people Even in the 90s there are some of us who still haven't ventured beyond our own churches and schools. Although that's strictly your choice, understand that being this insulated makes it difficult for conversations to flow easily. If there's a gap between you and the interviewer s/he will feel it, and your interview will not go as smoothly as it could.

Successful Interviewing Techniques

There's only one thing I can say about interviewing: Be prepared. Even if you have the gift of gab, practice will make you look crisp and sharp in your interview. If we realized how we sometimes sound in interviews we'd practice a bit more. The first time I saw and listened to myself on television I was mortified. I hoped I was the only one watching that day. (I wasn't—several people called to say they saw me!) I looked fine; it was how I sounded that turned my stomach. I didn't sound as polished as I actually was, and it was because I hadn't practiced. I basically knew what the questions were going to be, and I still didn't practice. Still, there were many positive things about the interview—I was comfortable in front of the camera, and for two or three seconds I even looked like a pro. For the next three seconds, I looked like an amateur—bobbing my noggin and eating my sentences. I made myself watch that clip at least twenty times to make sure I enhanced what was good and never committed any of those sins again.

Establish yourself as an interviewing pro and people from all over the world will want you on their shows. Botch up one stinking interview, and you may never get another chance; or worse, you'll develop a reputation for being a poor speaker or a bumbling idiot on the air waves.

Some people think that because they think fast on their feet they will automatically be a good interviewee. Not necessarily so. The more you know about the interviewing process the better your message will be delivered.

Black women, if we do anything, it's look good. However, looking good at the club is different from looking good in the paper or on television. Part of looking good is knowing what works and what doesn't. For instance, if you are posing for a newspaper photo be sure you're not sporting a fly girl or betty bouffant hairdo. The wrong camera angle or light reflection could make you look like you're wearing a lamp shade. For television, you need to get some theater makeup. If you've performed on stage, you know how those lights can mess with your complexion. If your makeup is too light you'll look really bad, even scary. You should get a foundation that's at least two shades darker than your face; otherwise, you will look like a corpse.

Look like you're having fun. Black women have the tendency to look real serious on television when they're being interviewed. While I don't recommend constant smiling, a simple, pleasant look will enhance your on-air appearance and make your voice more pleasant to hear. It's okay to joke or laugh during an interview, if it's appropriate. The more personality the interview has, the better your interview will be.

Go slow and low. Black folks have the tendency to either speak really fast or really slow when they're on the air. I saw a woman on a talk show who spoke so fast, I only caught one word of each of her sentences, which presents a problem if you're on radio or television. If you're doing a print interview and the reporter has to continue to say, "would you repeat that?" you know you need to slow down.

Sit up and look 'em dead in the eye. Posture says so much about people. Don't slouch, especially in an interview. Having good posture gives you a better overall appearance, helps you to speak from your diaphragm and gives the appearance of confidence. Eye contact during television interviews is critical. You want to keep the interview on equally playing ground. If your eyes are everywhere except on the interviewer, the perception is that you feel you are inferior.

Talk with your body. The tube is a medium of motion and movement. One of the most common mistakes African American women make when they're on television is to freeze—they don't move. Loosen up, no one's going to bite you. Use your hands and facial gestures as they feel natural for you. Be careful not to overuse them, you don't want to look like you're landing a plane! The best way to appear relaxed in an interview is to really listen to the interviewer and get into the conversation. Once you get into the questions, you'll automatically relax.

Interviewing Dos and Don'ts

Television

> Do eat an orange (not orange juice) before you go on the air. It helps vocal cords.
> Do prepare a list of things you want to say before the interview.
> Do relax and be yourself.
> Do make a conscious effort to open your eyes.
> Do enunciate.
> Do speak clearly and at a comfortable rate.
> Do smile sometimes.
> Do sit or stand up straight.
> Don't fold your arms.
> Don't frown.
> Don't pick your teeth.
> Don't lick your lips before every sentence.
> Don't suck your teeth.
> Don't roll your tongue over your teeth.
> Don't use profanity under any circumstances.
> Don't eat or chew gum while you're on the air.

Radio

> Do speak slowly.
> Do enunciate.
> Do smile (yes, even on radio it will help your voice).
> Do prepare a list of things you want to say before the interview.
> Do speak into the microphone.
> Do drink water before you go on the air.
> Don't eat or chew gum while you're on the air.
> Don't use profanity under any circumstances.

Print

> Do prepare a list of things you want to say before the interview.
> Do enunciate.
> Do listen to the questions.
> Do repeat the questions for clarity.
> Don't ever cut down anyone to the media.
> Don't use profanity under any circumstances.

The key to giving good interviews is practice and planning. In addition to the dos and don'ts you should also:

Set objectives. What do you want to accomplish in this interview? Do you want to tell the public about your new product or that you're opening a new business? Know what you want to say and then gear your answers to enhance this message.

Anticipate the questions. Before you go into any interview, make a list of questions most likely to be asked. You don't have to be a PR professional to devise this list. You can even have a friend practice asking you questions.

Be prepared. "I'll get back to you on that" is one of the worst things you can say to a reporter. It means you're not prepared, period. If you are holding a conference to talk about a new product, you'd better know all of that product's features and benefits. Reporters are not necessarily trying to put you on the spot by asking provocative questions, so don't be offended if one asks you a toughie.

Final Public Relations and Publicity Dos and Don'ts

Do map out specific and measurable publicity goals.

Do make a special effort to get to know as many media people as possible.

Do be willing to spend time shooting the breeze with media.

Do invite media to special events.

Do send media little company goodies when you have extras (T-shirts, key chains).

Do cosponsor an event.

Do work with a charitable organization so that your company name is associated with a good cause.

Do send releases in a timely fashion.

Do provide a contact name and phone number on all correspondence sent to media.

Do record, track and evaluate publicity your company receives.

Do measure effectiveness of the publicity you get.

Do recognize the potential and limitations of publicity.

Don't look at publicity as a substitute for advertising.

Don't confuse publicity with public relations. Publicity is done to gain exposure. Public relations is more encompassing and deals with the long-term image of you and your company.

Don't write a novel for a release when you can tell your story in a paragraph.

AND NOW A WORD FROM OUR SPONSORS

> *Good advertisement does six things: makes people see it, read (listen to/watch) it, understand it, believe it, want it or do it.*

Did you know that an ad for last year's Super Bowl went for a cool million dollars? Sure did, and I hear that cost continues to rise. Do you even remember the Super Bowl advertisers? People are *still* talking about the three Budweiser frogs who said "Bud," "Wei," "Ser." I don't know about you, but I didn't really like that commercial. Guess what? I may not have *liked* it but I *remembered* it—which is probably what all the good people at Budweiser wanted to happen.

While I'm thoroughly impressed if you have a thousand-dollar advertising budget to start out, most entrepreneurs are fortunate to have bite-sized ones. It doesn't matter if you're the mega or mini advertiser; if you don't craft a message that will deliver maximum benefits, your ad dollars are not living up to their potential. Can you afford not to do any advertising? Doing business without advertising is like writing a best-selling book but not sending it to an agent or publisher. You're the only one who knows how good it is.

Successful businesspeople know not only the what, why and how of advertising, they also know the when and where of advertising and to whom to direct their messages. But that's only half of effective advertising. You must also become intimately familiar with your present and potential customers' motivations—what they want and need.

What Is Advertising?

Ask fifty people what advertising is, and you'll probably get fifty different answers. Even advertising professionals differ in their definitions. It's mystical. You know good advertising when you *see* it. However, you're not always sure how the sender did such a good job of delivering the message. Since there's no simple definition of advertising, most agree that it is meant to

> persuade
> promote
> motivate
> inform
> change behaviors
> influence thinking and buying habits.

An effective advertisement makes people do six things: (1) see it, (2) read (listen/watch) it, (3) understand it, (4) believe it, (5) want it and (6) do it. If it fails in one, it fails in all.

What Can Advertising Do for Your Business?
>
> attract new customers
> reattract old customers
> build a new image in the customer's mind
> establish reputation in customer's mind
> promote specials (hours, prices, days) at your business
> help increase sales
> create excitement about a service or product
> tell people who you are
> get more people to come to your place of business
> introduce a new product or service
> let people hear from you directly

Do-It-Yourself Advertising

One of the main reasons many small businesses fail is that they lack the know-how to generate effective advertising. It doesn't take a truckload of money to launch a successful advertising campaign. This section will talk about developing your own advertising plan. Pay attention, and you'll save yourself some money, time and frustration.

What Is Rate of Return on Advertising?

That's a fair question considering you're pouring your hard-earned money into this enterprise. A better question may be, "How can I tell if I'm spending my advertising dollars wisely?" There are a few ways to measure your dollars:

Traffic: Has the number of customers or clients increased since your advertising started?

Awareness: Are people talking more about your business?

As a small-business owner your challenge is to find the most effective advertising vehicle for the most reasonable amount of money. Advertising affords you the opportunity to reach more prospects more practically and more effectively than through any other means now available, including personal selling. It helps you reach potential customers—people who might use your business or service if they knew about you. Before you spend one dime, you need to understand what advertising can accomplish for your business.

Steps to Successful Advertising

Where Are You Now?

Are you just in the contemplating stages or have you started your business recently? Take a long look at your company. In fact, I think you should devote a half to a full day of doing nothing but thinking about where you are.

Take a note pad, pencil or pen and highlighter and head to the most serene place you know. Serenity doesn't mean that you need to go to the library. A coffee shop or a park bench might be appropriate. Try to locate a place that is quiet but not somber. In a coffee shop there's usually an eclectic group of people. I've written some of my best work at the park where there's diversity of people and environment.

Once you get there, try to get a close-up shot of your business or business idea. Try to assess the business from a professional standpoint. Are people really ready for your business? Picture what doing business will be like. Write down all of your thoughts in the form that they come to you. Don't try to form an opinion or pass judgments on anything you write, just write. At the end of the session, review your notes and see what you see, hear, feel and touch as a result.

Know Your Customers

When I played ball my coach would always say "know your people" to us. What she meant was know the habits, strengths and vulnerabilities of the people on your team. Don't make a hard basketball pass to someone who has difficulty catching those kinds of passes. In your case, it means knowing the habits of your consumers. First, you have to identify who they are.

The biggest problem most small-business advertisers face is a lack of awareness that most of their work must be done before the pen is ever put to the paper. What you must do is learn as much as you can about the product or service you sell plus all you can about the person who would be buying or consuming it. Why? Because once you understand the product and all of its unique benefits and features, you can better devise a targeted message to your consumer.

Watch the Competition

Watch, fight and pray. Watch the competition, fight rising costs and pray that you develop a good plan the first time. Seriously, know your "comp." You may believe that you've got it going on and on and you don't need to know what your competition is doing. To this I say sssstupidddd. I don't advocate being obsessed with your comp, just aware of what they're doing—pricing, special promotions, and new technologies.

Your business is new, right? Does that mean that the competition knows more about your customers than you? Not necessarily. Another classic mistake of new entrepreneurs is imitating the competition. Don't copy what your competition is doing—she or he might not know any more than you. But if you're watching the competition, and what they're doing looks like it's bringing in basketloads of business, take good notes!

The primary reasons you should watch your competition is so that you can sell *your* products/services' benefits and features *over* the competition.

The second reason is to improve your product and stay abreast of what's in the market.

Know Your Budget

Set a budget, period. Even if it's a hundred dollars, that's a start. Pillsbury didn't build the Dough Boy campaign in a day, and your empire has to start somewhere. It's difficult to develop a budget without having any knowledge of the mediums available to you (we'll discuss them soon). Still, it's important to decide on a bottom-line figure for advertising.

Develop an Ad Plan

You need an ad plan that matches your company's goals and objectives. If you want to build your client or customer base by 20 percent then your ad plan should revolve around making that happen. You should spend your money and time trying to increase your customer count.

Investigate the Media

This is a biggie. Learn as much as you can about television, radio, newspapers, magazines, newsletters and advertising on the Internet.

Developing a Cost-Effective Advertising Plan

The following discussion is designed to help you develop a detailed, effective marketing/advertising plan that will net you the results from your dollar investment.

Creating an Image

Part of developing your advertising plan is knowing the image you want to convey. If you want people to think of you as a cutting-edge company, everything about you must say that—your business cards, letterhead, working environment, even your clothes.

What the public—your buying community—thinks about your company shows up on the financial statements. The question you need to be acutely aware of is "How much do the people need to know about your company before they are willing to do business with you?" For example, I bet there are few people who just think Exxon is a company that sells gas. We've heard about the oil spill troubles of Exxon and their involvement in South Africa. Exxon is more than just the tiger, and your company is/will be more than the product or service it sells.

Although you may not think that integrity is important to your customers, it is. Every chance you get you must convince them that you are honest and dependable. Since the public has come to distrust just about everything it hears or sees, your biggest challenge is convincing them that you are not out to take them to the cleaners.

Taglines and Slogans

You've read about Penny's Pastries already. I just love Penny's motto, "Penny's Pastries: Changing the world one bite at a time." Isn't that clever? It's simple, but it goes much deeper than just baking cookies. Penny is telling the public what she's about—change and empowerment through her tagline. Use taglines to help the public get to know you. The more information people have on you and your company, the easier it will be to distinguish you from the competition.

One day I was sitting at my desk wondering how I was going to increase my company's visibility this year. Hmmm . . . what do I do? I thought. I produce sporting and special events. "Yeah, but it's more than that," I thought. What does it do for people? Well, it gives them an opportunity to work together, have fun. (Snap the fingers!) I got it!

Nouveau
We Make Fun for a Living

It was brilliant (or so I keep telling myself), so I tried it on a few people. They loved it! I did a quarterly proposal and printed it on the cover, and people smiled as they got their copy of the report. I asked people from diverse markets and disciplines what they thought of when they heard it. All positive feedback. After I did my test market, I knew I was on to something. Now I use it on all kinds of promotional items.

What Makes a Good Slogan? Why is Nouveau's slogan so good? Because it's catchy, intriguing and it's easy to remember. As you think of your slogans remember that the best ideas say something about the company or product/service. See if you can match the company with the following slogans.

Slogan	Company

it just keeps going and going and
  going and going
the heartbeat of America
you're in good hands with _____
the pursuit of excellence
I love what you do for me
I love this game!
the standard of excellence

The best way to develop your own slogan is to relax. Don't focus on it. You really can think about something in your subconscious mind and bring it to your conscious mind when you need it. If you have trouble coming up with a tagline or slogan, use the brain power around you. Get a contest going among friends, employees and family members.

Comparing Media

Let me ask you a question. If you sell a product for women who are sixty-five years of age or older, would you put your ad on television at 1:00 in the morning? Probably not. If you were selling a children's item would you put it in the business section of *The Wall Street Journal?* I sure hope not. Part of choosing the right media is knowing your audience and when to talk to them. In order to do this effectively, you must know the advantages and effectiveness of each medium.

You have to do some homework in this area, there's just no other way to put it. If you don't know the ins and outs of each medium you will be bamboozled, swindled and plain ol' took! There are ad people out there who are forthright, honest people. And there are people who can spot a sucker ten miles away. Before we go any further, know that it is your responsibility to make media people put their money where their mouth is—make them prove everything they say. If they insist that they are the number one station in the area in terms of reaching the 18–24 market, ask to see a copy of the latest books—ratings, numbers or Neilsens. Don't let them get away with just telling you how wonderful they are.

Now, let's compare the media.

Newspapers

Using the papers as your main advertising media can be beneficial depending on who your audience is and where you live. If your market is the business audience then you already know where to place your ad—the business section. The important thing is to know your audience. If you are appealing to say, a business audience, you must know that business people read newspapers (especially during the week) faster than a speeding bullet. On the other hand the retired market generally has more leisure time to spend reading the paper. Know how your audience reads the newspaper.

Newspapers give extensive coverage of your market. In most markets the daily newspapers are read or taken by at least 60 percent of the area's population. By advertising in the newspaper you are reaching a potentially huge market.

You also get short lead times. Some newspapers only require a twenty-four-hour notice for an ad, depending on its complexity. Sometimes advertisers cancel, which means on occasion you may be able to get your ad in as a last minute insertion.

Advertising executives say that when developing ads you should follow the AIDA rule:

Attention (headline)
Interest (subheadline)
Desire (text and body copy)
Action (closing)

The *headline* is the most critical component in any newspaper ad. Its primary purpose is to attract attention and get readers to keep reading. Graphics in headlines are effective; sometimes pictures say what words can't. For even greater effectiveness, use a picture and a headline, that way the reader can see and get an explanation if they don't get the picture.

It doesn't matter how compelling your copy; if you don't catch the attention with your headline, your story will never be heard.

The type (font) you choose can have a great effect on how your ad will be received. Here are just a few examples of headlines. Which stand out more to you? Why?

(1) Clearance Sale

(2) EVERYTHING MUST GO!

(3) Beautiful Black Women

(4) Win $10,000

Would these headlines get your attention? Why? Size, message? Did the Beautiful Black Women headline attract your attention especially? Just remember, speak directly to your target audience and you will almost always pique their curiosity.

Some argue that a big ad is better. As an emerging entrepreneur you may have to settle for small initially. If your ad is written in a clear fashion with good use of font sizes and type, a small ad can be as effective as a larger ad.

Make the headline and copy easy to read. This is important. Sometimes when people discover computers and the world of word processing they go

Medium	Advantages	Disadvantages
Newspaper	Extensive coverage of market Low cost per 1,000 Short lead time	Competition from stories and ads Can't guarantee readership
Newsletters	Usually sent to target market Less competition from ads/stories	Limited space Limited distribution
Magazines	Good reproduction Target market Multiple readers	Long lead time Waste circulation Not very flexible
Television	Visual impact Extensive reach Fast results	Expensive airtime Expensive production Sometimes long lead time
Cable Television	Target market Relatively inexpensive	Unproven success
Radio	Target market Short lead time Audience loyalty Cheap	Limited to your ears Listener fragmentation Short message life Compete with car stereos
Billboards	Visual, big Hard to miss	Expensive Locations not guaranteed 5–7 seconds to read
Yellow Pages	Credibility Results measurable	Expensive
Direct Mail	Target market Can make copy highly persuasive	List reliability Expensive Junk mail syndrome
The Internet	Massive reach/target market Relatively inexpensive Fast results	Unproven results Being ready for response

crazy with fonts. It doesn't matter how cute you think a certain type is, all fonts are not easy to read. Here is an example of poor font choice: *If you want to help your reader, please type in a font that is readable.* If the reader has to work too hard to read your message, they'll move on.

Relevance to the reader is important. Would you read an ad that read "Are You 25 Years or Older?" Not unless you're twenty-five years or older.

Then and only then would this ad speak to you. If you are eighteen years old would you be *more* or *less* likely to continue with this ad?

Relevance has to begin with the headline. If your ad is about dogs or cars or allergies, then something in your ad must let the reader know that.

Newsletters
Advantages:

Target Market Entrepreneuring Women is sent to women who are entrepreneurs. If you choose to advertise your "Incorporation Kit: How to incorporate your business for $15," you can be sure that you are reaching a market that is interested in your product. Most newsletters are sent to people with a common interest, making this avenue a highly effective way to reach consumers.

Less competition from readers Because a newsletter is a letter about specific news, its main purpose is to inform. However, most newsletter publishers are wising up and taking advantage of the advertising opportunities (I'm one of them). Generally you may see two to three ads in a newsletter versus one hundred in a given section of the newspaper, and it's usually less expensive.

Disadvantages:

Since its primary purpose is to inform, there may not be much space for advertising. Also, unless you get hooked up with a newsletter with a huge distribution, you are reaching only a small piece of your market.

Tips for Creating a Good Newsletter Ad

Speak to the audience.
Make good use of small space.
Use a graphic or logo.
Don't cram too many words in a small space.
Print phone number or other important information larger than body
   text.
Use a border.

Magazines
Advantages:

Good reproduction You can get 1, 2, 4, 6-color reproduction in magazines, giving you a visually effective ad. I've also seen some ad people do some incredible things with black and white.

Target Market Like newsletters, magazines are for a specific group, so your dollars are well-invested if you select the appropriate publication.

Multiple readers How many times have you gone into the doctor's office and seen magazines on the waiting tables? All the time—which means that that single copy of a magazine is being read by hundreds of people over a month's time.

Disadvantages:

Long lead time Some magazines require ads to be placed months in advance. Some smaller ones have longer lead times than, say, an *Essence* or *Black Enterprise.*

Tips for good magazine ads

If you can afford it, use some color.

If you can't afford color be sure to make use of reverse types (white text on black background), shades, borders, etc.

Make good use of space, don't cram words in space.

Television

Advantages:

Visual impact Still our most visual medium, television utilizes two of the five senses, seeing and hearing. TV combines sight, sound, movement and color so that it resembles a real-life selling situation. You can actually talk to your audience.

Extensive reach It is estimated that 95 percent of U.S. homes have at least one television in them—that's incredible reach. Which means that if you buy the right time slot for your audience your message can be delivered.

Fast results If you're having a special or sale, you can greatly influence your traffic by using television. It's immediacy is probably one of its greatest assets. If something happens on the other side of the world at 11:45 A.M., we see and hear about it by 11:48. *Credibility* Being on television gives your product or service immediate authenticity and relevance.

Disadvantages:

Cost Television network airtime is expensive. An ad during the 10:00 P.M. news can cost thousands of dollars depending on where you are. Additionally, producing your ad can be expensive; sometimes stations produce public service announcements at no cost.

Lead Time Unlike newspapers, you can't always just call up the television station and say, "I'd like to run an ad tomorrow." Big advertisers buy weeks, months in advance, which means all the good time may be gone by the time you decide to buy.

Tips for good television copy

Be a part of the production process.

Tell the producer what kind of tone you're trying to set.

Give them all the information they need (phone number, correct spelling of names).

Ask for your schedule (when your ad will run).

Cable Television
Advantages:

Target market People are starting to recognize the power of advertising on cable. It's similar to advertising in a magazine in that you can be certain of the audience you're reaching. Imagine advertising on MTV, one of the most popular vehicles for reaching the young adult market, for much less than on network television.

Cost Cable television is at least a third less expensive than network advertising, depending on times and locations.

More freedom The content of advertising messages is less restricted than in network television. If you had a new beer, you could actually show your actors drinking beer, which is not allowed on network television.

Diversity of message length On cable your message doesn't have to be a 15, 30 or 60-second spot, it can be 2 minutes or a 4-hour training program.

Disadvantages:

Measurability Effectiveness of any message depends on the penetration at a local level. It's often difficult to get local market ratings and statistics.

Segmented audience Although the cable audience tends to be more educated and higher salaried, it's quite segmented. Because there are more than thirty stations, the audience for any particular program could be quite small.

Radio
Advantages:

Target market If you want to reach males 40+ who are conservative and who make $50,000 annually, there's probably a radio station that those men listen to. Radio is a magazine for your ears.

Cost You can buy a radio spot for one dollar! Isn't that amazing? Of course, it may be at 4:30 A.M. on Tuesday morning, yet it's still cheap time. Prime-time spots can run into the hundreds for sure. Just remember, everything's negotiable!

Short Lead Time Sometimes you can call a station and get on the next day, if they have the production capacity or if you already have the ad cut yourself.

Audience loyalty If I'm listening to the radio, my dial does not leave K-JUICE, an oldies station that cannot be beaten. Media reps can usually break down your market to a very low level, so make sure you're reaching the people you want to reach.

Disadvantages:

Limited to hearing If a radio ad gets you to see what it is saying, brava! Most of the time, radio spots are brief, so if you miss some information, oh well. Your ad has to ask listeners to do something other than, or in addition to, calling you. "Free T-shirts for the first one hundred people who stop by our grand opening" would pull some customers.

Tips for developing effective radio copy:

Know the intended outcome. Do you want people to flock to your place of business for this awesome sale you're having? Do you want to build a reputation or image?

Write a picture of your message. Have you ever known people who could tell a story, and you can visualize exactly what they're saying? That's what your radio copy must do.

You have thirty or sixty seconds to tell a story. Sometimes the most visual pictures are the ones you can't see.

Be in on the production of your copy. Don't just hand your money over to the radio station, give them your input as well. Get involved and make sure what you pay for is what you want.

Repeat Key Words Phrases. Since your message will be heard be sure important information is repeated several times (phone numbers, sales information, your name, whatever you want your audience to remember).

Make sure your company name is mentioned several times.

Use music sound effects, they are usually free. No one wants to hear all talk, nobody's voice is that melodious. Don't drown your message with music—use it strategically.

Build trust and integrity in your ad. The public's scared and skeptical. Help them by letting them know that they can trust you.

Call your audience to an easy action. *"Just call 1-800-U-GO-GIRL and we'll send you a free kit absolutely free."*

Sound conversational. Your mother or father may have taught you not to use slang—disobey them this time, say "can't" instead of "cannot," "it's" in place of "it is."

Ask for the times/schedule your spots will run.

Direct Mail
Advantages:

Target market reach If you can get the right mailing list, you are in business. You can deliver your message right to your potential customers' doorstep.

Persuasive tool If you design and develop compelling copy, the business will pour in. The key is in the design and language of your mail piece.

Disadvantages:

List reliability If you buy a list that is outdated and has tons of unde-liverables, you've wasted hard-earned or saved money. Be careful, check the credibility of your list company or broker.

Cost It is expensive to buy a list of rich white women over sixty-five who used to work in corporate America and who now travel to the Caribbean at least once a year. Do you get my point? The more specific a list you want, the harder someone has to work to put it together for you and the more your costs go up. As effective as direct mail lists are, they are expensive, so plan carefully. Another alternative is co-op advertising, which means that you can buddy with someone who's trying to reach the same audience. The watchout here is to be sure that there aren't one hundred mail pieces going to the same consumer—yours may get lost in the shuffle.

Tips for developing effective direct mail pieces:

Be eye-catching. Your customers get junk mail all the time. If your message is sitting on white paper, you'll be thrown in the evening trash bin.

Open with a bang! Maybe your piece isn't a letter, so make your opening statement or offer exciting. If you're sending a letter, address people by their first names. Fran, Betty's Cookies has a treat for you!

Be arresting. There's eye-catching, then there's arresting. Choose bright colors and unusual shapes for your pieces.

Be brief. You have about five seconds to make an impression. Give important information on the piece, but please don't go on and on, your reader will stop in the name of boredom.

Offer an incentive. Usually direct mail pieces are designed to get a rise out of the customer. So you must call the consumer to action. "Free T-shirt to the first 50 callers." *This is one of the most effective tools for getting people to do something. No one but you (and me, of course) has to know that after the fiftieth caller you're still handing out free T-shirts! The point is to create a sense of urgency and offer an incentive.*

Offer a guarantee. Only if you can. Guarantees make the customer feel better.

Add a P.S. Post scripts are believed to be the first thing read in a letter. Be sure that your P.S. states your primary benefit. For instance *P.S. Don't forget to call by May 25 and receive a 50% discount.* You can believe that if the reader hadn't planned to read the letter he will read it after seeing that P.S.

Make it easy to respond. Although it's expensive, return envelopes or postcards increase response rates tremendously. If you want your customer to do something, it must be easy or you'll affect your return rate. If you want them to call, print the number several times on your direct mail piece in different sizes, maybe even on the envelope.

Yellow Pages

This book is said to be the most frequently referred to publication—next to the Bible. *Yellow Pages* salespeople claim that more than 165 million people shop in their books. Does it mean that you have to be listed in the *Yellow Pages* in order to be successful? Not really. But if you decide to advertise

❖ Know that listings are less expensive than display ads.
❖ Get a bold listing.
❖ Negotiate your rate, don't accept the rate they quote.
❖ Go for size if you have the money. I think $1,000 is a big investment for someone just starting out, especially for an advertising vehicle whose results are questionable, unless you are an exterminator or printer with a half-page ad.

Two Important Questions:

Are you in a business that people understand, are familiar with?
Are you in a business that is more responsive to referrals?

Advantages:

Credibility People rely on *Yellow Pages* when there's no referral. It carries instant credibility.

Good source of supplemental business Ever so often someone will browse and will stumble upon you.

Disadvantages:

Cost It costs between $500 and $1,000 to advertise in the *Yellow Pages,* depending on what you choose.

Effectiveness The first year I was listed in the yellow pages, I got a total of fifteen calls—not great for a $1,200 investment. If you're in a business for which there is great demand, such as florists, then a display ad would probably be a good idea. However, if you're in a consulting business like me, where 90 percent of my business comes through referrals, you may not get much business because your work is based on credentials and trust in you and your experience.

Tips for creating effective Yellow Page ads:

If you can afford bold or a color such as red, do it.
If you can afford a display ad, do it. You'll have better visibility.
Negotiate your rate, don't accept the standard rate, at least without exploring the possibilities.

Billboards

They're everywhere, but are they effective? If you think about it, you have five to seven seconds to read a billboard—that's if you see it before you get right upon it. Billboards are great for announcements such as political campaigns—Vote for Christy Love on November 4, marriage proposals—Will You Marry Me, Terrence? and events information—Luther Vandross July 4 the Forum.

Billboards are useful and effective at image building. In other words, if you just want people to be familiar with you or you're interested in creating awareness of your unique services, billboards provide constant exposure without really selling something. Television stations and banks use them for this purpose all the time.

Advantages:
   High visibility if you get a great location.
   Make big and bold statements.

Disadvantages:
   Reach Not very targeted market; you'll never know if your market takes that route.
   Cost Billboard advertisements can cost between $500–$5,000+.
   Readability The reader only has a few seconds to get your message; they can't put the car in reverse if they missed it.

Internet

I won't even try to be impartial as I discuss this advertising vehicle. Its potential is phenomenal, and I strongly encourage you to introduce yourself to it. If you don't have a computer yet, start saving your money to buy one. I can't see becoming a booming enterprise without one. In case you're new to cyberspace, I'll give you some basic background information on the Internet.

Advantages:
   Reach The number of people you can send your message to is incredible—thousands, millions of folks. Statewide, worldwide markets.
   Access Easy to get set up and get hooked into other businesses.
   Cost It's relatively inexpensive to advertise on the Internet. For example, America Online, one of the services that hooks you up to the Internet, charges about twenty-five dollars a month for access. You can actually advertise to thousands for less than a penny in some cases.
   Credibility It sends a positive message when someone looks on your business card or promotional materials and you have an Internet address. The message is "hmm, this person is with it, progressive."

Rapid Expansion Potential The Internet keeps getting bigger and bigger, with more exciting capabilities each day.

Diversity Literally, anything you can advertise in the newspaper or on television can be advertised on the Net.

Disadvantages:

Response Rate You have to be ready for the massive response.

Home Page Creation Unless you're computer literate, you'll have to hire someone to create your page. Can be expensive.

Server Cost A server is where your home page is housed; can be expensive initially but cheap by the month.

Media Etiquette

Face it, media people are trying to get paid just like you. And that's fine. However, don't let them get paid completely at your expense. Remember, you're trying to build a business, and your decision-making process in all areas has to be on the money (no pun intended). You will meet some super aggressive in-your-pocket media reps, believe me. Remember, you control your money and you make the decisions.

Dealing with media reps is like buying a new car. You walk into the lot, you and the car salesperson both know that you're there to buy or at least look at a car—in other words, you are in the market for a car. S/he doesn't need to know at that moment anything other than the type of car you're interested in buying. Ever notice how the salespeople try to immediately draw you into a conversation? "What are you driving now? What were you looking to spend?" They are trying to size you up—your worth, your money, everything. Buying media is the same game. You can't go to a meeting with a rep unless you are ready, or you'll end up buying a Lamborghini when all you really needed was a GEO Metro.

Salespeople

All salespeople want one thing: to close, period. They want you to buy, buy, buy and buy. So, be careful. Implement these strategies in your meeting, and you'll be just fine (by the way, did I mention that I've sold media?).

- Call them and set the appointment.
- Meet on mutually foreign ground—away from your office and their office.
- Do your homework. Research the station in the market.
- Ask for references in your first phone contact.
- Call a competing station and ask for the latest numbers.
- Be cordial, not too friendly, in the meeting.

- Be assertive in the conversation, don't let them do all the talking.
- Insist on seeing numbers; if not in that meeting, request that they be mailed or faxed to you.
- Talk their language. Ask about ratings, demos (demographics) and events they've been involved in.

Questions to Ask the Media
❖ Why should I buy from you?
❖ Your rates are $10 higher than (insert competitor) for the morning drive time. I'd like to spend my money here—I'm interested in $55 for this time slot instead of $75." Boom! You haven't asked them to do anything, you've merely stated your desires and preferences (plus, told them that you've been shopping around). The ball's in their court, either they want your business or they don't.

Six Things You Should Know about Dealing with the Media
1. *Everything's* negotiable. Don't let them fax over a rate sheet that you automatically accept. Deals are made every second of the day; don't get left out of the game.
2. They are not always interested in achieving a win-win situation. They want you to spend, so approach with care.
3. They're salespeople. They don't make money if you don't buy.
4. Their business is highly competitive, so talk about the relationships and business you do with their competitors and watch them sit up in the chair.
5. They're not all shysters.
6. They have specials just like department stores. Ask about their special rates and frequency bonuses, such as do you get free commercials for running X number of ads?

This is one of the most critical parts of developing your ad plan. If you get this right you are way ahead of the game, and you will do quite well. Determining a medium's effectiveness can only be done after you've determined who your audience is.

Are You Down with OPP?
Have you ever seen an awesome ad and thought, what a great ad? This is called appreciating *Other People's Promotions, OPP*. If it's a print ad, I cut it out of the publication. If it's on television or radio usually I jot down what I liked about the ad. Then I put my snippets and notes from my television or radio ads in a file, my copy cat file. When I need to design an ad, I go to this file and go to town. I take what worked in these ads and incorporate them into an ad that is distinctly mine using what made theirs so good.

Starting Your Copy Cat File

The key to creating a successful copy cat file is not limiting yourself. If an ad makes an impression on you, it goes in the file. It's also good to jot a note on the ad or the back of it indicating what caught your eye. Don't copy their ad word for word or graphic for graphic—just ideas. Don't plagiarize or infringe on copyrights, just use their ideas. If you don't like filing, then buy an album and put them in there with tabs; or if you're into paperless and have a computer and scanner, just scan it into a computer file.

Creating Compelling Copy

Good advertising copy should first *attract*, then *inform*, then *call* your customers to action. Some argue about which is most important. I believe that if one fails, they all do. If my ad doesn't attract the reader, they'll never read it, which means they'll never be informed of me or my wonderful services, which means that I'll go out of business because I'll never get the chance to call them to action!

Good ads should also answer the following four questions:

1. What are you selling?
2. Why should I buy from YOU?
3. Where can I buy from you?
4. What is the price? (if you omit price, customers assume that it's too high.)

Additionally, good copy is warm and *friendly*—not necessarily fuzzy. The MADD (Mothers Against Drunk Driving) are not meant to make us feel good, instead they are to make us think about the danger in drinking and driving. Beer commercials usually make us think about what? Good times with our friends, right?

Good ad copy is "you" directed instead of "I" directed. It boils down to arousing reader interest.

I Raised $50,000 in One Week! You Can Too! 800-555-8329

Would you call that number? Why? Curious? Need money? I ran this ad in *Success, Inc.* and *Entrepreneur* magazines and got nearly 1,000 phone calls from entrepreneurs seeking capital to start their businesses. Did this headline arouse your interest? If you answered yes then I succeeded in part one of successful ads school—it caught your attention. Did it pique your interest even though it didn't really inform you? Finally, it definitely called people to action to the tune of several thousand dollars. I was selling tips on raising seed money plus a copy of my killer sample investment prospectus. Creating great copy requires thought. You have the words, you just need the practice.

Features Tell, Benefits Sell

When a salesperson calls you and tries to sell you that gorgeous oceanfront property in California, what runs through your mind? "Why should I do this?" Well, benefits. What we all want to know when anyone asks us to do something is "What's in it for me?" So your ad must speak loudly when it comes to answering this question. If you provide the fastest tailoring services in town, say so. That's a benefit to the consumer.

Do you know the difference between a feature and a benefit? Features are the *qualities* of your products or services. If you were a designer, a feature might sound like this: "We use only the finest materials from Italy." That is a feature, it *tells* about your product. Features are fine, however, they don't get people to buy from you consistently—unless they are accompanied by a benefit.

A more compelling sales pitch would go like this: "You will love these jeans when you get them, we use only the finest materials from Italy (feature), and since we buy them directly from the manufacturer, we can pass along a superior product at substantial savings to you (benefit—what's in it for the customer)."

Types of Ads

Children

Using children in your ads can be quite effective if they're used correctly. Have you seen the Frosted Mini Wheats commercial that begins with a woman talking about how she loves that cereal, and all of a sudden a child appears in the same clothes? Or the Oscar Meyer wiener kid? Or Bill Cosby and his Jell-O pudding kids? Be careful though, kids don't always work. Don't force it.

Humor

Most of us like to laugh, I know I do. When used well, humor is a powerful tool. Yet there is nothing worse than humor that isn't funny. Some say that when it's too funny people will remember the wit and forget the product. You decide which is most effective for your purposes. Remember, when using humor—make sure it's funny. A podiatrist once ran an ad that read:

Are your dogs barking?
(Here it had a picture of shoes that resembled dogs barking.)
Call 123-4567

This ad was a special on foot work.

Developing Ads

Use short words, short sentences and short paragraphs. Don't make reading your ad a chore. Keep it short and simple.

Short copy is usually better than long. You have only a few seconds of my attention, don't make me read an anthology.

Use adjectives sparingly. Adjectives tend to weaken copy. Words such as "very" mean nothing. If you must use an adjective, choose a descriptive one. For instance, if I were describing my skin tone I would say that I am a milk-chocolate diva instead of a brown woman!

Check your spelling and grammar. Don't turn off readers with dangling participles and double negatives. The only time you are allowed to break the traditional rules of grammar is for effect. An ad for an alarm system show-ing a house that has not been "burglar proofed" (papers in the driveway, mail and notices at the door and grass that resembles the emerald forest) might read, "Ain't Nobody Home," to let people know what messages they are sending would-be prowlers.

Proofread. Be sure that you have not used the incorrect word—their/there, whole/hole or others. This could be quite embarrassing.

Let's Talk Customers

The key to a successful advertising campaign is knowing your customers. Who are you trying to talk to, and what makes them who they are? How do you find out who your customers are if you're not already in business? You use the information you got from thinking about your product and who would use it (remember that exercise?). In 1991, a survey helped Greyhound Lines, Inc. determine who their customers were—who was riding their buses. That survey revealed the following:

- 22 percent were older than 55 years, 24 percent were 18 to 24 years and 21 percent were 25 to 34 years.
- 58 percent were female.
- 31 percent were married.
- 13 percent were unemployed, 62 percent were white, 24 percent were black and 10 percent were Hispanic.

Now can you see the value in having this information? By conducting this demographic profile, Greyhound could see who their current passengers were and, more important, who their potential or would-be passengers were.

What's All the Fuss about Demographics?

It's simple. If you know your customer's preferences and motivations then you are more likely to know (1) how to reach them (which media to use) and (2) how to develop ad messages that catch their attention, speak to their desires and needs, plus what will call them to action.

Surveys

Just because you may have a small-time budget doesn't mean that you should operate like a small-time operator. The method for finding out the demographic profile of your target market is the same for the Ford Motor Company as your company—ask the customers themselves. A survey is a simple method of acquiring information that can give you more insight into your customer's and client's needs and wants. And it's something you can do yourself.

Collecting data

Information about current or future customers can be purchased from research companies—usually at a substantial expense to you. This method might not be the best route at the start. Fortunately, you can get the information you need simply by listening to your customers whenever you come in contact with them.

Personal interviews are the most time-consuming and least productive in terms of number responses, but they may be the easiest to initiate. Even if it's a matter of developing a two-question questionnaire, this will tell you exactly what your customers are thinking. If you run a one-woman operation, use the student labor around you. Most cities, regardless of size, have a college campus nearby. Call the appropriate department and get an intern to work for you for college credit. Most of the time you can get quality work out of students, if you're a good leader and if you make the benefits apparent. Here are a few do-it-yourself methods of collecting data:

In store questionnaires Preferably this is a short list of questions that you have on postcards generally at the cash register or near the area where customers stand in line.

Advantages: Relatively inexpensive and easy to develop.

Direct mail You develop a survey/questionnaire that you send directly to a home or business.

Advantages: You don't have to wonder if you're talking to the right people. If they are on your list then they fit your target market.

Disadvantages: Often expensive because you have to purchase mailing lists, unless you already have the names and addresses of your market. Sometimes unreliable because people move or change habits.

In-person questioning This gives you an opportunity to ask open-

ended questions that give your customers the opportunity to elaborate on specific issues.

Advantages: Personal contact with customers gives them a chance to get to know you on another level. Open-ended questions.

Disadvantages: Takes time and takes you away from your business. Customers rarely have the time or desire to sit and chat.

Focus Groups This is a meeting of people to discuss a topic. It's usually better to make this an informal session—invite people to dress comfortably and casually if possible.

Advantages: Cheap. Usually only takes the cost of a large pizza. Gets people in an open forum for discussion, which usually generates more thoughts than a one-on-one session.

Disadvantages: It's sometimes difficult to get all the people there when you need them because of incompatible schedules. Sometimes turn into socials if you don't have a good facilitator to keep it on track.

Selecting a Medium

Once you've decided who your customer is, it's critical to know how to reach them. Over the last fifty years advertising has changed drastically. Remember when the word "period" was absent from the airwaves? Now the makers of Tampax and Stayfree have discovered that if they want to attract a loyal user, they have to speak to them—on their time and terms! These specific advertisers can now talk to their consumers by targeting their message directly to them.

When you know which medium to use to reach your customer you do more than just deliver an effective message, you make good use of your advertising dollars. Although the main three mass media—network television, radio and newspapers—are still going strong, there are more cost-effective means of advertising available to small-business women. Understanding the advantages and disadvantages of each will save you a lot of heartache and money down the line.

Starting a Home Base

❖ ❖ ❖

Starting out can be exhilarating enough as it is, you certainly don't need the potential headache of finding office space. Depending on where you live, it can be a downright nightmare. That's why working out of your home is a smart option. Of course there are challenges for anyone working out of their homes; it all depends on who your customers are and if they even have a need to see you. One of the first things people ask me is "where's your office?" Or they'd look at my card and see a street address and say, "oh that's near so and so. I of course agreed. They didn't have to know that it was a mailbox. Like everything else, working at home has its advantages and disadvantages. If you've never worked in a corporate office you can actually develop some good working-at-home skills. If you're used to the office environment, you may encounter some challenges with the transition. Let's examine some of these pros and cons.

WORKING AT HOME

First, you must take the time to get organized and, although this may sound like a simple task, it's one of the biggest ones you'll have. Your home is the center for so many **other** activities. Adding a business could potentially complicate it even further. Here are a few areas to consider.

Setting Your Own Hours

Advantage: No time clock to punch.

Disadvantage: No regular schedule.

Time management is of the essence for the home office professional. Not only are you juggling all of the activity of home, you can always find other things to do that have nothing to do with your work life. Working at your own pace is fine too, but you must set some definite hours of operation. If you don't you'll never be completely organized and you'll never realize your true potential.

My best work was sometimes done at 6:00 in the morning although my clients didn't get to work until 9:00 or 10:00. I could use this time for administrative work, doing memos or returning phone calls. Yes, returning phone calls—leaving a message on a recorder or voice mail. Sometimes all people need is an answer to a question or further information. This way, they get what they need and I increase my productivity during regular business hours.

No Dress Code

Advantage: You never have to get out of your pajamas or workout clothes.

Disadvantage: You may have a difficult time putting on the professional look when you really need to.

Sometimes I would go work out, come home, shower and never put on any more clothes. It was great! Comfort was never an issue. No panty hose or swollen feet from standing or walking all day.

People must still know that you're a serious businesswoman. I once spoke with a guy over the phone about his services. He sounded very professional, had a voice like a good radio personality. So I went to his house and I kid you not, here's what I saw when I got there. First, a four-year-old answered the door. Which is fine, but he wasn't the owner of the business— I hoped! The owner finally appeared in a suit, well groomed, so I felt a little better. However, as I got all the way into the house, I quickly saw at least five other kids under six and at least two who were between ten and twelve years of age. There were four other adults there—all women, performing various duties—cooking breakfast and cleaning. I went into his office, which was a separate area that he'd converted into an office. I think you know what happened after that. Kids invaded our meeting with their Power Rangers and runny noses. The television was glaring because "The Restless was about to come on," as one woman put it. It was a circus! I was completely turned off.

How did this guy ever get anything done? Was he going to be able to keep up with my information? By the time our meeting was over, I realized that he wasn't a serious operator—in fact, he turned out to be quite crooked! Lesson learned: Appearances do tell about a person's habits—don't ignore them and, more important, don't be like this shyster!

Being Your Own Boss

Advantage: No one looking over your shoulder or checking your work.
Challenge: Disciplining yourself.

When I left my corporate position, I was pretty lucky because that position required a home office, so I made the transition fairly easily. It takes a particular personality to succeed in a home-based business because of the obvious freedom. If you're good at motivating yourself, you're ahead of the pack. However, if you're one of these people who has a difficult time making yourself do something, I'd advise you to try to find office space.

Setting Up Your Office

Advantage: Low or little overhead.
Disadvantage Paying for all of your equipment.

If you have a desk, you will want the majority of the things you need to be in arm's distance. If you are constantly printing things out on your computer, wouldn't it make you more productive to have your computer paper stored nearby so that you don't have to get up everytime you want to print? Most people are amazed at how much time they spend getting up to get things.

Being at home affords you the luxury of not paying obscene office rents. Although deciding where you're going to put your office may stress you a little, it's really simply a matter of carving out a space in a section of your house, using an extra bedroom or the attic.

Home Address or Post Office Box?

Good question. It's probably a good idea to rent a mailbox versus using your home address; it gives you a more professional image. Most postal boxes can be rented for as low as ten dollars a month. Once you get a box, you'll have to decide whether to use the street or post office (P.O. box) address. Remember that Federal Express and UPS will only deliver to a street address, not a P.O. box.

You'll also need to consider the image issue centering around using P.O. boxes and street addresses: P.O. box addresses send a different message from actual street addresses with suite numbers/letters.

Executive Suites

An executive suite is generally a set of offices owned by a management company that are leased to a variety of tenants, much in the same way as an apartment building. The advantage of executive suites is that you can work out of your home and also have a variety of services ranging from an answering service to full secretarial and support services, conference rooms, workout facilities, copiers and fax machines. Services can start as low as a hundred dollars for a business address, mail service and answering services. Check in the *Yellow Pages* under "Executive Suites" and ask around.

Organization

Now that you're working at home, you may find the work and the space don't seem to be compatible. You have tons of paperwork and no place to store it all. The phone's ringing off the wall. The dog's barking like *Cujo*. How will you ever do it all? Believe me, there were days when I would just sit in my chair wondering how it got to that point in such a short time. The answer is simple. An ineffectual system. I've since moved to an office and tightened my system considerably. That's the key: developing an effective system.

Getting Started

First you must figure out the needs of your business. Do you need order forms more than you do bookshelves? Do you need an awesome answering device or do you intend to sit there all day and answer your phone? Here's a suggested list of things to get for your home office.

Basic Supplies (one-time purchases)

Business card holder
Calculator
Check endorsement stamp
Clear shoe boxes
Computer disk holders
Letter opener
Postal scale (can be leased)
Ruler
Scissors
Stamp moistener
Stamp holder
Daily planner
Date stamp

Drawer dividers
Electric pencil sharpener
Hanging file system for cabinet
Stapler
Staple remover
Tape dispenser
Three-hole punch
Vertical file holder
Wastebasket

Basic Supplies (need to be replenished)

Address labels
Business cards
Computer disks
Computer paper
Copy paper
Correction fluid
Correction tape
Erasers
Fax paper
Hanging file folders
Highlighter markers
Labels for file folders
Laser printer paper
Legal pads
Mailing labels
Overnight mailing supplies
Paper clips
Pencils
Pencil Sharpener
Pens
Rubber bands
Stackable filing shelves
Stamps
Staples
Stationery (your business)
Tape

Add to this list whatever else you need. This list will grow as your business diversifies and grows. Always buy these at a discount office supply store, and you'll save tons of money.

The Good Old "To Do" List

Everyone has done a "To Do" list. After all, how can you not have a To Do list? It's the eleventh commandment. The key is to making your To Do list *effective*. You say, "Good grief, Fran, how do you make an effective To Do list?" Check out the To Do list on the next page. What makes this list so special? The components of it. It's action oriented, it doesn't just let you make a laundry list of things to do—it challenges you to get them done! It helps you prioritize and decide what is important and what can wait. It tells you what action needs to be taken and when.

This tool is in my three-ring agenda and goes everywhere I go. Train yourself to have one central location for your To Do list. You're not being efficient when you write thousands of little notes on everything on your desk. The phone rings and you grab a sheet of paper. By having this sheet with you, you can put it immediately on the sheet, decide if it's an A, B or C task and then—the part I love—place that little check mark in the right ledger. It feels great at the end of the day to see all of those checks (my friends say that this is classic CAR—certifiability anal retentive). It may sound like a simple joy but it brings me incredible pleasure!

Anyone can compile a To Do list, but it takes discipline to make it an effective business tool. Your "to dos" can be weekly or daily. I use a combination.

Dr. Feelgood Bulletin Board

This could be a simple pin board used to hang or stick notes from friends or customers, but it's a nice reminder that people recognize and appreciate you and your work. Plus, it works wonders when you're having a rough day.

How Do I Deal with All the Paper?

I know what you mean. If it's not mail, it's proposals. Well, the answer is simple. File it. Touch each piece of paper only once. That means when something comes to your office you decide where it goes, stamp it and file it or respond to it. What most people do is place little stick 'ems on every single sheet of paper on their desk and then go back to it. What for? If it needs to be filed, just do it. If you need to pay it, pay it. But don't just let it sit on your desk. It creates a hazardous and unproductive work environment.

Here's a simple formula for dealing with the paper wars:

> Put it in your file.
> Act on it.
> Place it in a recycle bin or the trash.
> Enter it on your list of things to do.
> Rid yourself of it.

Sample To Do List

A = Most Important		Date _____	
A, B, C	Task	Date Due	✓
_____	_____	_____	_____
_____	_____	_____	_____
_____	_____	_____	_____
_____	_____	_____	_____
_____	_____	_____	_____
_____	_____	_____	_____
_____	_____	_____	_____
_____	_____	_____	_____

Why file it? The purpose of filing your paperwork is for simplification and to help you find it when you need it. Therefore, it's important to have a file system that works for you. If you have to spend ten minutes looking for something, your file system isn't working. Ideally, you should go right to something when you need it. Take some time to figure out which system will work best for you. I use a system down to the lowest possible denominator, "Sponsor Requests, May 95." That way if a company calls and says this is regarding our request of May 22, I can go to that file, pull it and know exactly what action we took in response to that request. "Yes, did you receive the sponsor packet?" Which reminds me, it's good to put notes (stamped or written) on your paper. Just a note to let you know what you did in response to that paper.

Handling Business Cards

If you network a lot, then you know how those business cards pile up. I put all of my business cards in a data base in my computer by category and throw the original business cards away. This works for me, but I also have 8½″ × 11″ plastic business card holder sheets in my organizer for those cards that I'd probably need with me when I'm not at the office—my attorney, CPA, printer.

The important thing is not to just keep every single business card you get. When you meet people, you usually know if you're likely to do business with them. Keep those cards and throw the others away. For example, you probably don't need ten printers' cards; five may be enough in case you want to get a bid on a job.

Your Mail

Did you know that it's estimated that Americans receive more than 63 billion pieces of mail? That's a lot of paper. What do you usually do when you get your mail? If you're like me, you open it in the car, the kitchen, the bathroom or some other inappropriate place. Instead of opening your mail just anywhere, discipline yourself to open it only in your office at your desk. Why? Because you stand less of a chance of losing it or parts of it. Don't do anything else while you're opening your mail. Don't eat, drink or be merry until you've finished. Sit next to a wastepaper basket so you can throw things away. Open it all at one time. This may seem like it will take longer, but it'll actually save you time in the long run.

Keep Receipts

The IRS may never come for you, but that's not the main reason you should organize receipts. The number one reason is organization and tracking of expenses. If you do your own bookkeeping as I do, receipts are extremely important. A smart businesswoman realizes the importance of this paper trail, plus you'll save time during tax season. Here are a few other receipt tips.

❖ When you take someone out to lunch for business, write their name and company on the receipt.
❖ Keep receipts for a certain time period together such as "April 1995" or "Week of . . ." If you don't have that many receipts the monthly system may work for you.

Leveraging Your Car as a Business Tool

Has anyone ever said to you, "oh, you live out of your car, too?" I've heard it at least five times, and it was because my car was full of "work stuff." Your car can be a valuable tool if it's organized. Regardless of which business you're in, you'll probably need some or all of the following: file box, pens, pencils, calculator, small stapler, paper clips, legal pads, letterhead, envelopes, stamps, napkins, rubber bands and the indispensable Dictaphone.

BUYING OFFICE EQUIPMENT

Shopping for your office can be as much fun as shopping for clothes. So don't get carried away. Just buy what you need. If you don't have a computer, why are you buying a computer table? If you know that you'll never have a meeting at your office, why are you even looking at that cute conference table? It's tricky. I'm guilty of buying things that I didn't need. I don't do that anymore mainly because I'm conscientious about hitting my financial forecasts. They don't always allow for my spontaneous shopping habits.

You'll discover that this is a good practice. Otherwise you may end up needing your money for something essential and you won't have it.

A word about comfort. This is a serious matter. Did you know that if your office surroundings do not provide you with the proper physical alignments and setup that you could cause yourself considerable physical *and* financial pain?

When I started writing this book, something changed. I had tremendous pressure and stress in my shoulder area. Why? Because I was writing every single day on my computer, yet I didn't have the proper setup to do that kind of intense writing labor. My chair was too low for my desk. My arm rests didn't allow me to pull directly up to my keyboard. Consequently, I wasn't supporting my hands and arms; instead I held up my shoulders. Plus, my neck was just too, too tight because it was supporting my big ol' head! So, recently I bought a wonderful chair that gives my entire body the proper support. It's amazing—my shoulders are better, my neck is loose and I can write for longer periods of time because I'm no longer in pain. If you can afford to have a consultant come out and inspect your work area, it's an investment well worth it. If you can't afford this starting out at least make sure:

- your chair has arm rests that can be the same height as your desk if you plan to write for long periods of time.
- your chair has adequate back support so that you don't have to slump or slouch in your chair.
- your feet are comfortable; they either touch the floor or get a foot rest.
- that you take breaks at least every thirty minutes to stretch and relax your limbs.
- that you drink plenty of fluids and eat healthy snacks throughout the day.

You don't want to damage your most precious natural resource—your body. I bought my chair at a place that sells products designed to help you operate more effectively in your work environment.

Answering Machines/Devices

When you're looking for an answering machine it's important to realize that your image is still on the line. I have a good friend who had an older answering machine. I kept telling her that she needed a new machine. True, her machine was, as she said, "getting the job done," but that's about all it was doing. Her outgoing message sounded like she was recording on the ocean's floor. I used to call her to just laugh. When you're looking for a machine, consider it an investment. No need to get extravagant, just practical, with the following things in mind:

- Good sound quality.
- Can it record all of the messages you expect to receive?
- Does it have remote access? New models allow you to call your phone while you're away, punch in a code and retrieve your messages.
- A time/date stamp lets you know when someone called.
- One tape or two? Have you ever called someone and after their outgoing message you thought you were listening to the American Broadcast signal? I have, and it's because they have a single tape machine. The main advantage of having two tapes is that one is for incoming calls, the other for outgoing.
- Tollsaver features tell you that you've received new calls since the last time you called your machine. I like this feature because it saves money and, if you travel, it's invaluable.

Make sure the message you record is professional. Avoid being cute or clever—it's a tell-tale sign that you're unprofessional and unpolished. The only exception is if your line of work is comedy and/or entertainment. Otherwise, avoid the sweet saxxy sounds of Najee in the background and record only a voice message. Use the following tips as recording guidelines.

- Include your company name.
- Let the caller know when s/he can expect to hear from you. My outgoing message is similar to this: "This is Fran Harris, I'm unable to receive your call. I return calls between the hours of 10:00 and 11:00 and 3:00 and 4:00 CST. Please leave your name, number and a brief message and I'll return your call." This has saved me so much time. As you probably know, returning calls can take all day. By telling people when I return calls, I increase my productivity and train them to either call me during those times or only expect me to call them during those hours.

  Of course, sometimes those hours don't work for them and they usually indicate this in their message by saying, "Fran, I'm going to miss your hours, could you please call me at 2:30, it's an emergency." Most people understand that if they miss these hours, the latest I'll get back with them is within twenty-four hours.
- Request that the caller leave a name, phone number and message and the best time to reach them.
- If your phone line is personal and business, your outgoing message could say, "Hello, you've reached 123-4567."
- Vary your message at least once a month.

Do You *Really* Need a Computer?

Not necessarily, it depends on your line of business. If your business requires a great deal of writing and reporting, the answer is obvious. You need some form of word processor. The conventional typewriter is nearly obsolete, plus you can't measure the value of being able to edit quickly. Well, you may say, you're going to keep using your typewriter because it gets the job done. And I'd say, that's your business, but understand that your image will be affected. Typewriters are like eight-track tapes; they are gone and anyone who's still hanging on to them will be seen as nonprogressive and outdated. Plus, typewriters don't allow for crisp and easy editing.

What Can a Computer Do for Your Business?

The question is more likely to be, what *can't* a computer do for your business? Aside from word processing, here are a few things that I use my computer for:

- ❖ Bookkeeping: tracking expenses.
- ❖ Accounting: reconciling my account, balance sheets, profit and loss statements.
- ❖ Financial analysis: how are this year's sales compared to this time last year?
- ❖ Spreadsheets: what percentage of my personal money is spent on travel?
- ❖ Marketing materials: developing brochures, fliers and posters.
- ❖ Voice Mail via Internet.

And this is only the beginning. I'm a software junkie basically. Computers fascinate and thrill me, so I'm always looking for ways to increase my productivity. In fact, I'm so fascinated by how much computers can help us in business that I did my own case study. For one day, I did all of my work manually—typed letters, balanced and reconciled my checkbook and did all of my financial statements manually. It took me ten hours—a whole work day *and* some! The next week, when it was time to do the same thing, I did everything on my computer. Are you ready? One hour and twenty minutes! I rest my case. That meant I had almost ten times as much time to be doing something else—writing this book!

So, no, you don't need a computer, but I don't think you will dispute how effective and efficient using one can make you.

Nothing to Fear but Fear

I've discovered that some black women "don't do" computers because they're intimidated. Here we go with fear again. It's the twenty-first century and, if you're planning to start a business, you've got to be able to keep up. I don't think you can keep up if you're pecking away on your typewriter. Plus, we all have to start somewhere.

Computer programs are now being developed to be more friendly. In fact, some programs even walk you right through and even give you hints about making mistakes. One idea might be to get a group of beginners together with a skilled computer person for training. There are usually community colleges and universities who offer informal classes that aren't usually expensive. So, go for it. You'll thank yourself later.

Always store floppy disks in a disk folder or holder. Don't just stick computer disks in a drawer or leave them lying around on your desk.

Printers

Even if you own a computer, do you need a printer? Not necessarily. If starting out you only have enough money to buy a computer, you can take a floppy disk to a computer/copy center and print your document. Again, if you are spending hundreds of dollars doing this, it's time to save your money for a printer.

Shopping for a Printer

Is the quality good? Print quality varies so look carefully and review samples.

How much paper does it hold? The more paper it holds, the less time you'll spend restocking.

How many pages does it print per minute? This was important to me. I don't like waiting too long for printouts, and some printers are slower than molasses on the coldest winter day.

Can it print envelopes? Professional looking envelopes are important from an image standpoint. Make sure that it does this if you're sending correspondence to clients and customers.

Is it compatible with your computer?

Does it print in color? Color may be important to you for presentations.

Is it affordable? Certainly not the least important. Printers are pretty competitively priced these days, so as Smokie Robinson says, "you better shop around."

Cellular Phones

There are basically two reasons that I vote for cellular phones: (1) safety and (2) efficiency. First, safety, especially for women, is a concern. If your business requires that you travel, you don't want to be stuck in the middle of nowhere and have something happen to your car. Having a cellular means that help is a phone call away. From an efficiency standpoint, it helps when you are running late or early for an appointment, as well as if you have car trouble—you can call clients or employees and update them. Only you can decide whether a cellular phone is a necessity. Be careful, though, it's very easy to get caught up in the convenience of having a phone at your disposal. Cellular phone rates aren't exactly cheap.

Types Available

- Mobile phones are mounted in your car and have three watts of power. Most have external speakers.
- Transportable phones also have three watts of power but are portable. They plug into the cigarette lighter of your car, or you may purchase a battery that allows you to use it for a period of time.
- Hand-held phones are portable and have six-tenths of a watt of power. They are small enough to slide into your briefcase or purse.

Cellular phones have all the features of your home or office phones: call waiting, call forwarding, paging and voice mail. Shop around for the best deals and buy only what you need.

Fax Machines

Again, only get what you need. Fax machines are almost a necessity for most businesses, but not all. Fax machines afford us the luxury of communicating in a matter of minutes. Things that would normally be mailed can now be faxed. Plus, most mail places charge you between three and four dollars to send faxes and two to four dollars for incoming ones. If you're spending a fortune on fax charges, start saving your money to purchase a fax machine. They can start as low as two hundred dollars and go as high as several thousand.

Fax Machine Features
As with cellular phones and computers, the market is saturated with fax machines with a wide array of features. Get only what you need. The basic fax machine should have a minimum of ten-page automatic document feed. Here are other options:

- Document feeder
- Copier
- Automatic paper cutter
- Delayed transmission. You can preprogram your fax machine to send documents later in the day when rates are lower.

- Plain paper. Regular fax paper has a finish that some people dislike. Or you can simply copy your faxes onto plain copy paper.
- Document memory. If your machine runs out of paper, it will save a certain number of pages in memory.
- Broadcasting. This feature allows you to send the same document to several locations instead of repeatedly feeding it into your fax machine and dialing the phone several times.

You may also use your computer to send or receive faxes. This saves paper, as you can read them on your screen and only print out those you want in paper files.

Fax Efficiency Tips

- ❖ Buy fax paper in bulk if possible.
- ❖ Keep your fax machine area uncluttered.
- ❖ Send fax transmissions after prime-time hours. You'll save money on phone charges.
- ❖ Buy fax labels and simply attach to the top of your first sheet. This will save you money because you don't have to send an extra cover sheet.
- ❖ Keep a fax log. When your phone bill arrives, you'll have a record of what you've sent.
- ❖ Always place your name, phone number, number of pages and brief description of what you're faxing so that the recipient will know what to expect.

Copiers

Again, only you can decide if you need a copier. I encourage you to log how often you go to the local copy center along with how much money you're spending on copies and gas. If you're spending hundreds of dollars a month at the copy center, you may need to invest in a copier. It's not only about how much money you spend on copies, it's also about how much of your work day is spent going to make copies.

Investigate if you're going to purchase a copier; there are hundreds to choose from. The following are features to look for:

- *Size:* Do you have the space for a copier?
- *Copy sizes:* Would you need enlargements or reductions?
- *Paper tray:* If you make lots of copies, an automatic feeder and paper tray may come in handy.
- *Copy quality:* Just because you purchase Canon's top of the line, doesn't

mean that it has the better quality. Check several models to be sure you're getting the best for your money.

REVIEW

Tips for Working at Home

- *Rest regularly*. Don't sit at a computer or your desk indefinitely. Get up and stretch and move at least every thirty to forty-five minutes.
- *Drink plenty of fluids*. Don't dehydrate your body. Even if you're just sitting there, have a beverage, preferably water or sports drink, handy to sip.
- *Eat healthy snacks*. One of the worst things about working at home is the temptation to sit and eat all day. Buy plenty of fruit, carrot or celery sticks, low-salt pretzels and other healthy snacks.
- *Set regular office hours*. This doesn't mean just saying, "I'm going to be in my office from seven till three." It means outlining what you're going to do on an hourly basis. I get into my office on most days around 7:30 A.M. The first thirty minutes are spent reading and expanding my knowledge base. At 8:00 I review my To Do list from the previous day to see what I need to do today. I then make my Today's To Do List and start working on unfinished tasks. At 10:00 I return phone calls. You get the point—*plan* and *execute*.
- If you have time, confirm appointments.
- Have an administration day or at least administration hours. Mine are from 8:00 to 9:00, the beginning of each day. The tasks vary, sometimes it's balancing books, other days it's filing.
- Have a separate personal and business checking account. Not only will this save you time at tax time, it will help you keep track of what's business versus what's personal.
- Snip and clip. If you're an avid reader like me, you probably have tons of magazines and papers all over the place. Now I just clip the articles from my favorite publications, then toss or recycle them. You can even create a file for your clippings. Don't keep the publications in your office, they take up valuable space.
- Use stick 'em's sparingly. Try to use them to write little notes on documents you're sending to people instead of reminders to yourself—get in the habit of using your planner for this.
- Plan when you're going to the post office, don't just go when the mood strikes you. Once you've decided which day and time is your post office day, go only on that day(s).

Dos and Don'ts for Home Office Professionals

Do remember that you are a professional.

Do remember that people will see you as a professional only if you put forth the effort to build confidence and produce quality work.

Do remember that your home is your home; get away from the work on nonwork hours.

Don't allow your home and office environment to become one.

Don't let anyone tell you that because you're a home office professional you're not a serious businesswoman.

Avoid Unprofessionalism

- Keep your office setting businesslike, especially if clients are coming to see you.
- Activate the answering machine and turn off the ringer when a client visits.
- Spend money on your business cards and letterhead. With all of the modern technology with preprinted materials, there's no reason for you to look miserly and unprofessional on paper.
- Consider using a post office box or mailbox location for business mail.
- Be confident and personable.

Five Things You Should Never Say

I know it's here somewhere!

Darn kids probably did something with it!

If I could just get out of bed in the morning.

My clients know that I'm never on time.

You'll have to excuse the mess.

PART FOUR

❖ ❖ ❖

Work It, Girl!

Is Your Net Working?

❖ ❖ ❖

Life is 10 percent what happens and 90
percent how you respond to what happens.

Perhaps the most underutilized and unsung talent among beginning, and even some more mature, black businesswomen is networking. My Terrie Williams story can be used in many ways; however, it is perhaps the biggest testament to the power of networking. Just what is networking and why is it important to our success? Networking is the act of making contact with an individual or individuals who are in a position to enhance your professional or personal standing. Notice that I didn't say this person was responsible for sending your ship to you. Notice that it's not called Net-sit or Net-rest, it's Net-*work*. Work! Work! Work! No one can network for you. Even if someone gives you a great contact, you still have to do the work if you want it to work.

Here are some common networking flaws of black women.
- ❖ They don't do it.
- ❖ They refuse or are hesitant to attend networking functions, such as chamber of commerce events, networking group meetings, seminars, town meetings, city council sessions and professional parties.
- ❖ They don't know how to work a room.
- ❖ They are afraid to be in a room of strangers, white people or men.
- ❖ They are afraid of "important" people.
- ❖ They do not have good presentation skills.
- ❖ They don't set networking goals before they attend an event.

- ❖ They don't recognize important contacts.
- ❖ They don't mingle once they get to an event—they stay in the comfort zone.
- ❖ They mingle too much, having no purpose once they get to an event.
- ❖ They go unnoticed because they don't know how to be seen.
- ❖ They think that networking is for salespeople, schmoozers and butt kissers.
- ❖ They don't bring enough or any business cards.

WHAT IS THE MOST EFFECTIVE NETWORKING TOOL?

Word of mouth is the world's best known marketing secret. You say how can it be best known and a secret at the same time? It's simple, most people know how powerful word-of-mouth advertising is, yet few actually put that knowledge to work for them and their businesses. I believe in the power of word-of-mouth advertising, and I've seen it do wonders for me and my businesses. I believe if you'll implement some of these techniques you'll reap similar benefits.

Take a look at the basic four ways to market your business.

Strategy	Initial Goal	Real Goal	Cost	Advantages
Advertising	Create awareness	Image, sales	Moola	Wide coverage
Public Relations	Awareness	Image, sales	Moola	Wide coverage
Word of Mouth	Get leads	Sales	Time	Wide coverage quality leads, inexpensive
Cold Calling	Get leads	Sales	Time	Who Knows?

From just looking at this chart, which seems to be the most cost-effective way for a small-business owner to generate business? Networking, right? I'm not knocking the other methods, and we'll get into some of them later. But I believe you can clearly see where your bread will be buttered—at least starting out. As you make more money, it may make sense to integrate some of the other strategies into your plan. In fact, we'll talk about how to create synergy between advertising, marketing, public relations and word of mouth later on.

Before we get into the different types of networking contacts, let's find out where you are.

Are you a star or couch potato when it comes to networking? Circle a or b.
1. When you go to a networking function, are you more likely to
   a. go alone?
   b. go with a girlfriend?

2. When you arrive at a networking function, are you more likely to
   a. split up even if you did go with a friend or colleague?
   b. hang on the coattail of your friend or colleague, staying committed to Siamese twinship?

3. When someone you don't know walks up to you, are you more likely to
   a. immediately find a discussion topic?
   b. have a difficult time striking up a conversation of any substance?

4. When you get to a function, are you more likely to
   a. have distinct goals of how many contacts you'd like to make?
   b. go just to show face?

5. When you leave a function are you more likely to
   a. leave without saying a word?
   b. make one last round of the room, in case you missed someone?

6. How many boards or committees have you been asked to serve on?
   a. more than five.
   b. less than two.

7. How many times have you been asked to speak in the last year?
   a. more than five.
   b. less than two.

If you have more *a*s than *b*s, way to go, girl! Keep sharpening those skills. If you have more *b*s than *a*s, get off your can and get out there! There is much business to be had and you're not getting your share.

I asked another pool of black women why we don't network, and here's what they said:

- I don't meet people well.
- I don't feel like it.
- When I get home, I'm too tired to go back out.
- Networking is for white people.
- I won't know anyone there.
- There will be no blacks there.
- I don't see the benefits.

TYPES OF NETWORKING CONTACTS

In order to be a savvy networker, you need to have goals. First you need to understand the kinds of networking contacts available to you. There are at least nine kinds of networking contacts: casual-casual networks, strong casual networks, strong personal contacts, community service clubs, professional associations, social/business groups, women's organizations, ethnic organizations, religious organizations and special interest networks.

Casual-Casual Networks

These are general business groups that allow many people from various overlapping professions. There are no restrictions on the number of people represented in any profession. These organizations usually meet monthly and hold networking mixers. Examples include chamber of commerce functions.

Benefits: Chamber functions often offer a unique opportunity to meet and make contacts with people from a diverse background. I met a representative for my long distance carrier at a chamber function and probably would have never heard of this company (which incidentally gave me some killer rates!) had I not gone to this event. Large companies are usually members of the chambers and are sometimes looking for black women to do business with as service contractors or to provide products. If you are there, you have a competitive edge over other subgroups who might want this business. So, go! Being the only black woman at a function could be a big plus if you play your cards right.

Strong Casual Networks

These are professional associations in which you develop strong ties with the members. They may be leads groups—groups that require members to bring leads to other members. These groups can be phenomenal boosts, particularly for you as a black woman. Why? Because leads groups are extremely effective at bringing you business if you develop strong relationships and, of course, you will.

Strong Personal Contacts

These are friends, relatives and the like. These people know you better than anyone. If you have quality products or services, these contacts can prove effective.

Benefits: The strongest referral you can have.

Community Service Clubs

Rotary clubs, YWCA or MADD are a few examples of community service clubs. These group members generally have a broad background and are often quite connected. Obviously what unites you is the cause. However, there are bound to be other connections. Learn to maximize these contacts. Get involved in these clubs and be committed.

Benefits: Visibility. People like do-gooders. If you're involved in something for a good cause, people like that.

Professional Associations

This is a potentially powerful contact on a broad-based scale because it could potentially put you in touch with people from different geographies. They tend to be specific in profession, such as The National Association of Black Journalists.

Benefits: Tapping into potential clients or target markets.

Social/Business Groups

Sometimes combining business and pleasure is the right thing. Groups like the Jaycees and singles business organizations are examples of social/business clubs. In these organizations the focus, in my experience, seems to lean more toward the social side, so don't join if you're looking for serious business building opportunities at meetings.

Benefits: Mixing business and pleasure is encouraged.

Women's Business Organizations

These organizations have been catalysts for our professional development in the last twenty years. They are an excellent way to meet professional women, build your business and network in general. Examples include Women Architects of America or The National Association of Women Sportscasters.

Benefits: Women can be good to and for other women when it comes to networking. This could give you the big break you've been looking for. They also give you the opportunity to learn in a sometimes nonthreatening, friendly environment. Some do allow men into the clubs provided they behave themselves.

Ethnic Organizations

The Black Women's Business Caucus is an example of leveraging ethnic business associations. You probably have some ties to some nonbusiness, black group. These are excellent opportunities to network among "family." Be careful not to fall into the trap of thinking that just because you're black someone will refer you to someone. You've got to be good too.

Benefits: Empowerment is the biggest opportunity—for yourself and other black women/people. You will be directly contributing to our emotional, psychological and financial wellness.

Religious/Church Organizations

Believe it or not, church is a gold mine of business opportunities. We are all consumers. It's probably a good guess that you see these people at least four times a month, sometimes more. You've probably even grown up with some of them. Use your church as a test market for your business idea. You can probably at least get an audience fairly easily. Be careful, if you dump on a church member, you know everyone will know it by mid-week prayer service!

Benefits: Frequency of contact is important for any networking group. You will have more chances to show your stuff in this arena. Familiarity and opportunity to test market.

Distant Contacts

Terrie Williams is a distant networking contact for me. She lives in New York, I live in Austin. We can both work for each other even though thousands of miles separate us. Don't be afraid to network with the seemingly "untouchables." Believe it or not, celebrities and rich people are human, and they won't bite—most of the time. Polish your approach and go for it!

Benefits: The biggest benefits are the incremental contacts. These contacts spread your message and name around the globe. I have referred Terrie Williams' book to more than fifty people. I am working Terrie's net. She is mentioning my motivational catalog in her book, so she is working my net. You too can establish a relationship with someone in or out of your industry and start reaping the benefits.

Now that you have all of this information, how do you choose which networking contacts you should make? My recommendation is to select three groups to belong to, more than three will leave you with little time to build that empire. Here are a few things to consider when choosing an organization.

First, ask around, listen to what people say about the groups they belong to.

Decide what you want to achieve. Is it more clients, visibility, connections to important people?

Know your commitment level. Are you going to go to meetings? Can you spare ten or twenty hours a month for networking organizations?

Don't join anything until you've visited at least once.

But I don't have time! I hear this all the time. I look at those sisters and say, "then you don't want your business to grow." You see, it's simple. Either you network, increase your advertising budget by X dollars, or worse, get on the phone and start making cold calls. Take your pick. Networking doesn't have to be a chore if you select careful organizations. But you do have to do it. I don't know any successful people who won't testify in the name of networking.

EFFECTIVE NETWORKING

Work that room, girl! Here are some dos and don'ts for effective networking:

- ❖ Do walk with a purpose. Don't look timid or like a lost puppy.
- ❖ Do look confident and poised. Comb your hair, straighten your clothes.
- ❖ Do have your business cards in your jacket or pocket.
- ❖ Do not bring a purse or briefcase, these things weigh you down. If you just don't feel secure without a purse, invest in a "wallet on a string," one that's svelte enough to hold just the basics.
- ❖ If you're at a trade show, don't just drop your card in a fish bowl, talk to the exhibitor, try to get her or him to remember who you are.
- ❖ Do dress comfortably, smart. Wear comfortable shoes, you'll probably do some walking.
- ❖ Don't overdress for any event. If it's a business affair, don't wear a velvet dress, you'll stand out the wrong way.
- ❖ Don't shove your hand out at anyone. Introduce yourself and confidently extend your hand in a comfortable fashion.
- ❖ Don't be so eager to give someone your business card. In fact, it is polite to ask someone if you may give them a card. Accordingly, don't expect someone to just give you a card; if you want one, ask for it.
- ❖ Don't bring your mobile phone, put your pager setting on vibrate. No one wants to hear a piercing tone in the middle of an event.
- ❖ Do have fresh breath yet avoid chewing gum. Breath mints are fine provided you're not the type to shift them around in your mouth and crunch them in people's faces.
- ❖ Do have soft or at least moisturized hands. People remember hard, rough hands, and they expect soft ones.
- ❖ Do dress appropriately, not like you're going to a club.
- ❖ If you want to get into a conversation, don't just stand around the outside of the group. Don't barge in and interrupt. Simply walk up, smile and you'll be invited into the conversation. If no one brings you in, simply say, at a break in action, "good evening, I'm __."
- ❖ Do say excuse me before leaving a networking circle. Don't just walk off.
- ❖ Don't hang too long at the buffet table and try not to go back too many times, even if you are starving.

❖ Don't stay with one group too long (two or three minutes is plenty); mix and mingle.
❖ Don't walk around with the same person all night or day.
❖ Do have a sense of humor.
❖ Do know what's going on in the world around you.
❖ Do listen intently when people speak to you.
❖ Do bring cash. Parking lots and bartenders don't always take checks.
❖ Don't be the first one there or the last one to leave.
❖ Don't pile your plate with hors d'oeuvres.
❖ Don't lick your fingers.
❖ Do RSVP when requested.
❖ Do confirm appointments before going.
❖ Do get to the point quickly.
❖ Do say "thank you."
❖ Do say good-bye to the hostess or host before leaving.
❖ Don't say, "let's do lunch," dinner or any other meal that you actually eat.
❖ Don't say, "I'll call you next week," if you don't mean it.
❖ Don't gossip, period.
❖ Do wear a name tag.
❖ Don't cancel an appointment unless you're dying.
❖ Do read these tips at least one more time.

Breaking the Ice

Here are ten things to say to begin a networking conversation:

1. What's your biggest challenge these days?
2. How do you deal with the rigors of such a fast-paced business?
3. Tell me about your family.
4. Taken any fun trips lately?
5. What do you do for fun besides work?
6. What an exciting business to be in, how did you get involved or start it?
7. What kind of year are you anticipating?
8. What brings you out tonight/today?
9. Have you ever attended one of their conferences/seminars?
10. What did you do before you started your business (got into this company)?

Remembering Names

It's pretty embarrassing to forget names. Do some people just have a knack for remembering names? I personally don't think people are born with great memories. Remembering names, like everything else, requires effort. When people say they are lousy at remembering names what they really mean is that putting forth the effort to improve this skill is not a good use of their time. Here are a few tips to help you remember the people who could bring you millions of dollars of business! (When you look at it that way, you kinda want to try a little harder, right?)

1. Repeat the names, in your head and then aloud, first and last.
2. Mentally paste the name across the person's forehead. We remember what we hear at least 50 percent more when we see it as well.
3. Think of someone you know who has the same name and then say that your dad's name is Robert.
4. Ask the person to spell the name: "Is that Kelly with an i or y?"
5. Help people remember your name, "It's Fran, like Tarkenton." (In fact, at least three men call me Tarkenton.)
6. Compliment someone on their name if you sincerely like it.
7. Write the phonetic spelling of the name on their business card.
8. Ask for name origin in a tactful manner. Say, "that's unique, were you named after someone special?" versus "hmm, that's an odd name."
9. Visualize a picture that would make you remember the name.
10. Repeat the name, as in: "Janice, it's a pleasure meeting you."

Things Not to Say

The following questions and comments are not recommended:

1. Where did you go to school?
2. How's business?
3. Are you married?
4. Got any kids?
5. Are you having a good year in business?
6. I think he's a fag (or she's a lesbo).
7. What a "different" name.

Don't call someone by the wrong name. (If you don't remember, just say so.) Don't talk negatively about anyone—you may unknowingly be discussing a mutual acquaintance!

TWO MUSTS OF NETWORKING

Before you take off on the go network, let's cover the two most important aspects of developing your word-of-mouth campaign: (1) developing a powerful, diverse network of contacts; and (2) creating a powerful, positive message, delivered efficiently and effectively.

Your Networking Base

The first of these strategies is developing a solid base of people who will tell other people about you and your company. A network is no good if they can't put you in contact with people who can move your business. The only way you can develop this network is by getting out there and meeting people.

Delivering Your Message

You're like a candle in the wind if you get out there but can't deliver your message effectively. That's one reason we went through that "What Business Am I In?" exercise earlier. You have to become proficient at telling your story. The more you tell it, the better it becomes. The better it becomes, the easier it is for *other* people to tell it—which is the key to what I call the *Perpetually Connected*. When done right, networking is like flowing water. It spreads and spreads without your help.

How Do You Develop Your Story?

Most black women—most people—are not skilled at standing before a group and saying who they are, what they do and who their customers are. All three of these are important components of your story. If you leave out anything your message will not be delivered effectively. Let's practice. Write your introduction. What do you say when you introduce yourself in professional settings?

If you are like most people, you go on for days like Cliff on Cheers. In conversations, you lose people and you leave them with an unfavorable impression of you. Here's an example of two introductions for around-the-room group functions. Which do you think people are more inclined to remember?

1. Good morning, I'm Fran Harris. I'm a small-business consultant. I help small businesses with sales, marketing and public relations strategies.

2. Good morning, I'm Fran Harris. As a consultant, I've worked with small-business owners and entrepreneurs for ten years, helping them increase their sales by helping them develop effective, low-cost marketing and advertising plans.

Which would you remember? Probably the second. It took less than twenty seconds to deliver, yet it told you who I am, what I do, who my customers are and asked you to share with me. Now the people who heard me can tell somebody else what I do.

Let's try another approach. If you have a catchy tagline, that tends to grab people or make them remember who you are.

Hi, I'm Fran Harris. Nouveau Sports Marketing is my company. We produce events.

Hello, I'm Fran Harris. Our motto at Nouveau is that we make fun for a living. We produce sporting events including golf, softball, volleyball and basketball tournaments for amateur players.

Everytime I've said, "we make fun for a living" people laugh. They remember it. They remember that I produce sporting events for two main reasons. One, they know I'm a former basketball player and two, I tell them every time they see me.

Of course, you can adapt the introduction depending on the function. When I introduce myself one on one, I don't say the entire spiel at one time, but at some point in the discussion it all comes out.

As a budding entrepreneur, it's important for you to realize the importance and effectiveness of networking. People ask me, "how do you do it?" Most of the times I don't know what they're talking about. How do you get asked to be on these boards and committees, featured in magazines and newspapers? I network, I answer—an answer that tends to boggle most people's minds because they think they're doing the same thing. Here's a list of Ten Commandments to help you become a better networker.

THE TEN COMMANDMENTS OF NETWORKING

1. Thou shalt have specific networking goals in mind before the event.
2. Thou shalt carry business cards everywhere you go.
3. Thou shalt not spend more than five minutes with one person or group.
4. Thou shalt describe your business in thirty seconds or less.
5. Thou shalt be well groomed.
6. Thou shalt appear as eager to give a referral as to receive one.
7. Thou shalt act like you're the hostess, not the guest.
8. Thou shalt write comments on the business cards you collect.
9. Thou shalt ask questions and listen intently.
10. Thou shalt follow up and follow through.

Commandment 1: Thou shalt have specific networking goals in mind. This means that you will determine how many contacts you will make, and you will not leave until you've reached your goal. If you know that you need to meet a certain person, don't leave until you've done it.

Commandment 2: Thou shalt carry business cards everywhere you go. Everywhere. When I go running, I have my cards. When I go to the gym, I have at least one business card. You never know who you're going to meet. It doesn't make sense to have a pen in your jog bra because you've got to have paper too. A business card does the trick. Whip that girl out and you are set!

Commandment 3: Thou shalt not spend more than five minutes with one person or group. Get moving! You don't have all night to reminisce about the good old days. A networking function is not the place anyway. If you see someone you haven't seen in a while, arrange to have lunch and you can talk until the cows come home. While you're at this networking mixer, you've got to work the room. Move, move and move. Circulate. There are at least ten people who need to meet you!

Commandment 4: Thou shalt describe your business in thirty seconds or less. Spit it out, girlfriend. We don't have all day to listen to you ramble. A good networker knows how to condense her message and deliver it with punch and power. Remember also that your words are only a part of the delivery. Maintain good eye contact and develop a firm (not bionic woman) handshake.

Commandment 5: Thou shalt be well-groomed. Don't go to a function with your clothes unpressed, hair looking like you've been standing in front of a fan and garlic breath. It won't work. In fact, you'll have people delivering an undesirable message about you. If possible, make a trip to the restroom to gather yourself. Remember, *you* are a part of your message.

Commandment 6: Thou shalt appear as eager to give a referral as to receive one. This is the commandment that has gotten me hundreds of referrals. Be eager to give and people will be eager to give to you. Don't attend a networking function solely to see what you can gain. Set goals for how many referrals you can give.

Commandment 7: Thou shalt act like you're the hostess, not the guest. When you give a party how do you behave? You're proactive, right? You check to see if people are having a good time. It's the same with a networking mixer. You have to move and groove. Smile, grip, grin and make your presence felt.

Commandment 8: Thou shalt write comments on the business cards you collect. I use the 1, 2, 3 out system. One is for strong contact, follow up immediately and start developing a rapport with this person; regular monthly contact with this person. Two is a medium contact, could be a good intermediate contact. May know a few people, so follow up and stay in touch at least once every two months. Three is for people who you probably won't do business with but are good people to know. Invite these people to functions and touch base quarterly. Additional comments might include notes to you for follow-up. The out group is for people who you will probably never do business with or people who turn you off.

Commandment 9: Thou shalt ask questions and listen intently. Don't just stand there like a bumpkin. Engage. Ask questions. Show people that you are listening. Nod (not too much). Make affirming statements such as "yes," "I see," whatever.

Commandment 10: Thou shalt follow up and follow through. Although this is at the end of the list, it is definitely not the least important. Few people are good at following through, white or black, men or women. As a black businesswoman, you put yourself in a strong position when you follow up and follow through. This means doing what you say you'll do. Calling on time. Sending information in a timely fashion.

HOW DOES NETWORKING AFFECT YOUR BOTTOM LINE?

Okay, let's take a real example. How many people do you know? A hundred? Two? Let's say you get one person to tell your story to 20 percent of the people they know. How many people does that one person know? A hundred? That's fifty people who know who you are and what you do. Of course, at least three of those fifty will tell people they know. And if they know at least 300 people total and we follow the 20 percent rule, then your business has been advertised to sixty more people and it costs you nothing! That, my friend is effective networking—you've developed your contacts and you've delivered your message well.

Remember: effective networkers realize the importance of building solid relationships based on trust, not necessarily friendship. When you provide an outstanding service and you've earned the trust of your colleagues and friends, the referrals will flow.

Action Plan: Make a list of ten people you need to contact to plant the networking seed. Beside their name place a target date for the contact and what you hope to gain specifically.

Name	Give	Gain	Date

TIPS FOR NETWORKING WITH NON-BLACKS

1. *Remember, we're all just people.* Don't put anyone on a pedestal. If you don't view the playing ground as equal, neither will they.
2. *Don't assume that all white people are flaming racists.* Train yourself to give people the benefit of the doubt. Sometimes when we take statements the wrong way, it has to do with how we feel about ourselves.
3. *Don't be so defensive.* You may be perceived as insecure or incapable of working in diverse environments.
4. *Go to events that you know will be all white attended.* Enter their world, you'll find that aside from the complexion, there's not much difference.
5. *Avoid making stupid comments that we hate*—you're not like other white people I know.
6. *Offer to womentor a white person.* Let people know that you are confident and competent and that you are willing to share your experience and resources.
7. *Don't tell any jokes, especially racially based ones.* You may think that you're letting them know how it feels when actually you put yourself in a position to be viewed as uncouth and unprofessional.
8. *Be who you are.* Some black folks change their walks and Lord, their talks, when they interact with white folks. Do Ice Cube proud, be yourself.
9. *Use opportunities to bridge the cultural gaps.* If you want to discuss BeBe Campbell's latest novel just do it. I once bought a 60ish white woman (who incidentally had had limited interaction with black folks) *Waiting to Exhale* for her birthday. It took her a while to get into it, but she finally finished.
10. *Invite them to black functions.* Even if you feel sure they won't attend, invite them anyway. If a black speaker is coming to town, make sure they know about it.

Are You Etiquettely Fit?

❖ ❖ ❖

As black women entrepreneurs enter the new millennium, it's really important that we be equipped for all business situations. Etiquette, or proper behavior, in personal and business affairs is critical to our success. Don't be embarrassed if you don't know all of the rules and regulations of protocol; no one knows what to do in every situation. This chapter should be fun and beneficial. It's designed to help you avoid the kingdom of etiquette misfitness.

WHY IS ETIQUETTE IMPORTANT?

How we behave in professional and business social settings is an extension of our images. You can be the most beautiful sister in the world and if you don't know that that itty bitty fork is for your shrimp cocktail or which beverage is yours you could knock yourself out of the race to land a huge account. That's why it's important!

Whether you're conducting business from your home or a plush downtown suite, good manners and grace are critical to your success. Of course, performance will always be an important part of succeeding in business and building a client base. However, in the twenty-first century, knowing how to dress, speak and act are playing an equally important role.

Nothing makes you soar faster than knowing how to handle clients, colleagues, VPs and customers with style, class and tact. In contrast, being socially inept can rain on even the brightest parade.

What About Manners?

There is no substitute for good manners. They are essential to building healthy, good relationships with other people. When we come in contact with people with good manners we remember them, right? "She was such a gracious host" or "He was so polite." Good manners leave favorable impressions. By the same token, we talk for days about people who are uncouth and unpolished—no matter how good they are at their businesses.

What Can Mastering Basic Etiquette Do for Me?

This chapter will challenge you and hopefully enlighten you. Even if you believe that you are "all that" and then some, I believe you will be challenged on some level to examine yourself. This section gives you tools to rise to the top in any business or social setting.

Good manners affect your entrepreneurial journey in the following ways:

- Enhances your professional image.
- Gets people engaged in positive talk about you.
- Increases the number of social and professional contacts you make.
- Increases visibility in the community.
- Creates positive image in your customers' eyes.

INTRODUCTIONS

You can get an early indication of where people fall on the etiquette scale within five seconds. How you introduce yourself tells a lot about you. Although introductions are far more casual these days, as black women we need to make sure that the first impression we make is a positive one. When introducing yourself, say, one on one in a networking situation, it's appropriate to walk up to someone and extend a firm, warm handshake.

Some people think that they should walk around with a stiff arm, when actually doing so makes you look like an amateur. When you see someone you want to meet, simply walk over to them and casually extend your arm. Don't shoot your arm out like a quick draw. Actually people are shaking hands less frequently these days. Forty years ago, all you saw were people sticking out their hands, now we see more pats on the shoulders, high fives (my personal favorite) and even hugs.

For black women, however, I recommend that you maintain a professional edge to your introduction until you've established a relationship such that the other options are expected and accepted.

Janet . . . Ms. Jackson If You're Nasty

Using first names is an interesting choice, especially for black women. Society expects us to defer to anybody who's not black. In today's highly dress-down environment, there is nothing wrong with calling someone by their first name. In fact, if you don't call someone, especially a man, by his first name, you'll immediately put yourself on unequal playing ground—and you do not want to do that. You are a businesswoman, you deserve the same respect that you give others. Even when you're calling someone (for business) who has fifty years more experience than you and who's won an Academy Award, they have a first name, so use it. If they need to be called Ms. or Mr. So and So, let them hear it from their personal assistant—you use their first name.

OFFICE PROTOCOL

Guests

Whether you work in your home or have an outside office, it's important to exhibit protocol when someone visits you. If you're in an office setting where there's a reception area and your guests are screened, it's proper to go out to meet your guest. Once your meeting is over, it's also good to walk him/her back to the reception area or the door if that's appropriate. You should never leave someone to wander around aimlessly in your office area.

Your Secretary

If you are fortunate enough to have a secretary or personal assistant, please treat him/her with the utmost respect and courtesy. Don't yell for things to be brought to your office. Don't ask him/her to bring you *anything* without attaching a please to it. Don't ask him/her to get you coffee or any other beverage unless they are getting themselves some. Don't ask him/her to lie for you.

TRICKY RELATIONSHIPS

Office Affairs

If your office is in a complex or environment with your significant other, be careful to maintain a professional image. Don't display affection publicly and don't argue, fuss and fight in front of employees.

Gays and Office Life

There is a tremendous amount of interest in equal treatment in the workplace. Regardless of your chosen business endeavor, you will encounter people who are different from you. As a professional you must make a commitment to be professional at all cost. Regardless of your personal stance on interracial dating, homosexuality, religion and cohabitation, you are in business to make a profit. It is not your place to judge the choices, orientations and habits of those around you. You will surely encounter a gay client or customer, a tattooed supplier or an interracial couple and, when you do, your reaction to that situation could make or break your business. Remember, everything is about image and if you send the message that you are a bigot, you may as well forget about building an empire in this lifetime. Bigotry is not limited to race relations, so don't be ignorant.

Dealing with Sexual Harassment

You don't have to tolerate it, period. If you believe that you are being sexually harassed, the best way to handle it is directly. I once had a guy who continued to comment (rather sheepishly) about my physical appearance. While I appreciate compliments, the degree to which he elaborated was inappropriate. On one of our regular meetings, I told him that before we got into our meeting I wanted to discuss something with him. I told him politely, tactfully that I perceived his comments to be sexually offensive and inappropriate. Notice that I didn't tell him that *he made me* uncomfortable. I merely stated that our relationship was of a professional nature, therefore, the conversation should center around professional issues, and the length of my legs didn't fit that description as far as I could tell. He responded by blushing and saying that I was gracious and that he was way out of line. We closed the matter, we continue to do business together and I've never had to slap his wrist since.

The last thing you want to do is joke around with anyone who's making sexual advances at you. Don't think that when *you* want it to end, it will. If you get involved, even if only by snickering when a comment's made, then you are fueling the fire. Remember in the movie *Disclosure* when Michael Douglas's character gave Demi Moore a back rub? He'd crossed the line already. Actually the game began when he agreed to meet her in her office after hours. So, take a tip from Mike. Don't play with fire, especially in an office setting that has glass walls!

Bringing Your Drama to Work

We all have had relationship issues, it doesn't matter if it's a lover, mother or child. They are inevitable. When they come up, leave them at home. Is it possible to leave your troubles at home? Not really . . . it's more possible to leave the drama at home—the emotional symptoms—the crying, gnashing of teeth and grouchiness. If you don't think it's possible to contribute to or create a positive, upbeat atmosphere for your employees, clients or customers, just stay home. Don't come to work.

Pregnancy and Children

I know women who worked hard and long during their pregnancies. They adapted their schedules and turned in stellar performances despite the emotional and psychological distress that sometimes accompanies pregnancy. The key is to do what's best for you, your baby and your business. If you're not feeling well, you are doing a disservice to all three of these by coming to the office.

Speaking of children, they really should be in day care or extend-a-care, if at all possible. It is unprofessional to have children in an office setting. It's different if it's once every purple moon. However, if it's everyday, you'll start to adversely affect your image. If you work out of your home, be sure your child/children are not affecting your work—crying, screaming or playing while you're speaking on the phone with a client or when a client comes to your home. Even if you can only afford day care for half a day, take advantage of having complete silence, minus interruptions or distractions.

EXECUTIVE COMMUNICATIONS

Sometimes the only contact we have with people is through the telephone and our business correspondence. How you come across on paper and the telephone are critical to your success.

Business Letters

Not everyone has the gift of prose and fluidity with the pen, that's why there are books on how to write effective letters. If you are good at writing, great. If you have trouble ending a sentence or knowing where to put a period or comma, consult a "how to," because you don't want someone to think you're a complete idiot before you get the chance to possibly prove it in person!

Successful business writing takes three things: *a desired outcome in mind, good mastery of the language and personality.*

Desired Outcome What is it you want? Sometimes people hire me to write letters for them. They send over their drafts and I look at them and think, what? I can't tell what they want. They want me to work some magic. The problem is that I can't work any magic because I don't know what the hell they're trying to say! The question you must answer before you put the pen to the paper is, "What do I want to happen when this person receives my letter?" Do you want someone to write you a check for $10,000? Do you want someone to feel good that they gave you $10,000? Do you want someone to join something? Do you want someone to come by your shop or office to see your fabulous products? Do you want someone to pick up the phone and call you to get you as a speaker? This must be clear to you first. If it's not clear to you, it'll never be clear to your reader, and guess what? If I get a letter from you and I can't tell what you want from reading the letter, I'm going to toss your letter on that beautiful ivory, linen paper right into the trash!

Mastery of the Language Knowing what to say and how to say it is key. Letters should be written based on your audience's listening level. If I have to pull out a dictionary to read your letter, you haven't written it for my hearing. So, skip the big words, nobody's impressed with your extensive vocabulary—save it for your thesis or dissertation. Keep your vocabulary on a seventh-grade level and you should be okay.

Personality Have you ever read a letter and thought, booooooooring? I have, and boy, I wonder if the author of it thought that it was good. Spice up your letters, use action words and sentences. Avoid run-on sentences unless it's for effect. Avoid clichés and other overused phrases such as "we live in interesting times" and "don't put off for tomorrow what you can do today."

Letter Structure

There truly is a wrong and right way to write a business letter. This is the recommended way:

April 1, 1995
Whomever You-Are
123 Write Now Way
Pen, Ink 12345

Dear You-Are,

It was good to see you at the recent Chamber of Commerce function at Liberty Bank. Congratulations again on your recent promotion to vice president. As promised, here is the information regarding the upcoming speaker series at The Marriott on October 21.

If after reviewing it, you have additional questions, please don't hesitate to call me at the office. I will be out of town for the next three days; however, my assistant, Chad, is heading this project and will be able to answer your questions.

Thanks again, Whomever, and I look forward to our meeting on April 10. Say hello to Penelope for me.

Sincerely,

Fran Harris
President, Nouveau Sports Marketing

Parts of a Business Letter

Heading On most business letters your company name and address are preprinted, so the first thing you need to type is the date.

Acceptable greetings include

Dear Fran:
Dear Ms. Harris:

I recommend refraining from "Gentlemen or Ladies and Gentlemen" or "To Whom It May Concern." If you don't know the person's name at least find out a position: Dear Human Resources Director:

Body The body is the meat of the sandwich—it's where your business is done. Remember, we're all business, so do your thing quickly or you might not get to do it at all! We're all busy with too many projects as it is, so make sure your letter is short and to the point. A good business letter is not more than one page—two pages maximum. If your letter starts running longer than two pages, then you need to pick up the phone and call somebody.

Closing Don't get cute, just say good-bye! The most common closings are "Sincerely," "Regards," "Cordially" or "Best regards." Some formal closings include "Very truly yours" or "Very sincerely."

Remember, your closing should match the tone of your letter. Don't craft a nice, informal letter and then say "Very truly yours" at the close—it's like wearing a pair of Reeboks with a black formal.

The Personal Touch in Business Correspondence

Maintain a personal flair in all of your correspondence. And please, please, send informal notes of sympathy, congratulations and thank you to clients, customers and employees.

A sample condolence note to a business acquaintance might go like this:

Dear Fran,

I was saddened to hear of the sudden death of your mother. Please accept my sympathy for you and your family and please don't hesitate to call me if I can help in any way.

Sincerely,

Morgan Leahy

A sample congratulations note:

Dear Jackson,

Congratulations on your new business! It seems like it was just the other day that we were both brainstorming about business ideas— I'm so proud that you just did it! Let me know how I can help you. I know you will do well, Jackson. Congrats again.

Take Care,

Fran

Sending and Receiving Faxes

I personally am against unsolicited faxes from just anybody. In fact, there is some interest in getting legislation to curtail such activity. The bottom line is that it's rude to send someone something that they didn't ask for—unless you know them and have an agreement. So don't get fax-happy and start faxing folks your stuff unless you get prior permission from them. It's courteous to include a cover sheet or at least a line on the top sheet that says:

(1) To: (2) From: and (3) number of pages in fax transmittal.

Writing Memos and Reports

Memos are actually a great substitute for letters, and they're quite acceptable. Memo writing is easier than letter writing in many regards. It can be less formal, yet more information-driven. Memos are usually shorter and take less time to craft. Memos should be written when you need to explain something quickly.

Your Writing Style

Anytime you send any written communication out of your office, it should reflect the best English and grammar you know. Again, keep the language simple. I impressed many a panel and professor with my developed vocabulary in high school and college, however, I would never take twenty seconds to say something that I could say in two and neither should you.

The purpose of business writing is to save busy people, like you and me, time. Time is money and money is time. Make sure you give consideration to your audience, their time constraints and needs.

Telephone Manners

The way you answer the phone tells me whether I really want to do business with you. People on the east coast (no offense) tend to be quite short on the phone, whereas Southerners (no offense taken) can't ever get off the phone! The important thing is to be courteous. If you, yourself, are not a pleasant and polite person on the phone, then hire a secretary. The first voice a potential client or customer needs to hear should be positive and energetic. All it takes is one rude encounter and your business will come trickling down.

Did You Get That?

That's one of the rudest things you can say to someone over the phone. Instead of asking someone if they "got it" or "if they follow you," develop communication tools such as repeating a figure/statistic or spelling, "Was that 555-2020?" or "Let me repeat that back to you."

Speaking of Success

Not speaking well can truly destroy potential business relationships. Poor speech patterns, mumbling and not enunciating can kill even the best business idea. If you think about it, speaking is our main vehicle for communication. Do it well and you win followers. On a certain level, speaking tells you a great deal about a person. For African American women our speech can sometimes knock us out of the boat for clients and customers. There are certain things that we must understand about the role of speaking as it relates to entrepreneurship.

Rule 1: Even though you may be highly educated, having a poor speaking voice and delivery will hurt you and your business.

Rule 2:   The world is watching and listening. Ever notice
                    how excited the world gets when it discovers the tal-
                    ents of a black speaker? Les Brown is a good exam-
                    ple. There are few circles, black or not, where Les's
                    name is not recognized.

Rule 3:   If you don't speak well, hurry and remedy the situa-
                    tion.

Rule 4:   Reading improves speaking.

Watch Others

If you want to know how effective you are as a verbal communicator, watch
how people respond or react to you when you do it. If people are constantly
saying, "I didn't catch that" or "what did you say?" something is definitely
wrong with your speech patterns.

Black Vernacular

"It's da bomb!" "It's all good!" "Make sure you're representing." All of
these are a part of our—or an acquaintance's—speech patterns. I have nothing against slang, I just think it has its place and that place is not in the business arena.

Grammar

An occasional slip with grammar or the misuse of a word is not a big deal.
However, consistent mistakes will leave people with an unfavorable impression of you. This is a big telltale sign of a person's attention to personal/pro-
fessional development. African Americans have a tendency to relax in our
speaking much more than we should. If we understood how deadly gram-
matical mistakes are, we'd pay closer attention to what we say.

Vocabulary and Diction

Diction refers to the choice of words a person makes and how they are spoken. Use the wrong word at the wrong time and you will flat out embarrass
yourself. Don't try to impress people by using words not in your vocabulary.
I'd hate to hear you say something was *nefarious* when you mean it's *nebulous*. Or that something was *erotic* instead of *exotic*. Stick to what you
know. Mistakes cost.

Dos and Don'ts of Speaking

Do practice what you are going to say.
Do speak slowly and clearly.
Do use common, simple words.
Do listen when someone else is speaking so that you can answer ap-
    propriately.

Do buy an English grammar book if you need to.

Do hang around people who use correct English grammar.

Do understand that if you frequently violate the rules of grammar your image will be tarnished.

Do correct yourself when you make a mistake.

Do allow others to correct you.

Do listen to great speakers every chance you get.

Do read books that expand your mind and vocabulary.

Don't be offended when someone corrects your grammar.

Don't worry if you make a mistake, just correct it.

Don't think that you'll get a second chance to prove that you're intelligent.

Don't take this section of the book lightly.

Language

Avoid racist, sexist, ageist, and other types of comments that reveal ignorance or lack of social grace. This includes jokes about religion, sexual orientation or other human conditions.

EXECUTIVE DINING

The only thing I have to say about eating and entertaining is be sure you know which utensil to use. There's a sample formal and informal place setting on the next page. Study them and don't forget them. Remember, always work from the inside out!

Tipping

One of the most controversial issues of today's black woman. We've all been faced with the tipping dilemma. How much should we tip, 15 or 20 percent? What if our server was rude and idiotic, should we still tip? Here is a guide for tipping.

Person	Service	Amount
Headwaiter	S/he shows you to your table	-0-
Waitperson	S/he takes drink order, tells you about the specials and takes your food order	Between 15 & 20 percent depending on the level of service and number in your party
Bartender	Serves drinks at the bar	Between 10 & 15 percent
Restroom Attendant		$1 minimum if service is provided
Door Person	Opens door	-0-
	Parks car	$1 minimum
	Hails cab	$1 minimum
Taxi Driver		When fare is more than $1.25 give 15 percent
Skycap	Handles bags in airport	$1 per bag; more for larger bags

INFORMAL place setting

FORMAL place setting

Informal Setting: An informal setting is much easier and the way to go when having clients over for a dinner party. This setting is for bread and butter, soup, the main course and dessert.

Formal Setting: Like I said, from the inside out is always right. Working from both sides of the plate, you start with the salad knife and fork, then the meat knife and fork, followed by the fish fork and soup spoon. Nesting in the soup spoon is the oyster fork. The dessert spoon and fork are above the plate. You also have a bread-and-butter dish. Usually the menu will be placed above the plate as well. As you are served, you will soon see the glasses disappear in the order of what you have had to drink.

Check, Please

If you invite someone to lunch, you pay, period. Someone in this case means a client or colleague. If you invite, you are the hostess and you are *expected* to foot the bill. Don't embarrass yourself by handing the check to your guest.

Drinking

I recommend that we (black women) drink minimally in social settings, especially if we're entertaining a client. Even if your client and everyone else is drinking, take it easy. One drink or a glass of wine, maybe. When the server comes to take your drink order always *first* ask your guest what they would like. If you are not a drinker, don't make a fuss over this fact or the fact that your guest *is* a drinker.

Smoking

There are many issues with smoking in business/social settings. People are allergic to it, people don't like the smell or people are fanatic about health hazards. The best thing to do is not to do it. If you must smoke, at least ask your guest(s) if they mind.

Eating Tricky Foods

If you're faced with a dish that's unfamiliar to you, simply ask someone how you should proceed. This shouldn't be embarrassing. What's embarrassing is doing something in a completely inappropriate manner, causing a scene and then asking for help.

Shrimp Cocktails
Use your seafood fork. Use your fingers to eat the shrimp in one bite if it's small; in two if it's large. Place the tails on the seafood plate, not on the table and not on a napkin to the side.

Chicken
Unless you're at your family reunion or a similar event, eat it with a fork and a knife.

Baked Potatoes
They are to be eaten in the skin. Do not take them from their home to make mashed potatoes on your plate. The skin may also be cut and eaten.

French Fries

These deliciously sinful things are finger foods when you pull up to your friendly fast food restaurant, otherwise they are to be eaten with a fork. Do not bite a piece of the French fry from your fork. Instead, cut the fry into smaller sections, then eat with your fork.

Sauces

Béarnaise, horseradish, mint jelly, ketchup, and other sauces are usually placed on your meat or to the side. If you order a sauce such as ketchup, do not put it on your French fries—put it on the side of your dish.

Bread

It's okay to use bread to get a difficult piece of food. It is not okay to get your plate squeaky clean with your bread.

Pasta

There are two ways to eat pasta. First, take your fork and twirl the pasta against a spoon until the desired amount is achieved. Or wrap it around your fork against your plate or bowl.

Tea

You may steep your tea in your cup or in the pot provided by the server. Never put tea bags on a napkin or tablecloth, they will stain it permanently.

Soup

Just don't slurp it. It's acceptable to drink from a soup dish that has two handles or no handles. If the soup is hot, don't blow it. Just wait a few seconds. Of course, you may use your soup spoon too.

Desserts

Eat them with dessert forks or spoons. Never scrape your dish with your utensil in an attempt to get every little bit that's left. Even if the dessert was to live for, don't order a second.

Toothpicks

Never use them in public.

Excusing Yourself

When you're in a dinner or lunch setting and you must be excused, just say so.

Using Your Napkin

Technically your napkin should go into your lap shortly after you take your seat. In a formal dining situation, wait for the server to put your napkin in your lap. Once you've finished eating, simply place the napkin to the side—do not refold it.

Pests in Food

"There's a fly in my water!" Surely at some point you will encounter something undesirable in your food or drink. When this happens don't scream or get excited, simply bring it to the attention of the server quietly. You don't need to announce it to the people at your table. The same rule applies to dirty utensils.

Talking to Servers

Be polite.

Reaching and Asking

If there's an item on the table that you need, ask someone to pass it to you. Never reach over people's food.

Removing Food from Your Mouth

If you have something undesirable in your mouth—bones, eggshells, pits and seeds that can't be swallowed, remove them discreetly.

EXECUTIVE GIFT GIVING

A scarf or tie are both acceptable gifts. Avoid giving jewelry, furs, leather or other expensive gifts that should only be given to personal friends and family. Food is a good gift provided it fits the occasion and the client's taste. Chocolates, holiday gift baskets and similar items are corporate favorites. And, of course, flowers are always acceptable.

Debra's Story

I decided to start my publishing company because it was cheaper than using a vanity press or subsidy company or waiting for a real publishing house to decide that they wanted my work! With a little research, I discovered that I could, via self-publishing, save money and have more control over the inner workings of my publication.

Of course, making my own money and controlling my destiny were big pluses, but I really decided to go into business for myself because I enjoy the freedom of planning my day and working toward my own goals.

The spirit of entrepreneurship runs rampant in my family. My greatest inspiration comes from my parents. My father was a self-taught tilesetter. My mother started her own cosmetology business at the tender age of forty. And, of course, my sister, your tour guide through *About My Sister's Business,* has inspired me beyond expression. She has always believed in me, and provided candid and enthusiastic input on my publishing business and where I could take it.

Writing and publishing gives me the chance to express my thoughts with little censorship, which I like . . . no, love. As an independent thinker, I am always looking for exciting ways to enhance my life; if I have a good idea, I move forward on it. Plus, as your own boss, you always get credit for your ideas and accomplishments—which also means when things go wrong, you're the one who shoulders the blame. That's okay, it's part of it.

Either way, entrepreneurship is exhilarating, and I know that whatever it is you aspire to do you will soar above the highest clouds.

Do Good!

Debra A. Nixon, MB Publishing

Ft. Lauderdale, Florida

Team Building Basics

❖ ❖ ❖

When a man gets up to speak people listen,
then look. When a woman gets up, people
look, then, if they like what they see,
they listen.
—*Pauline Frederick*

Besides being one of the buzz words of the decade, team building is actually one of the most important skills you can have as an entrepreneur. Why would you need to be effective in team settings if you're going into business by yourself, for yourself? Because no one does anything alone and neither will you. Successful people understand and practice effective team building. What exactly is team building? *Team building* is leveraging the unique talents of two or more people who are working toward a common goal. Said another way, if you and I collaborate on a project, there are certain behaviors that will make us highly effective—those are qualities that build great teams. *A team is a group of individuals working toward a common goal.*

WHIRLWIND TEAMWORK

When I finally decided to write this book, I decided to have a smooth, successful ride into authorship. I had already written and published one book; however, I wasn't interested in another do-it-all experience. So on one of my weekly trips to the bookstore, I passed Terrie Williams' book, *The Personal Touch*. I had bought about $200 worth of books and decided to get Terrie's book the following week. When I got home that night, a good friend called and said, "You need to get *The Personal Touch*, it reminds me of you." I told her that I'd seen it but decided to get it another time. Long story short, she already had it and said she'd pass it on to me because she had finished it. As I read Terrie's book I was warmed by her homegirl style and impressed by her business acumen. Then it hit me. Terrie was hooked, connected that is. She might be willing to help me. So, first I finished her book. Then I wrote her a letter explaining who I was and how much I needed a literary agent. Terrie put me in touch with a few agents, and you're reading the results of that networking contact. At the time, I had never met Terrie. I'd seen her in *Essence* and *Working Woman* magazines being advertised as a speaker for a national women's conference.

MENTORING VERSUS WOMENTORING

I'm a huge fan of mentoring, yes. However, I love what *womentoring* does for black businesswomen in particular. When we want to we can take care of each other. What is womentoring? It is taking a woman—younger or older or your age—and sharing your contacts, resources and most important, the benefit of your own skills and talents. Womentoring is really no different from mentoring, except I'm trying to get us to be conscious of our language.

I'd like to think that what went down between Terrie and me happens everyday. I would if I didn't hear from so many sisters that it doesn't. I asked a random pool of black women this question, "Why do black women avoid womentoring relationships with other black women?" Here's what they said. A black woman:

- Is afraid to share resources because it may mean she loses some of them (resources).
  Example: You call me and ask me to put you in contact with prospective investors for your company, and I refuse to do it because that's money I could be getting!
- Thinks that if she helps another black woman the protégé will be better than she, get the promotion/raise or will take her place as "the black woman."
  Example: If I show you the ropes, you become better skilled or at least as skilled as me and may subsequently take my job or status, whatever that is.
- Wants to avoid competition with another black woman.
  Example: There's one board seat left on somebody's board, and if I help you improve your presence in the community you may be chosen for this seat; or worse, you and I may be in constant competition with one another, and I'm not comfortable competing.
- Feels insecure professionally and/or personally.

What this means: This woman is insecure in all areas of her life. There's no telling what she will do to avoid feeling "less than." Common behaviors of these sisters include talking behind your back but smiling in your face and sabotaging everything you do.

- Doesn't feel empowered to help, doesn't realize that she's in a position to help.
- Is proud, doesn't want to help anyone, not even a sister.
  What this means: This sister may appear to be quiet, even aloof. When actually she just doesn't want to help you because she's stubborn and selfish—wants it all for herself.
- Is ignorant, doesn't know how to help anyone, not even a sister.
  What this means: Sad but true, there are black women who simply don't know how to support or womentor. She may appear to ignore obvious opportunities to share her wealth of knowledge when actually she doesn't even recognize what is right in her lap.
- Is angry because she had to fight to achieve success and believes everyone ought to have it just as hard.
  What this means: The chips stacked on this sister's shoulder are higher than any of my Las Vegas winnings! She has fought hard, yes, and she wants everyone to know it. Plus, she wants you to suffer as long and hard as she has, so she's determined to make your trip as tedious as hers. She won't return your call or is belligerent when you do speak to her.
- Doesn't want to be viewed by whites as nondiverse—concerned only with the plight of black women.
  What this means: This black woman not only doesn't help you, she avoids interaction with you in white settings. She doesn't really speak and may not sit at the black table at functions, which wouldn't be a big deal if she weren't all over you in a one-on-one setting acting as if the two of you are straight-up girlfriends.
- Perceives herself as superior.
  What this means: You can hear and see this in the sister who thinks she's better, smarter. She appears to not identify with the struggles of the black race. She has arrived—or so she would like for you to believe, when actually she's often having an inner struggle on some level. She may not speak and she certainly is not listening when you talk.
- Says she's too busy moving her own career forward, doesn't have time to hand hold.
  What this means: This sister is so cool at the women's conference. She says she'll call you next week but doesn't. She says "let's do lunch" but really has no intention of getting together. When you follow up with her she tells you how swamped she is and asks you to (again) call her in a few weeks. Of course when you call again, her assistant says she's unavailable.

What do you do? If you really want the benefit of her wisdom and experience, be persistent until you meet. You may discover that she really is extremely busy and a nice person (then again she may actually be a witch).

- Afflicted with an acute case of the Crab Syndrome, doesn't want the sister to succeed, so she's not going to help her climb the mountain of success.
  What this means: This woman appears to have it together. The secret is that she thinks she's the only one who does! No matter how good your life is going, she'll find a way to rain all over your parade. She's negative, unhappy and insecure.
  What to do: Avoid this person. She is dangerous.

Perhaps you are one of the few black women who works to make sure that we all get over, but I'm here to tell you that you're a rare gem. Even if there is a fair amount of support among the sisterhood, there's still a long way to go.

Two Flavors of Womentoring

There are basically two types of womentoring relationships: (1) womentoring someone who's trying to jump-start a business/career and (2) womentoring between women who are on the same path; for instance, a friend of mine who is an aspiring novelist. We provide womentoring opportunities for each other. She's helping me break into the freelance industry, and I'm helping her approach agents and publishers as well as put her book proposal together. We are on different, yet similar paths. We are each other's womentor.

Doing Business with Other Black Women

Womentoring is just one way we can help each other become more successful. Another obvious way is to do business with one another. My literary agent is a black woman, and I'm too thrilled. How often do we seek to do business, not just with black folks, but with black women? In general, not often enough. Let's take a survey.

How many of the people who provide you with professional services are black women? Your gynecologist, doctor, dentist, hairdresser, agent, graphic artist or printer? Well, you say, what's the big deal? I look for the *best* professional available. I say what are you saying about black women when we are not among your best list? You'll never know whether she is worth your consideration unless you give her a chance. Perhaps you will indeed discover that your person is better—I still think we deserve a shot at your business.

I'm reminded of a story I read about our reaction to being emancipated from slavery. Some of us gave all of our business to black businesses and others gave none of it to black businesses. The writer goes on to say that the reason we didn't keep the business in the family is because we had been trained to think that white people were the only people who knew how to take care of us. Some of us still think that. Unless we can break the shackles of oppressive thoughts and give each other the opportunity to win our dollars, black women entrepreneurs will never experience the true joys of entrepreneurship.

Economic empowerment among black women is a whole other issue. I want us to address why we fail to do business within our culture and gender. What do you think? Let's assess your beliefs about doing business with other black women. I asked several black women why they didn't do business with other sisters. Check this out.

- Don't know any black (fill in the blank). There aren't any black doctors in town.
- Don't trust black people. We think we're going to run off with our money.
- Services in the past were not up to high standards.
- Haven't been trained to support and patronize each other. We were all we had during slavery, black doctors took care of us when there were Blacks Only and Whites Only signs everywhere, but as soon as we could go into white hospitals we did.
- We're more inclined to think that white people can do anything, but we wouldn't think that we would find, say, a black neurosurgeon.

Now, look at this list again. Pitiful. Absolutely sad. What are we saying about ourselves by saying these things? Because that's exactly what we need to realize. When we say that black women business owners don't deserve our business for any of these reasons and others, we're saying the identical things about ourselves. We're saying that we are not competent professionals ourselves. I know that we've been burned by each other, but that's life. I have at least fifty horror stories involving business dealings with sisters and brothers. Each time, I get so disappointed, mainly because I want so desperately for us to wake up and start doing the right thing.

While there are mess-ups in every culture, my energies are hardly focused on what's going on in the Hispanic or Japanese communities. Speaking of the Japanese, we as black people should sit up and take note of how they continue to build thriving enterprises. First, they take care of their own. They cultivate leadership from within. They pass their businesses from one generation to the next. They adhere to a strict regime that cultivates integrity and persistence. The Japanese are simply utilizing the foundations that are inherent in all people.

Even though we continue to be burned by our own, I refuse to give up on black people. That would mean that I'm giving up on me and the young, black women who want to do exactly what you and I are doing and more. I can't turn my back on black women, I don't care how many times they cheat me, beat me down and try to keep me from climbing that last mountain.

Choosing Black Women

When I was with my Fortune 500 outfit, I was limited to the black professionals in our medical and health network. Sure, I could have gone outside of the network but from a financial perspective that wasn't real smart in my mind. You'd better believe as soon as I left, I got on my black female mission, and I'm proud to say that in all my years of going to the gynecologists, I just got my first black woman. In all my years of dealing with financial advisors and stockbrokers, I just found a prospective sister. In all of my years of going to the dentist (and believe me, I am a teeth freak!), I have finally found a black female orthodontist.

I feel good about this for several reasons. First, I am contributing to the economic empowerment of our people. Second, I am contributing to the economic empowerment of black female entrepreneurs of our time and those to come. Third, I am role-modeling the behavior that I believe should be prevalent throughout our culture. Fourth, these professionals are competent, conscientious people, and I like dealing with the best.

BLAME SHIFTING

Sometimes I think we give white folks too much credit and power. We blame them for our skin color woes. We blame them for our inferiority complexes. We blame them for almost all of our failures, big or small. What we need to do is hold ourselves and each other accountable for the shape our lives are in. In one of my focus groups for this book I enlisted the feedback of black women from various backgrounds and ages. When I asked the question, "why don't we support and help each other more?" one participant said that it was hereditary—not genetically but behaviorally—that we continue to pass these dysfunctional behaviors through generations. This, no doubt, is quite true. I was never unclear about the cause. I am, however, more interested in the solution.

SPORTS ARE A POWERFUL BUSINESS TOOL

Since I'm an athlete, it probably comes as no surprise that I'm a big advocate of sports participation, especially for black women. Why for us? Because by understanding the elements of effective game playing we give ourselves a tremendous advantage as business owners.

How We Play

First let's talk for a second about what sports are. Games, right? What is the object of the game? It varies depending on who you talk to. Some will say *winning*, others maintain *competing*; yet another group will say it's not whether you win or lose, it's *how* you play the game. For me, winning and competing are a tie for first. Competing *is* how I play the game. Winning doesn't mean that my score is always higher than my opponent's. Winning for me happens when I play hard and smart. When I play a sport, my goal is to compete—not necessarily against the other person—but with myself. That doesn't mean that I vote for winning at all cost. I'm not going to pull a Tonya Harding on my lowest day.

The good thing about sports is that it's never too late to learn to play. The same is true for business. My mother didn't start her own business until she was forty years old; quite a remarkable feat considering she was reared to believe that women were to glorify their roles as mother and wife. So it doesn't matter if you have some true sports experience already or if you've never attempted to participate in any sport. You'll soon discover that there's an athlete and a winner in all of us.

Take Your Pulse

First we need to take a look at your conditioning—how you were trained to play as little girls. What you'll discover throughout this exercise is that many of us are just little girls in bigger bodies.

Take this short quiz, which will tell you how much work there is to be done to make you a champion businesswoman.

What games did you play when you were a child? Check all that apply.

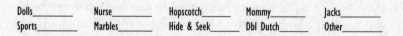

| Dolls_____ | Nurse_____ | Hopscotch_____ | Mommy_____ | Jacks_____ |
| Sports_____ | Marbles_____ | Hide & Seek_____ | Dbl Dutch_____ | Other_____ |

Without knowing much about you, I bet most of you grew up playing traditional girl games—dolls, nurse and hopscotch. Now, I'm not knocking girl games. I've played my share, and they have taught us a great deal about sharing and caring. However, they have not prepared us for business at all.

Decide for yourself. Write what you consider the purpose of each game beside it.

Dolls_____   Nurse_____   Mommy_____

Most of these games were designed to create harmony. They did not teach us about strategy and planning.

     Here's what we learned by playing traditional girl games.

❖ Girls should avoid conflict.
❖ Girls should be caring.
❖ Girls should share.
❖ Girls are not leaders.
❖ Girls shouldn't be aggressive.
❖ Girls are to be helpers and nurturers.
❖ Girls are helpmates to men (nurses).

     Now let's reflect on the games our brothers and male cousins played as youngsters. I bet most boys played sports when they were growing up. They played football and marbles. By the time they were seven years old, they had learned early about aggressive play, winning, losing, strategizing and disappointment, among other things. All of these elements are a part of being in business for yourself. In fact, they're essential for the game of life. Does that tell you how black women can potentially be at a disadvantage going into business?

     I once did a Team Building for Women seminar and used an adaptation of this exercise. Most of the women "got it," yet a few initially thought I was trying to tell them to be like men. I wasn't advocating imitating men, I was merely showing them how the game of business is played. I don't always play the game the way my brother does but I sure understand his approach to the game. What's more important, I can enter the ring with men in business and not get my head boxed!

     Both genders bring unique talents to business. What will help you is to learn about the game—if you don't like the current rules of business, change them. Unless you have developed these skills and learned these lessons in other arenas, you are not equipped for entrepreneurship. The good news again is that these are skills that can be taught—to a willing heart and body. If you didn't grow up playing sports or if you still are missing the sports experience, here are the messages you probably received.

❖ Girls should avoid contact, don't get dirty.
❖ Girls cannot be leaders.
❖ Girls are not good under pressure.

❖ Girls are not smart enough, not strategic.
❖ Girls should avoid difficult tasks.
❖ Competition is bad.

These are just a few of the messages society has tried to instill in us. Sadly, some of us have fallen prey to this sexist brainwashing. Even if you were encouraged to play a sport, it is quite possible that the rules surrounding your participation were "softened" to compensate, per say, for your femaleness. For example, how many times did you hear someone say to a male playmate, "don't be rough with her—she's a girl"? Probably all the time. In fact, we send the identical messages to our daughters today. Do you realize that we are training another generation of women to feel that they are not tough enough, good enough or smart enough?

When the Going Gets Tough

One of my favorite stories involves my five-year-old niece, Miki, and her brother, my six-year-old nephew, Jon Michael. While baby-sitting on Christmas Eve a few years ago, I decided to play a word association game with them. I asked them things such as name something that's green, or name a kind of meat. The games began and, since they are both extremely bright and energetic, at first they were both doing well. Then all of a sudden, my nephew got a couple of right answers in a row. He was fired up. He was rubbing his palms together saying how good he was and how he was winning. Meanwhile, my beautiful little niece had sunken into the chair and faded into the decor of my old bedroom. She was despondent, unmotivated and had literally checked out of the game because she had fallen behind.

I was amazed, though hardly shocked. I had given each of them the same rewards, an enthusiastic high five, each time they got a correct answer. Finally, after Jon Michael got another right answer, Miki blurted out, "I raised my hand!" Now, I had never said that in order to give an answer they had to raise their hands. In fact, Jon had never raised his hand and neither had Miki. She started to whimper and, what I call, weenie out. So, I called a time-out and said, "Miki, what's up?" She gave me those puppy dog eyes and said, "Jon's winning and *I* want to win." I almost laughed it was so pitiful and cute. Jon, who has a smile that is sure to win many hearts and help him land some major business deals in about twenty years, was just sitting there smiling. Triumphant. Victorious. He was hungry. He knew he had Miki just where he wanted her. Doubting herself and feeling sorry for her poor little soul.

What I was seeing in Miki is what I see in black women every day—a lack of drive and motivation and an unwillingness to hang in there! I said to myself, "Miki's not going out like this." "Okay, Miki, look, you are as smart as Jon, aren't you?" She nodded yes. "Well then, get in there and show him!" She straightened up in her seat, looked at Jon as if to say, "here I come, Mister." The game resumed and although Miki didn't win according to the scoreboard, she held her own. What I'm proudest of is that she didn't back down to the competition after our little pep talk. She had to be reassured of how good she was, but she wasn't about to let her brother win without a fight.

How many Mikis are out there? Millions. Everything about our upbringing says that we should have felt just as Miki did. Wounded and helpless, right? How many times have you been in the battle and it got tough, so you just gave up? Sure, we all feel a bit beaten down sometimes, yet the key is in having the courage and strength to pick ourselves up. You see, Miki's not going to have me to give her a pep talk each time she gets behind in the game of life. And you're not going to have your spouse, parents or friends each time you get kicked around on the playing field. That's why you have to train for the entrepreneurial race every single day of your life. You have to realize that business is a contact sport, and little girls will get run over, not only by the boys, but also the big girls!

Be Aggressive, Step Up to the Plate

What black women don't realize is that the opportunity to get the business has never been better. African American women's enterprises are at an alltime high. There's no reason why you shouldn't do it if you want it. You can't be timid. If you snooze, you lose. When I was getting my consulting business going in full force, I realized that there are at least 200 people in my city doing some aspect of training and development. So, how was I going to get the business over them? By being aggressive, by seizing opportunities, by *making* opportunities.

Black women have been known to be aggressive when it comes to telling someone off, but when it comes to networking and making business contacts, we can be wallflowers. If you want the business, get ready to play and go after it!

GOOD GIRLS FINISH LAST

I don't care what you've been told, good girls are not winning in the real world. Good black girls are way behind in the E-race. Why? Because good girls don't know a thing about playing the game of business. Think about what we were taught about being good. Good girls were rewarded for avoiding conflict, for kissing and making up, for avoiding risks. Face it, that kind of behavior will get you nowhere as an entrepreneur. Sure, people may like you, but they won't necessarily respect you and they surely won't want you to go to war with them. So let's dispel the myths that some of us are still perpetuating: Good girls may make their mommies happy, but they won't last in the sport of business or the game of life.

Should You Be a Bad Girl?

Depends on how you define bad. To this question I'd love to say no boldly and loudly, but the reality is that you may think being bad means that you shouldn't compete and ask for what you want. So I can't say no just yet. What I am *not* saying is that you should abuse and disrespect people or that you should be disloyal and bowl people over with your boldness and competence. I *am* saying that in order to be even remotely successful as entrepreneur you will need to abandon some of that good girl nonsense that society has fed you for so long.

How Do I Know If I'm a Good Girl?

Glad you asked. Good-girl stuff includes trying to do everything even when you can't (which is most of the time). It's always following the rules even when they don't make sense or when they lead to unproductive and unhealthy lives. It's waiting patiently while the bad girls get all the glory, money and fame. It's worrying what people think and say so much that you're afraid to take a tiny step without someone's permission or approval. It's never ever ruffling any feathers.

Can you see clearly now? These are just some of the good-girl baggage we've been lugging around. When you bought this book you were probably looking for a nice little "how to" guide. Well, forget it. This book is to help groom phenomenal success stories, not moderate ones, and I can't begin to help you build your empire if you're not willing to push yourself.

Here's a good girl, bad girl comparison. You decide which one will yield the greatest business results.

A good girl	An empowered (bad) woman
Lets people walk all over her	Commands respect
Takes care of everybody all the time	Takes care of herself first
Relies on other people to motivate her	Is self-motivated
Keeps a low profile	Is out there for all to see
Avoids confrontations	Is proactive in difficult situations
Engages in negative self-talk	Feeds herself positive, empowering talk
Questions her abilities	Believes in herself
Takes all the credit	Shares the glory

What are you? A good girl or bad girl? I don't know about you, but side two looks pretty good to me!

TEAM TRAITS CAN HELP YOU

Having been a member of a state, national and world championship team I feel quite qualified to talk about team synergy and the qualities of great teams. If I've learned anything through my varied team experiences it's that there are a few fundamental principles that are inherent in all championship teams. I developed this model about four years ago and have gotten positive responses from people of all ages, colors and disciplines. The same qualities that are present in championship teams are needed for successful entrepreneurship. Where do you fall on the CALUPA™ scale?

> CALUPA:™ *Communication, Accountability, Leadership, Unity, Persistence, Attitude*

Communication

Ever been in a relationship where there was a communication gap? If you haven't, keep living, you will. As far as I'm concerned everything starts or ends with communication or the lack thereof. Ask people what good communication looks like and folks start to stumble all over their words. When you've been in a relationship where the communication patterns are fluid and at the same time tight, it is an incredible experience. *Good communication is an open, honest and constantly flowing exchange of words, body language and other physical messages.*

What about you? Are you a good communicator? Do you give and accept honest, direct feedback? Do you have a difficult time telling people how you feel? Can you discuss difficult subjects without getting defensive? Can you hear negative things about you from other people without going off?

Accountability

This is one of my most favorite words. Self-accountability means that you hold yourself responsible and answerable for your actions. That means that when something happens you don't immediately look to blame someone else for the predicament you're in. Instead you ask, "how did I contribute to this mess?" In effective team settings, accountability is critical. Other-accountability is equally important. Not only must the players on your team hold themselves responsible, they must hold each other accountable. In other words, when a player violates code or team standards, the team has a right to initiate a conversation about that person's actions. As an entrepreneur you will develop relationships with vendors, suppliers and customers. You must be ready to accept your part in the victories and losses. Doing so makes you look like a mature, responsible businesswoman.

What about you? Do you hold yourself accountable most or only some of the time? Do you find yourself whining about the cards life has dealt you? When people offend you, do you hold a grudge until (sometimes after) they apologize to you? Do you find yourself saying that people owe you—an apology, an explanation?

Leadership

A team without any leadership won't go anywhere fast. As an entrepreneur you are already thrust into a leading role. How you accept this role will determine how successful you are. Many people start new businesses without any leadership experience—they don't know how to lead people, manage projects or take a business from one mountain top to the next.

What about you? Would you call yourself a leader? Do other people call you a leader? Does being in charge scare or intimidate you?

Unity

One of the biggest challenges you'll face as an entrepreneur is unifying a group of different people. Even if you start out as a one-woman show, at some point you will need to develop skills that successfully bring people together.

What about you? Can you work with people you don't like? Can you bring a group of diverse individuals on a project?

Persistence

When it's late in the game, great teams don't feel tired. If they do, they run on anyway. Your ability to persevere in the face of racism, sexism and any other ism will determine how high you fly. Be sure you have the support system in place to help you hang in there.

What about you? Do you find yourself giving up when things get tough? Do you frequently call your friends crying about your plight in life? When faced with a difficult task, is your first thought somewhere along the lines of how in the world will I ever do this?

Attitude

There's attitude and then there's *attitude*. You need both. The first refers to a good, positive attitude. One that inspires greatness and unconventional thinking. The second is a style, a flair for doing business, and it's equally important. You've seen people with attitude, right? In every movie actress Jada Pinkett has played in she's had *much* attitude, and I'm not talking about a bad attitude. I'm talking about a presence, an energy that says step correct or don't step at all. We tend to have a natural aptitude for this.

What about you? Do you have a positive outlook on life in general? Can you charm a plant?

HOW TO TEAM WITH ANYONE, ANYWHERE

Be yourself. If you decide to be someone else, what will happen when the real you shows up?

Extend yourself. Don't always expect your potential teammates to come to you. Invite someone to lunch, to golf or some other event where talking seems natural.

Be honest about who you are. If you have a bad temper, tell people so that they'll understand your behavior and perhaps even help you develop in this area.

Communicate openly. Don't let issues build up in your mind. If someone on your team does something that pleases and excites or irritates and offends you, tell them.

Have a sense of humor. Learn to laugh. There's enough seriousness out there, an occasional laugh is good for you and your team.

Come to practice. A sure way to upset your teammates is to miss meetings or important events. If you commit to something, say, a committee or board, attend functions. It's part of being on the team.

Play hard. Once you get on the team, play hard, concentrate and focus on the team's objectives.

Respect the other players. Don't be a big shot or a know-it-all. Everyone on the team has a unique talent.

Respect the coach. It really doesn't matter if you like or even agree with the authority in your situation; as a good team player, respect her/him.

Follow rules set by team or suggest amendments. If the team decides that the meetings will be on Mondays from 7:00 A.M. to 8:00 A.M. then it's your duty to be there. If those times don't work for you, bring it up in the meeting—don't just miss the meetings.

Always put the team first. In team settings, remember, your personal agenda is not the dominant theme.

Closing Ceremonies

❖ ❖ ❖

One day two friends were traveling in the Colorado mountains. It was a cold, blizzardy day with very little visibility. They'd been warned of hiking in the mountains because of the bears and other animals. While walking, one of the friends heard something rustling in the woods. "Did you hear that?" The other person answered, "yes." The two looked around and sure enough it was a big bear. They took off running for safety. For the first thirty yards they were side by side. Then one friend fell to the ground. The other friend looked around and saw her friend in the snowy path, then glanced up and saw that the bear was gaining on them both. She continued to run, leaving her friend behind. The fallen friend, badly hurt, couldn't get up and, by the time she had gained enough strength to stand, the bear was breathing down on top of her. "Are you going to kill me?" the woman asked. The bear, herself out of breath, looked down the road then back at the woman. "No, of course not, but if I were you I would never travel with a friend who'd leave me at the first sign of danger."

Sisters,
You are embarking on a journey that is as exciting as it is potentially tumultuous. One that is full of rewards and good times. One

that has its share of lions and tigers and bears. The good news is that you have this book as your friend. Use it. It's your traveling buddy. It will be with you as long as you use it as a resource. I've warned you of the hilly areas and speed bumps. I've taken meticulous notes, and I've even included some short cuts for you. Remember to work smart and hard, not long.

About My Sister's Business will not change your life—no book can do that, I don't care what anyone says. This book does contain *life-changing principles*. Adhering to and implementing those principles in your daily life will result in an energy that can be seen and felt, but will be difficult to explain. This book will challenge you to change, yes. However, only *you* can change you.

It is with pride and joy that I share these entrepreneurial lessons with you. I guarantee that if you will take advantage of the creeds, tools and insights on the preceding pages, your life will be spiritually enhanced, financially abundant, emotionally prosperous and physically exhilarating! That's my pledge to you. You have to promise me that no matter how rocky the mountain or how murky the waters you will persist and prevail. Deal?

You have the talent and tools for successful entrepreneurship. Thank you for letting me contribute to your empire. Pass your knowledge and blessings on to other sisters. Let me know how you're doing and, if I can help, pick up the phone and call me. Until then, stay strong in the race, and I look forward to hearing about your many victories.

Respectfully,

Fran

African American Women Entrepreneurs in History

❖ ❖ ❖

1856   A California court affirms the freedom of Biddy Mason, a slave who remained in California when her master returned to the South. Mason later became a prosperous landowner and a community and civil rights activist.

1866   Mary A. Warren was the first known professional female photographer.

1878   Austinite Emma Jones Hodge was the first traveling black woman photographer. She received her first camera at the age of eighteen and for the next forty years traveled in her husband's wagon taking wedding pictures and portraits. She lived to be 119 years old.

1890s   Jane (Mrs. Mose) Johnson Calloway, widowed former slave with nine children, opened one of Dallas County's largest and most profitable coal businesses.

1897   Mrs. S. H. Norris of Dallas organized the Grand Court, Order of Calanthe, the only fraternal insurance organization owned and controlled by black women.

1903   Financier Maggie Lena Walker becomes the first black woman bank president in the United States.

1904   Mary McLeod Bethune founds the Daytona Norman and Industrial School in Florida.

1906   Madame C. J. Walker starts a black hair-care business in Denver, CO, altering curling irons that were popularized by the French to suit the texture of black women's hair. At her death, she was thought to be the wealthiest black woman in America. She is arguably the first woman millionaire in United States history.

1906   Dr. Ollie L. Bryan, one of the first black women to practice dentistry in the South, was also the first female graduate of the Meharry Dental College. She had offices in Dallas from around 1906 to 1915.

1909   Nannie Helen Burroughs founds the National Training School for Women in Washington, D.C. Renamed the Nannie Helen Burroughs School, it now provides elementary education in missionary and industrial training.

1909   *The Galveston City Times* of May 1, 1909 listed a host of businesses run by women. Mrs. W. D. Lewis had five employees in her Lone Star Restaurant; Mrs. James Blair employed three in her furniture store; Miss Gertrude Shirley had a successful barbershop; Mrs. M. E. Webb owned an ice cream parlor; and Miss G. H. Freeman was a milliner.

1916   Kitty House Pollard was almost fifty when she opened her own restaurant in Austin's downtown Sixth Street area. A few doors down, Elizabeth Glasco, the mother of eleven children and the wife of a minister, opened a series of restaurants, each progressively larger, over a twenty-year period.

1916   Lauretta Green opens the Butler Dance Studio, the first black-owned professional studio for children. Although it was established mainly for black students, Butler Studio also trains whites, including cast members of *Our Gang* and *The Little Rascals* films.

1916   Mrs. C. H. (Lena Hamilton) Graves opened her home to the sick in Temple, TX, in 1916. Later, as a nurse, she founded the Memorial Colored Hospital, which operated until the 1950s.

1918   Actress Anita Bush cofounds the Lafayette Players (also known as the Anita Bush Players), one of the first black theater groups to perform nonmusical theater.

1920s–1930s   Madam N. A. Franklin opened her Franklin School of Beauty Culture in Houston as well as beauty shops in other cities.

1930   Fannie B. Peck organizes the Housewives' League of Detroit, an organization committed to "support black businesses, buy black products, patronize black professionals and keep money in the black community."

1931   Katherine Dunham, a modern dance performer and teacher, founds the Negro Dance Group in Chicago, IL.

1932   Miss Erma Jewell Hughes founded the Hughes Business College in Houston after the demand for business education grew with the development of urban business.

1941   Mary Caldwell Dawson founds the National Negro Opera Company in Pittsburgh, PA, the first permanent black opera company in the United States.

1947–48   Louise Martin, the first black member of the Southwestern Photographers Convention, ran a successful portrait studio in Houston for almost forty years. She was a graduate of Denver University and began her business after World War II. "You have to have confidence in yourself," she said at the end of her forty-year career. "I didn't get rich, but I made a good living."

1948   Doris Akers forms the Simmons-Akers Singers, a gospel group, with Dorothy Simmons; they later establish the Simmons and Akers Music House to publish and distribute their songs.

1959   Ruth Bowen opens Queen Artists, a talent agency for black artists. By 1969, Queen Booking Corporation is the largest black-owned entertainment agency; their talent roster includes Aretha Franklin and Ray Charles.

1975   Marva Collins founds the Westside Preparatory School, an alternative educational institution in Chicago.

1981   Byllye Avery founds the National Black Women's Health Project.

1982   Annette Hamilton and her husband, Bill, founded Annette 2 Cosmetiques in Dallas. Within ten years, the direct marketing firm grew to a multimillion-dollar business.

1983   One black woman-owned business that was turned down for a loan guarantee by the Small Business Administration was Amistad Bookplace in Houston, founded by Denise Armstrong and Shirleye Bridgewater. A publisher's representative who refused them credit said, "Black folks don't read." The women raised $2,000 by asking friends to donate $5 each. By 1993, the store had been teaching children about black history and showcasing black writers, poets and artists for ten years.

1984   Clara J. McLaughlin said that if blacks "wanted to have any real power we would have to be involved with the media. It is so important to our survival . . . because it helps develop our minds." She took advantage of a then-existing Federal Communications Council preference for granting broadcast licenses to women and minorities to launch the East Texas Television Network, a chain of four stations in Longview, Nacogdoches, Paris and Denton. McLaughlin raised more than $10 million from loans, personal funds and investments. In 1984, she became the first black woman in the U.S. to own a national television network affiliate.

1989   Oprah Winfrey buys Harpo Productions, becoming the first black woman—and the third woman—to buy a television and movie production studio.

Recommended Reading and Resources

❖ ❖ ❖

The Personal Touch
Terrie Williams

Success Runs in Our Race
George Frasier

Entrepreneurship and Self-Help Among Black Americans
John Sibley Butler

Inc. Your Dreams
Rebecca Maddox

Lions Don't Need to Roar
D. A. Benton

Shut Up and Sell
Don Sheehan

Think and Grow Rich
Dennis Kimbro and Napoleon Hill

Women, Mentors and Success
John Jeruchim and Pat Shapiro

The Corporate Coach
James Miller with Paul Brown

The Winner Within: A Life Plan for Team Players
Pat Riley

You Just Don't Understand—Women and Men in Conversation
Deborah Tanner, Ph.D.

Mail Order Success Secrets
Tyler Hicks

Tested Advertising Methods
John Caples

Treasury of Humor
Isaac Asimov

The World's Best Known Marketing Secret
Ivan Misner, Ph.D.

How to Succeed as an Independent Consultant
Herman Holtz

Word Smart II
Adam Robinson

INDEX

For You!

❖ ❖ ❖

Sisterpreneur
If you like the principles espoused in *About My Sister's Business,* I invite you to receive *Sisterpreneur,* the newsletter for today's enterprising black woman. You'll receive information on the issues that are affecting existing and would-be entrepreneurs.

Working Black Mothers
This newsletter will address the challenges you face as a working mom raising twenty-first-century children. How do you balance your life so that you get what *you* need, are a strong role model and instill in them the principles that will promote a healthy, productive life? You'll find out!

_____ YES! I will take advantage of this great opportunity. Send my subscription to *Sisterpreneur,* the newsletter for today's enterprising black woman, immediately! Enclosed is my check or money order for $9.99.

_____ YES! I will take advantage of this great opportunity. Send my subscription to *Working Black Mothers* immediately! Enclosed is my check or money order for $9.99.

Send to:

Fran Harris

c/o AMSBz
P.O. Box 5806
Austin, TX 78763
(512) 472–7465

Mail my subscription(s) to:

_____
_____
_____